Gathered Gold

GATHERED GOLD

A treasury of quotations for Christians

compiled by
JOHN BLANCHARD

EP
EVANGELICAL PRESS

EVANGELICAL PRESS
16-18 High Street, Welwyn, Hertfordshire, AL6 9EQ, England.

First published 1984
Second impression 1984
Third impression 1985
Fourth impression 1987

ISBN 0 85234 186 5 (Paperback)
ISBN 0 85234 197 0 (Hardback)

Other books by John Blanchard

Read Mark Learn
Right with God
Learning and Living
What in the World is a Christian?
Luke Comes Alive!
Truth for Life
Pop Goes the Gospel
How to Enjoy Your Bible
Ultimate Questions

Typeset in Great Britain by Inset, Chappel, Essex.
Printed at the Bath Press, Avon

Affectionately dedicated to

FRANK FARLEY

Brother and Friend, Example and Inspiration

Introduction

Ever since my conversion I have had a trawling eye. From my earliest days as a Christian I devoured books, magazines and other papers and gathered from them a growing harvest of statements that impressed themselves upon me. I soon began to arrange them into a simply indexed system and as time went on their growing numbers were joined by hundreds of other statements I heard in live preaching or on radio or television. Within a few years my files were bursting at the seams and I occasionally toyed with the idea that in my dotage I might assemble some of the material into a published anthology which I could usefully bequeath to others.

Two things encouraged me to advance the schedule. The first was in 1978 when I came across *The Golden Treasury of Puritan Quotations,* compiled by Dr I. D. E. Thomas. I had acquired several books of quotations over the years and by and large had found them very disappointing, but this one was superbly different. The following year I had the privilege of preaching at First Baptist Church, Maywood, California, where Dr Thomas is the pastor. In thanking him for his book, I mentioned my own thoughts about a more widely based collection. He immediately encouraged me to press ahead and graciously invited me to make free use of any of his material.

This unexpected bonus was followed some time later by another, when Rev. Robert Horn, editor of *Evangelical Times,* gave me an ageing copy of *The Puritan Remembrancer,* edited by his great-uncle Rev. H. J. Horn, and out of print for over half a century. Browsing through its tiny, packed pages was like discovering a private gold-mine and provided the final spur I needed to get to work on the augmented treasures at my disposal.

My debt to the Puritans goes far beyond this book and their prominence here was always a foregone conclusion. Who could fail to be fascinated by meeting people like Thomas Brooks, John Flavel, William Secker, John Trapp and Thomas Watson, with their agile army of aphorisms? These men and their ilk were spiritual giants and we can still benefit from their wit and wisdom today. However, it will soon be seen that the quotations in this book are drawn from much wider circles. Some are from people with whom I would have substantial doctrinal differences – and the inclusion of any quotation does not thereby imply endorsement of the author's stance on any matter of faith or practice. To go even further, not all those whose names appear in these pages are even Christians, but this in no way invalidates their words. Any reader who questions my rightness in using non-Christian sources is hereby referred to Acts 17:28! My concern in these pages is with the relevance, truth or usefulness of the quotation, rather than with the spiritual or doctrinal position of the author. It is not even suggested that all the quotations have the same depth or tone; mingled with the deeply serious are those in which wit or humour provides the vehicle to convey the message.

In assembling the material for publication I have avoided cluttering up the pages with titles, ranks, positions and dates, thus leaving the quotations to stand on their own. For ready reference, a subject index has been provided. As many subjects could be listed under various headings, the index includes a cross-reference showing where each subject will be found.

I have deliberately excluded from the material at my disposal hundreds of quotations which are of a negative nature – statements reflecting anti-Christian attitudes about life, man, death, eternity and so on. These have their place, but I wanted this book to be wholly positive and more widely useful than as a technical reference book. It will obviously be a source of quotations for preachers, teachers and other Christian communicators, but I trust that it will also be a means of direction, inspiration, insight, encouragement and help to countless 'ordinary' Christians in the rough and tumble of their daily lives.

Material from my own written and spoken ministry has been included where it was felt this might be helpful (though with no suggestion that it qualifies as 'gold'!). This always appears in italics at the beginning of a section.

If the stimulus of the words of men leads their readers to the substance of the Word of God, all the effort involved in producing this volume will be more than amply rewarded.

John Blanchard
Banstead,
Surrey.
August 1984

ABANDONMENT

(See also: Consecration; Submission; Zeal)

The greatness of a man's power is the measure of his surrender. *William Booth*

I have this day been before God and have given myself – all that I have and am – to God; so that I am in no respect my own. I have given myself clean away.
Jonathan Edwards

I will place no value on anything I have or may possess, except in relation to the kingdom of Christ.
David Livingstone

Before we can pray, 'Thy kingdom come', we must be willing to pray, 'My kingdom go'. *Alan Redpath*

Christianity is the total commitment of all I know of me to all I know of Jesus Christ. *William Temple*

Were the whole realm of
  nature mine,
That were an offering far
  too small;
Love so amazing, so divine,
Demands my soul, my life,
  my all. *Isaac Watts*

ACTIONS

(See also: Duty; Good Deeds; Service)

Practice is the soul of knowledge. *Thomas Adams*

Every action of our lives touches on some chord that will vibrate in eternity.
E. H. Chapin

Man's practices are the best indexes of his principles.
Stephen Charnock

Action is the proper fruit of knowledge. *Thomas Fuller*

Practice is the very life of piety. *William S. Plumer*

ACTIVISM

(See also: Service)

It is dangerously possible for activity to be no more than a dizzy whirl around a central emptiness.

Let us beware of feeling that unless we personally are up and doing the Lord is not at work.

In too many churches today we have the motion but not the unction.

Busyness in the King's business is no excuse for neglecting the King. *Anon.*

No man has a right to lead such a life of contemplation as to forget in his own ease the service due to his neighbour; nor has any man a right to be so immersed in active life as to neglect the contemplation of God. *Augustine*

It is possible to be so active in the service of Christ as to forget to love him.
P. T. Forsyth

We have been too busy chopping wood to take time out to sharpen the axe. *Vance Havner*

To concentrate on service and activity for God may often actively thwart our attaining of the true, God himself. *Roy Hession*

It is difficult to see Jesus when you are in a hurry.
Joel Horne

One of the greatest dangers in the spiritual life is to live on your own activities. In other words, the activity is not in its right place as something which you do, but has become something that keeps you going.
D. Martyn Lloyd-Jones

Beware the barrenness of a busy life. *Len North*

We won't get rid of the malady of sin by increasing our activity. *Alan Redpath*

Of what use is it to have many irons in the fire if the fire is going out?
Eric Roberts

To be always preaching, teaching, speaking, writing and working public works is unquestionably a sign of zeal. But it is not a sign of zeal according to knowledge. *J. C. Ryle*

Sometimes I think the church would be better off if we would call a moratorium on activity for about six weeks and just waited on God to see what he is waiting to do for us.
A. W. Tozer

Many a Christian worker's activity is the grave of his spiritual life. *C. J. Vaughan*

ADOPTION

Adoption gives us the *privilege* of sons, regeneration the *nature* of sons.
Stephen Charnock

Adoption . . . is the highest privilege that the gospel offers: higher even than justification. *J. I. Packer*

Adoption is a greater mercy than Adam had in paradise.
Thomas Watson

ALCOHOL

(See also: Drunkenness)

Alcohol does not make people able to do things better. It makes them less ashamed of doing them badly. *Anon.*

Alcohol never drowns sorrows; it irrigates them. *Anon.*

Drink like a fish only if you drink what a fish drinks. *Anon.*

The youth who stands with a glass of liquor in his hand would do well to consider which he had best throw away, the liquor or himself. *Anon.*

Wine is a turn-coat: first a friend, then a deceiver, then an enemy. *Anon.*

If we could sweep intemperance out of the country, there would be hardly poverty enough left to give healthy exercise to the charitable impulses. *Phillips Brooks*

I have better use for my brain than to poison it with alcohol. To put alcohol in the human brain is like putting sand in the bearings of an engine. *Thomas Edison*

Whisky is a good thing in its place. There is nothing like it for preserving a man when he is dead. If you want to keep a dead man, put him in whisky; if you want to kill a live man, put whisky in him. *Thomas Guthrie*

I never see a sign 'Licensed to sell spirits' without thinking that it is a licence to ruin souls. *Robert Murray M'Cheyne*

No drug known to man is more widely used nor more frequently responsible for deaths, injuries or crimes than is ethyl alcohol. *S. I. McMillen*

Wine has drowned more than the sea. *Publilius Syrus*

AMBITION

If there is anything worse than social climbing in the world it is ecclesiastical climbing in the church.

The man who desires honour does not deserve it.

Ambition, like the grave, is never full. *Thomas Adams*

Ambition is a gilded misery, a secret poison, a hidden plague, the engineer of deceit, the mother of

hypocrisy, the parent of envy, the original of vices, the moth of holiness and blinder of hearts, turning medicines into maladies and remedies into diseases. High seats are never but uneasy and crowns are always stuffed with thorns.
Thomas Brooks

When we seek honours we depart from Jesus.
Hugh of St Victor

Ambition is but avarice on stilts. *W. S. Landor*

You may get to the very top of the ladder, and then find it has not been leaning against the right wall.
A. Raine

ANGELS

Angels mean messengers and ministers. Their function is to execute the plan of divine providence, even in earthly things.
Thomas Aquinas

Angels will never be kings. They will always be servants. *Andrew Bonar*

Angels are the dispensers and administrators of the divine beneficence towards us. *John Calvin*

An angel is a spiritual creature created by God without a body, for the services of Christendom and of the church.
Martin Luther

If two angels were sent from heaven to execute a divine command, one to conduct an empire and the other to sweep a street in it, they would feel no inclination to change employments. *John Newton*

ANGER

(See also: Hatred; Revenge)

It is better to swallow angry words than to have to eat them afterwards.

Anger is a wind which blows out the lamp of the mind. *Anon.*

Anger is just one letter short of danger. *Anon.*

One thing that improves the longer it is kept is your temper. *Anon.*

The anger of today is the remorse of tomorrow.
Anon.

The worst of slaves is he whom passion rules.
Phillips Brooks

The worst thing we can bring to a religious controversy is anger.
Matthew Henry

It is the great duty of all Christians to put off anger. It unfits for duty . . . a man cannot wrestle with God and wrangle with his neighbour at the same time.
Philip Henry

When angry, count ten before you speak; if very angry, count a hundred.
Thomas Jefferson

When you are in the right, you can afford to keep your temper; and when you are in the wrong you cannot afford to lose it.
G. C. Lorimer

People who fly into a rage always make a bad landing.
Will Rogers

There is no old age for a man's anger. *Sophocles*

Passion is the drunkenness of the mind. *Robert South*

It is not a sin to be angry, but hard not to sin when we are angry. *John Trapp*

ANNIHILATION

(See also: Death; Eternity; Judgement)

What men fear is not that death is annihilation but that it is not. *Epicurus*

The wicked will not be annihilated by the second death as judgement for their sins any more than Christ was annihilated when he paid the penalty for our sins. *R. A. Killen*

ANTINOMIANISM

The person who claims he can live carelessly because he is not under law but under grace needs to be sure that he is not under wrath.

Antinomianism sets up the grace of God in opposition to his government.
Richard Cecil

To argue from mercy to sin is the devil's logic.
James Janeway

Such as will not have Christ to be their King to rule over them shall never have his blood to save them.
Thomas Watson

ANXIETY

(See also Fear; Worry)

Anxiety never strengthens you for tomorrow; it only weakens you for today.

Anxiety and prayer are more opposed to each other than fire and water.
J. A. Bengel

Anxiety is the fundamental phenomenon and the central problem of neurosis.
Sigmund Freud

Anxiety is the natural result when our hopes are centred in anything short of God and his will for us.
Billy Graham

To carry care to bed is to sleep with a pack on your back. *Thomas Haliburton*

The beginning of anxiety is the end of faith, and the beginning of true faith is the end of anxiety.
George Muller

Unquiet minds and hearts will be uncertain in decision and unsettled in grace.
J. Charles Stern

Anxiety is a self-contradiction to true humility.
Kenneth Wuest

APATHY

(See also: Complacency; Indifference)

Still water and still religion freeze the quickest. *Anon.*

When God has spoken, apathy is evidence of practical atheism.
Joyce Baldwin

The only thing necessary for the triumph of evil is for good men to do nothing. *Edmund Burke*

Some Christians are not only like salt that has lost its savour, but like pepper that has lost its pep. *Albert George Butzer*

If we once become listless to duty, we shall quickly become lifeless in it.
Stephen Charnock

If the doctrine of sinless perfection is a heresy, the doctrine of contentment with sinful imperfection is a greater heresy.
A. J. Gordon

Never before have we had so many degrees in the church and yet so little temperature. *Vance Havner*

APOSTASY

Apostasy is a perversion to evil after a seeming conversion from it. *Timothy Cruso*

None sink so far into hell as those that come nearest heaven, because they fall from the greatest height.
William Gurnall

Apostasy must be called what it is – a spiritual adultery. *Francis Schaeffer*

He falls deepest into hell who falls backward.
Thomas Watson

ART

All arts proceed from God and ought to be held as divine inventions.
John Calvin

Art is a collaboration between God and the artist, and the less the artist does the better.
André Gide

Art is the gift of God, and must be used unto his glory.
Henry Wordsworth Longfellow

Art is here because God meant it to be here.
Hans Rookmaaker

ASSURANCE

That faith which is never assaulted with doubting is but a fancy. Assuredly that assurance which is ever secure is but a dream.
Robert Bolton

A soul under assurance is unwilling to go to heaven without company.
Thomas Brooks

Assurance is glory in the bud, it is the suburbs of paradise.
Thomas Brooks

Assurance makes heavy afflictions light, long afflictions short, bitter afflictions sweet.
Thomas Brooks

The more the soul is conformed to Christ, the more confident it will be of its interest in Christ.
Thomas Brooks

Though no man merits assurance by his obedience, yet God usually crowns obedience with assurance.
Thomas Brooks

Assurance is the fruit that grows out of the root of faith. *Stephen Charnock*

Assurance is from God every bit as much as faith is.
J. C. P. Cockerton

Assurance hath a narrow throat, and may be choked with a small sin.
Thomas Fuller

Assurance is, as it were, the cream of faith.
William Gurnall

A well-grounded assurance of heaven and happiness, instead of puffing a man up with pride, will make and keep him very humble.
Matthew Henry

I think the first essential mark of the difference between true and false assurance is to be found in the fact that the true works humility.
A. A. Hodge

Sin can never quite bereave a saint of his jewel, his grace; but it may steal away the key of the cabinet, his assurance.
William Jenkyn

The Holy Spirit is no sceptic, and the things he has written in our hearts are not doubts or opinions, but assertions – surer and more certain than sense or life itself. *Martin Luther*

Faith is our seal; assurance of faith is God's seal.
Christopher Nesse

Assurance of hope is more than life. It is health, strength, power, vigour, activity, energy, manliness, beauty. *J. C. Ryle*

No less a person than God is needed to assure us of God's love. *Richard Sibbes*

If the priesthood of all believers is the first fruit of justification, 'assurance' is the second.
John R. W. Stott

A letter may be written, when it is not sealed; so grace may be written in the heart, and the Spirit may not set the seal of assurance to it. *Thomas Watson*

Sanctification is the seed; assurance is the flower which grows out of it.
Thomas Watson

The jewel of assurance is best kept in the cabinet of a humble heart.
Thomas Watson

ATHEISM

(See also: Impiety; Unbelief)

The world is still waiting for the first wise atheist.

To be an atheist requires an infinitely greater measure of faith than to receive all the great truths which atheism would deny.
Joseph Addison

Atheism is the death of hope, the suicide of the soul. *Anon.*

For an atheist to find God is as difficult as for a thief to find a policeman . . . and for the same reason.
Anon.

One trouble with being an atheist is that you have nobody to talk to when you are alone. *Anon.*

No man says, 'There is no God' but he whose interest it is there should be none.
Augustine

He that doth not believe that there is a God is more vile than a devil. To deny there is a God is a sort of atheism that is not to be found in hell.
Thomas Brooks

An atheist is a man without any invisible means of support. *John Buchan*

A denial of God is practically always the result of shutting one eye. It may be for this reason that God gave us two. *C. A. Coulson*

It takes no brains to be an atheist.
Dwight D. Eisenhower

An atheist is got one point beyond the devil.
Thomas Fuller

It has always seemed to me utterly absurd for the atheist to profess such deep regard for the random products of a universe where chance is king.
Michael Green

It amazes me to find an intelligent person who fights against something which he does not at all believe exists.
Mohandas Gandhi

The devil divides the world between atheism and superstition. *George Herbert*

Atheistic morality is not impossible, but it will never answer our purpose.
Roswell D. Hitchcock

I can see how it might be possible to look down upon the earth and be an atheist, but I cannot conceive how he could look into the heavens and say there is no God. *Abraham Lincoln*

The best reply to an atheist is to give him a good dinner and ask him if he believes there is a cook.
Louis Nizer

Atheism is a cruel, long-term business.
Jean-Paul Sartre

The religion of the atheist has a God-shaped blank at its heart. *H. G. Wells*

Atheism

There are no atheists in foxholes and rubber rafts.
James Whitaker

ATONEMENT

(See also: Cross; Forgiveness by God; Jesus Christ – Death; Redemption)

Just as surely as there was an actual cross, an actual body, actual blood, an actual death, an actual tomb, an actual resurrection – so there was an actual atonement, not merely the possibility of one.

The death of Christ was an atonement which totally succeeded, not an attempt which partially failed.

The cross of Jesus Christ is a two-way street; we have been brought to God and God has been brought to us.
Donald Grey Barnhouse

Bearing shame and scoffing rude,
In my place condemned he stood;
Sealed my pardon with his blood:
Hallelujah! what a Saviour!
Philipp Paul Bliss

When the Lord Jesus Christ . . . had our sins laid upon him, he did give more perfect satisfaction unto divine justice for our sins than if . . . all of us had been damned in hell unto all eternity.
William Bridge

The simplest word of faith is the deepest word of theology: Christ died for our sins. *James Denney*

God in his love pitcheth upon persons . . . Christ died not for propositions only, but for persons . . . He loved *us*, not ours.
Thomas Goodwin

The wrong that man hath done to the divine majesty *should* be expiated by none but man and *could* be by none but God. *John Howe*

Our answer to the devil's charge is not an alibi, but a plea of guilty and a claim that the demands of justice have been satisfied in the blood of the Lord Jesus Christ.
J. Russell Howden

Christ did not die for any upon condition, if they do believe; but he died for all God's elect, that they should believe. *John Owen*

The Redeemer's death actually saves his people, as it was meant to do.
J. I. Packer

It cannot be over-emphasized that we have not seen the full meaning of the cross till we have seen it ... as the centre of the gospel, flanked on the one hand by total inability and unconditional election and on the other by irresistible grace and final preservation.
J. I. Packer

The atonement was not the cause but the effect of God's love. *A. W. Pink*

Do not believe the devil's gospel, which is a *chance* of salvation; a chance of salvation is a chance of damnation. *Adolph Saphir*

God requires satisfaction because he is holiness, but he makes satisfaction because he is love.
Augustus H. Strong

Payment God cannot twice
demand;
First at my bleeding
Saviour's hand,
And then again at mine.
Augustus M. Toplady

Christ's blood has value enough to redeem the whole world, but the virtue of it is applied only to such as believe. *Thomas Watson*

Well might the sun in
darkness hide,
And shut his glories in,
When God, the mighty
Maker, died
For man, the creature's sin.
Isaac Watts

AWE

(See also: Fear of God; Worship)

We are encouraged to come freely to God but not flippantly.

Awe is the primary religious emotion. *Anon.*

We should give God the same place in our hearts that he holds in the universe. *Anon.*

The world will never starve for want of wonders; but only for want of wonder.
G. K. Chesterton

Where there is no awe the highest love is surely lacking. *Peter Green*

When we cannot, by searching, find the bottom, we must sit down at the brink and adore the depth.
Matthew Henry

The greatest need of the moment is that light-hearted, superficial religionists be struck down with a vision of God high and lifted up, with his train filling the temple. *A. W. Tozer*

BACKSLIDING

Backsliding never begins with a loud bang . . . it begins quietly, slowly, subtly, insidiously.

It is possible to be back-slapping and backsliding at the same time.

If thou wilt fly from God, the devil will lend thee both spurs and a horse.
Thomas Adams

Never look back unless you want to go that way.
Anon.

A declining Christian must needs be a doubting Christian. *William Gurnall*

Grace in a decay is like a man pulled off his legs by sickness. *William Gurnall*

We are so sub-normal that if we ever became normal people would think we were abnormal.
Vance Havner

For some of us, our greatest ability seems to be the ability for getting away from the Shepherd.
Geoffrey King

The backslider is a man who, because of his relationship to God, can never really enjoy anything else.
D. Martyn Lloyd-Jones

We are all constantly backsliding but for the grace of God. *Dick Lucas*

Backsliding is caused by slack abiding. *Ernest Plant*

Backsliders begin with dusty Bibles and end with filthy garments.
C. H. Spurgeon

Unsaintly saints are the tragedy of Christianity.
A. W. Tozer

BIBLE – Authority

The authority of the Bible comes not from the calibre of its human authors but from the character of its divine Author.

The faith will totter if the authority of the Holy Scriptures loses its hold on men. We must surrender ourselves to the authority of Holy Scripture, for it can neither mislead nor be misled.
Augustine

The Bible is the sceptre by which the heavenly King rules his church.
John Calvin

Whether we happen to like it or not, we are closed up to the teaching of the Bible for our information about *all* doctrines in the Christian faith, and this includes the doctrine of the Bible's view of itself.
Edward John Carnell

The Word of God is above the church.
Thomas Cranmer

God's Word is its own best argument. *Vance Havner*

The Word of God is either absolute or obsolete.
Vance Havner

There is only one real inevitability: it is necessary that the Scripture be fulfilled. *Carl F. Henry*

The Bible is the statute-book of God's kingdom.
Ezekiel Hopkins

All experience must be subservient to the discipline of Scripture. *Erroll Hulse*

The Bible was the only book Jesus ever quoted, and then never as a basis for discussion but to decide the point at issue.
Leon Morris

Our vision of God must be controlled not by what we *see* in the world but by what Scripture authorizes us to *believe.*
Iain H. Murray

The religion in which our Lord was brought up was first and foremost a religion of subjection to the authority of a written divine Word. *J. I. Packer*

The ordinary Christian with the Bible in his hand can say that the majority is wrong. *Francis Schaeffer*

The truth of Scripture demolishes speculation.
R. C. Sproul

The Bible, the whole Bible, and nothing but the Bible is the religion of Christ's church. *C. H. Spurgeon*

The truly wise man is he who always believes the Bible against the opinion of any man. *R. A. Torrey*

BIBLE – and Christ

Ignorance of the Scripture is ignorance of Christ.
Jerome

There is not a word in the Bible which is *extra crucem,* which can be understood without reference to the cross.
Martin Luther

As we go to the cradle only in order to find the baby, so we go to the Scriptures only to find Christ. *Martin Luther*

When you are reading a book in a dark room, and find it difficult, you take it to a window to get more light. So take your Bible to Christ.
Robert Murray M'Cheyne

Jesus saw himself as the key to Scripture and it as the key to himself.
J. I. Packer

The deity of Christ is the key doctrine of the Scriptures. Reject it, and the Bible becomes a jumble of words without any unifying theme. Accept it, and the Bible becomes an intelligible and ordered revelation of God in the person of Jesus Christ.
J. Oswald Sanders

Christ is the scope of the Scripture. *Richard Sibbes*

BIBLE – Divine authorship

(See also: Revelation)

The Bible does not say that its words were inspired by God but that they were expired by him.

The shortest road to an understanding of the Bible is the acceptance of the fact that God is speaking in every line.
Donald Grey Barnhouse

The Bible is none other than the voice of him that sitteth upon the throne. Every book of it, every chapter of it, every syllable of it, every letter of it, is the direct utterance of the Most High.
John William Burgon

Observe . . . that the same reverence that we have for God is due also to the Scripture, because it has proceeded from him alone, and has nothing of man mixed with it. *John Calvin*

The Bible is a letter God has sent to us; prayer is a letter we send to him.
Matthew Henry

The very words of Scripture are to be accounted the words of the Holy Ghost.
Matthew Henry

God has favoured us with his autobiography so that we might know and think his thoughts in every department of our lives.
Robert Horn

Divinity is nothing but a grammar of the language of the Holy Ghost.
Martin Luther

The sacred Scriptures come from the fulness of the Spirit; so that there is nothing in the Prophets, or the Law, or the Gospel, or the Epistles, which descends not from divine majesty. *Origen*

The biblical writers invented not their words themselves, suited to the things that they learned, but only expressed the words they received.
John Owen

The Bible appears like a symphony orchestra, with the Holy Ghost as its Toscanini; each instrument has been brought willingly, spontaneously, creatively, to play his notes *just as the great conductor desired,* though none of them could ever hear the music as a whole. *J. I. Packer*

Inerrancy affirms that the Bible is nothing less than revelation, revelation that comes to us from a transcendent personal God.
R. C. Sproul

The Bible speaks to you in the very tones of God's voice. *C. H. Spurgeon*

The Scriptures sprang out of God. *William Tyndale*

Scripture is the library of the Holy Ghost.
Thomas Watson

BIBLE – Fulness

The completeness of the Bible is as full as any other gift of God. *Anon.*

The difference between John's Gospel and the book of Chronicles is like the difference between man's brain and the hair of his head; nevertheless the life of the body is as truly in the hair as in the brain.
A. A. Hodge

The Bible is an inexhaustible fountain of all truths. The existence of the Bible is the greatest blessing which humanity ever experienced.
Immanuel Kant

I have made a covenant with God that he sends me neither visions, dreams, nor even angels. I am well satisfied with the gift of the Holy Scriptures, which give me abundant instruction and all that I need to know both for this life and for that which is to come.
Martin Luther

In Scripture, every little daisy is a meadow.
Martin Luther

One gem from that ocean is worth all the pebbles from earthly streams.
Robert Murray M'Cheyne

In the divine Scriptures, there are shallows and there are deeps; shallows where the lamb may wade, and deeps where the elephant may swim.
John Owen

If when I get to heaven the Lord shall say to me, 'Spurgeon, I want you to preach for all eternity,' I would reply, 'Lord, give me a Bible, that is all I need.' *C. H. Spurgeon*

We do not expect any new worlds in our astronomy, nor do we expect any new Scriptures in our theology.
Augustus H. Strong

The Bible is a rock of diamonds, a chain of pearls, the sword of the Spirit; a chart by which the Christian sails to eternity; the map by which he daily walks; the sundial by which he sets his life; the balance in which he weighs his actions. *Thomas Watson*

All the knowledge you want is comprised in one book, the Bible.
John Wesley

BIBLE – and the Holy Spirit

Proper understanding of the Scriptures comes only through the Holy Spirit.
Martin Luther

He who has the Holy Spirit in his heart and the Scriptures in his hands has all he needs.
Alexander MacLaren

If the Holy Spirit guides us at all, he will do it according to the Scriptures, and never contrary to them.
George Muller

BIBLE – Inerrancy

There can be no falsehood anywhere in the literal sense of Holy Scripture.
Thomas Aquinas

I believe most firmly that no one of those authors has erred in any respect in writing. *Augustine*

If the Bible contains errors, it is not God's Word itself, however reliable it may be.
James Montgomery Boice

I have learned to ascribe infallibility only to the books which are termed canonical, so that I confidently believe that not one of their authors erred.
Martin Luther

No sciences are better attested than the religion of the Bible.
Isaac Newton

I will put down all apparent inconsistencies in the Bible to my own ignorance.
John Newton

God writes with a pen that never blots, speaks with a tongue that never slips, acts with a hand that never fails.
C. H. Spurgeon

We must never edit God.
A. W. Tozer

If there be any mistakes in the Bible, there may as well be a thousand. If there be one falsehood in that book, it did not come from the God of truth. *John Wesley*

BIBLE – Influence and Power

The Word generates faith and regenerates us.
Joseph Alleine

Our faith is fed by what is plain in Scripture and tried by what is obscure.
Augustine

The Lord does not shine upon us, except when we take his Word as our light.
John Calvin

Unless God's Word illumine the way, the whole life of men is wrapped in darkness and mist, so that they cannot but miserably stray.
John Calvin

The foundation of every reformation of the Holy Spirit is the Word of God made plain to the people.
Frank Cooke

What though no answering
voice is heard?
Thine oracles, the written
Word,
Counsel and guidance still
impart,
Responsive to the upright
heart.
Josiah Condor

The only true reformation is that which emanates from the Word of God.
J. H. Merle d'Aubigné

The Scriptures teach us the best way of living, the noblest way of suffering and the most comfortable way of dying. *John Flavel*

There is no devil in the first two chapters of the Bible and no devil in the last two chapters. Thank God for a book that disposes of the devil!

Vance Havner

God's Word is the instrument by which God's Spirit transforms the Christian. *Robert Horn*

If half the strength spent in attacking or defending the Bible were spent in releasing it, how the level of ordinary life would be raised!

Will H. Houghton

The divine law, as seen by the Christian, exhibits liberty, gives liberty, is liberty. *Robert Johnstone*

I have done nothing: the Word has done and accomplished everything.

Martin Luther

While other books inform, and some few reform, this one book transforms.

A. T. Pierson

Scripture is not only pure but purifying.

William S. Plumer

A Bible-reading laity is a nation's surest defence against error. *J. C. Ryle*

The sum of all the counsel I can give you, necessary for the regulating of your behaviour towards God and man, in every station, place and condition of your lives, is contained in that blessed Word of God.

Isaac Watts, Senr.

BIBLE – Preservation

It is a miracle how God has so long preserved his book! How great and glorious it is to have the Word of God!

Martin Luther

The Christian feels that the tooth of time gnaws all books but the Bible . . . Nineteen centuries of experience have tested it. It has passed through critical fires no other volume has suffered, and its spiritual truth has endured the flames and come out without so much as the *smell* of burning. *W. E. Sangster*

When the dust of battle dies down we shall hear all sixty-six books declare with the apostle Paul, 'Do thyself no harm, for we are all here.'

W. H. Griffith Thomas

BIBLE – Purpose

There are two dominant themes in the Bible: the one is the story of man's seduction by sin; the other, man's salvation by Christ.
S. Barton Babbage

The Bible, as a revelation from God, was not designed to give us all the information we might desire, nor to solve all the questions about which the human soul is perplexed, but to impart enough to be a safe guide to the haven of eternal rest. *Albert Barnes*

Salvation, the salvation of man, is the final purpose of the whole Bible.
J. H. Bernard

The Bible is a window in this prison world through which we may look into eternity. *Timothy Dwight*

The storehouse of God's Word was never meant for mere scrutiny, not even primarily for study but for sustenance.
Vance Havner

The Bible calls itself food. The value of food is not in the discussion it arouses but in the nourishment it imparts.
Will H. Houghton

The Scriptures were not given to increase our knowledge but to change our lives. *D. L. Moody*

The Scripture is both the breeder and feeder of grace.
Thomas Watson

I want to know one thing, the way to heaven . . . God himself has condescended to teach the way . . . He hath written it down in a book. Oh, give me that book! At any price give me the book of God!
John Wesley

BIBLE – Relevance

Do not try to make the Bible relevant; its relevance is axiomatic.
Dietrich Bonhoeffer

The doctrines of the Bible are all practical and its laws all reasonable. Every doctrine has its practical *therefore* and every law its doctrinal *because.*
John Brown

The Bible never grows old.
Edith Deen

The Holy Scripture, as it is a rule both of our duty to God and of our expectation from him, is of much greater use and benefit to us than day or night, than the air we breathe in, or the light of the sun.

Matthew Henry

Scratch the surface of Scripture wherever you wish and you will uncover a slice of life.

Arthur Skevington Wood

There is no ancient history in the Bible.

Dinsdale T. Young

BIBLE – Submission to

The man who is not prepared to heed the Word of God obediently will not even be able to hear it correctly. This is why the parables become windows to some people and walls to others.

There are parts of the Bible which cause me difficulty, but none which cause me doubt.

The primary qualification demanded in the reader of the Bible is not scholarship but surrender, not expert knowledge but willingness to be led by the Spirit of God.

Martin Anstey

To the canonical Scriptures alone I owe agreement without dissent. *Augustine*

Beware of reasoning about God's Word – obey it!

Oswald Chambers

Of all commentaries upon the Scriptures, good examples are the best and the liveliest. *John Donne*

The more reverence we have for the Word of God the more joy we shall find in it. *Matthew Henry*

Before the Word everyone must give way.

Martin Luther

My conscience is captive to the Word of God.

Martin Luther

Few *tremble* at the Word of God. Few, in reading it, hear the voice of Jehovah, which is full of majesty.

Robert Murray M'Cheyne

I'm tired of hearing people say, 'I'm standing on the Word of God.' We should be standing under it.

Stephen Olford

To defer to God's Word is an act of faith; any querying and editing of it on our own initiative is an exhibition of unbelief.

J. I. Packer

Where the Scripture hath no tongue we must have no ears. *John Trapp*

Doers of the Word are the best hearers.
Thomas Watson

I am a Bible bigot. I follow it in all things, both great and small. *John Wesley*

BIBLE – Supremacy

The Bible among books is what Christ is among men. *Anon.*

As God is the only holy person, so Scripture is the only holy book.
William Gurnall

In regard to this great book I have but to say it is the best gift God has given to men. All that the good Saviour gave to the world was communicated through this book.
Abraham Lincoln

The Bible is not only the book of God but also the god of books.
John Ruskin

Many books in my library are now behind and beneath me. They were good in their way once, and so were the clothes I wore when I was ten years old; but I have outgrown them. Nobody ever outgrows Scripture; the book widens and deepens with our years.
C. H. Spurgeon

Had I the tongue of angels, I could not sufficiently set forth the excellency of Scripture.
Thomas Watson

BIBLE – Unity

All Scripture is the context in which any Scripture is to be considered and applied. *Anon.*

The Bible is a unity, and this unity is such that the New Testament functions as an infallible interpreter of the Old.
Richard B. Gaffin

The doctrines of the Bible are not isolated but interlaced; and the view of one doctrine must necessarily affect the view taken of another. *A. A. Hodge*

God's truth always agrees with itself. *Richard Sibbes*

The same Testator made both Testaments.
Thomas Taylor

BIBLE STUDY

Hit-and-run Bible reading can often become hit and miss.

There is more to Christian growth than knowing what the Bible says; nobody is ever nourished by memorizing menus.

Scripture knowledge is the candle without which faith cannot see to do its work.
Anon.

Study the Bible to be wise; believe it to be safe; practise it to be holy. *Anon.*

The devil is not afraid of the Bible that has got dust on it. *Anon.*

The study of God's Word for the purpose of discovering God's will is the greatest discipline which has formed the greatest character. *Anon.*

To reject study on pretence of the sufficiency of the Spirit is to reject the Scripture itself.
Richard Baxter

Apply yourself to the whole text, and apply the whole text to yourself.
J. A. Bengel

I have sometimes seen more in a line of the Bible than I could well tell how to stand under, and yet at another time the whole Bible hath been to me as dry as a stick. *John Bunyan*

I was never out of my Bible. *John Bunyan*

Sin will keep you from this book, or this book will keep you from sin.
John Bunyan

Explain the Scriptures by the Scriptures.
Clement of Alexandria

The difference between reading and study is like the difference between drifting in a boat and rowing toward a destination. *Oscar Feucht*

Compare Scripture with Scripture. False doctrines, like false witnesses, agree not among themselves.
William Gurnall

The Christian is bred by the Word and he must be fed by it.
William Gurnall

No one ever graduates from Bible study until he meets its Author face to face.
Everett Harris

The Bible that is falling apart usually belongs to someone who isn't.
Vance Havner

They who would grow in grace must be inquisitive.
Matthew Henry

If the Bible is to get into us we must get into the Bible. *Robert Horn*

The jewel of the Word should not hang in our ears, but be locked up in a believing heart.
William Jenkyn

Let us never forget that the message of the Bible is addressed primarily to the mind, to the understanding.
D. Martyn Lloyd-Jones

Pause at every verse of Scripture and shake, as it were, every bough of it, that if possible some fruit at least may drop down. *Martin Luther*

What we take in by the Word we digest by meditation and let out by prayer. *Thomas Manton*

Devout meditation on the Word is more important to soul-health even than prayer. It is more needful for you to hear God's words than that God should hear yours, though the one will always lead to the other. *F. B. Meyer*

I never saw a useful Christian who was not a student of the Bible. *D. L. Moody*

If all the neglected Bibles were dusted simultaneously, we would have a record dust storm and the sun would go into eclipse for a whole week.
David F. Nygren

Meditate on the Word in the Word. *John Owen*

The Spirit is not given to make Bible study needless, but to make it effective.
J. I. Packer

If I were the devil, one of my first aims would be to stop folk from digging into the Bible. *J. I. Packer*

The Scriptures make prayer a reality and not a reverie.
Austin Phelps

Partial examination will result in partial views of truth, which are necessarily imperfect; only careful comparison will show the complete mind of God.
A. T. Pierson

What is needed, in times when crisis assaults faith

and difficulty spawns doubt, is a fresh examination of the New Testament, that utterly amazing book of realism and hope.
Paul S. Rees

The longer you read the Bible, the more you will like it; it will grow sweeter and sweeter; and the more you get into the spirit of it, the more you will get into the spirit of Christ.
William Romaine

The Bible is the one book to which any thoughtful man may go with any honest question of life or destiny and find the answer of God by honest searching.
John Ruskin

Knowledge of the Bible never comes by intuition.
J. C. Ryle

If such a diligent study of Scripture should interfere with our reading of religious literature, we may rest satisfied that we shall not be the losers, to say the least of it.
Adolph Saphir

Blame none but yourself if all the Bible you get is that little bit from under the calendar hurriedly snatched as a sop to conscience. *David Shepherd*

Salvation comes by faith, but knowledge of the Bible by works. *Charles Simeon*

Inerrancy is never a licence for superficiality. It is not a ticket to skate lightly over the surface of the text.
R. C. Sproul

The Word of God is deeper than a flannelgraph. It demands the closest possible scrutiny. It calls for the most excellent scholarship. It makes the finest point of technical analysis worth the effort. The yield of such effort is truth. *R. C. Sproul*

Backsliders begin with dusty Bibles and end with filthy garments.
C. H. Spurgeon

An honest man with an open Bible and a pad and pencil is sure to find out what is wrong with him very quickly. *A. W. Tozer*

Nothing less than a whole Bible can make a whole Christian. *A. W. Tozer*

Leave not off reading the Bible till you find your hearts warmed . . . Let it not only inform you but inflame you.
Thomas Watson

Nothing can cut the diamond but the diamond; nothing can interpret Scripture but Scripture.
Thomas Watson

You can only understand Scripture on your knees.
Maurice Zundel

CHANCE

If life is an accident, it cannot conceivably have any purpose, for accident and purpose are mutually exclusive.

The doctrine of chances is the bible of the fool.
Anon.

There is no such thing as chance or accident; the words merely signify our ignorance of some real and immediate cause.
Adam Clarke

I cannot believe that God plays dice with the world.
Albert Einstein

CHARACTER

Circumstances never create character; they merely reveal it.

Everything in life is a test of character.

A man's character is accurately measured by his reaction to life's inequities.
Anon.

No amount of riches can atone for poverty of character. *Anon.*

Reputation is precious, but character is priceless. *Anon.*

Reputation is what men think you are; character is what God knows you are.
Anon.

What thou art in the sight of God, that thou truly art. *Thomas à Kempis*

Happiness is not the end of life; character is.
Henry Ward Beecher

The character wherewith we sink into the grave at death is the very character wherewith we shall reappear at the resurrection.
Thomas Chalmers

The fruit of the Spirit is not excitement or orthodoxy: it is *character.*
G. B. Duncan

A character, no more than a fence, can be strengthened by whitewash.
Paul Frost

Men and brethren, a simple trust in God is the most

essential ingredient in moral sublimity of character.
Richard Fuller

The finest test of character is seen in the amount and the power of gratitude we have. *Milo H. Gates*

The Lord knows them that are his by name, but we must know them by their character. *Matthew Henry*

Many a man's reputation would not know his character if they met on the street. *Elbert Hubbard*

Material abundance without character is the surest way to destruction.
Thomas Jefferson

Character is like a tree and reputation its shadow. The shadow is what we think of it; the tree is the real thing.
Abraham Lincoln

Character is what a man is in the dark. *D. L. Moody*

Orthodoxy of words is blasphemy unless it is backed up by superiority of character. *Blaise Pascal*

Men best show their character in trifles, where they are not on their guard.
Arthur Schopenhauer

The grace of God will do very little for us if we resolve to do nothing for ourselves. God calls us to co-operate with him in the perfecting of character.
W. Graham Scroggie

Human character is worthless in proportion as abhorrence of sin is lacking in it.
W. G. T. Shedd

The actions of men form an infallible index of their character.
Geoffrey Wilson

CHARITY

(See also: Generosity; Giving; Kindness)

Charity gives itself rich; covetousness hoards itself poor. *Anon.*

The word 'alms' has no singular, as if to teach us that a solitary act of charity scarcely deserves the name.
Anon.

Charity is the very livery of Christ. *Hugh Latimer*

The greatest charity in the world is the communication of divine truth to the ignorant.
Alexander Maclaren

The brightest blaze of intelligence is of incalculably less value than the smallest spark of charity.
William Nevins

The place of charity, like that of God, is everywhere.
Francis Quarles

Charity is the best way to plenty; he gets most that gives most.
George Swinnock

CHASTENING
(See also: Trials)

God always warns before he wounds.

When God takes away correction, damnation enters the doors.
Thomas Adams

God's corrections are our instructions, his lashes our lessons, his scourges our schoolmasters.
Thomas Brooks

God would not rub so hard, were it not to fetch out the dirt and spots that be in his people. *Thomas Brooks*

Where God loves, he afflicts in love, and wherever God afflicts in love there he will, first or last, teach such souls such lessons as shall do them good to all eternity. *Thomas Brooks*

There is nothing more to be dreaded than that the Lord should allow us loose reins. *John Calvin*

God denies a Christian nothing but with a design to give him something better. *Richard Cecil*

God never strikes except for motives of love, and never takes away but in order to give. *François Fenelon*

There is comfort to be found even in God's condemnations.
François Fenelon

God kills thy comforts from no other design but to kill thy corruptions; wants are ordained to kill wantonness; poverty is appointed to kill pride; reproaches are permitted to destroy ambition.
John Flavel

God's wounds cure; sin's kisses kill. *William Gurnall*

When we are chastened we must pray to be taught, and look into the law as the best expositor of providence. It is not the chastening itself that does good, but the teaching that goes

along with it and is the exposition of it.
Matthew Henry

Believer, think not of undisturbed repose until the flesh be dropped. There is a ceaseless cycle of sorrow and temptation here. But despise not the scourge. It has a teaching voice. It is held by a loving Father's hand. *Henry Law*

The bitterest cup with Christ is better than the sweetest cup without him.
Ian MacPherson

If nothing else will do to sever me from my sins, Lord, send me such sore and trying calamities as shall awake me from earthly slumbers.
Robert Murray M'Cheyne

The heavenly Father has no spoiled children. He loves them too much to allow that. *Fred Mitchell*

The rough hewing of reproof is only to square us for the heavenly building. *D. L. Moody*

Our heavenly Father never takes anything from his children unless he means to give them something better.
George Muller

The sword of justice no longer threatens us, but the rod of parental correction is still in use.
C. H. Spurgeon

The painful pruning knife is in safe hands.
John R. W. Stott

It is in mercy and in measure that God chastiseth his children.
John Trapp

God parts that and us which would part us and him. *Ralph Venning*

God punishes most when he does not punish.
Thomas Watson

CHRISTIAN

(See also: Christianity)

A Christian is not a person who has made a new start in life, but a person who has received a new life to start with.

A Christian is a man possessed. *Anon.*

Christ's sheep are marked in the ear and the foot; they hear his voice and they follow him. *Anon.*

The best Christians we have among us are only Christians in the making. They are by no means finished products. *Anon*

The Christian is called upon to live a supernatural life, and he has been given the power to live that life.
Donald Grey Barnhouse

No true Christian is his own man. *John Calvin*

The Christian family is entered by calling and evidenced by character.
Herbert W. Cragg

If you were arrested for being a Christian, would there be enough evidence to convict you?
David Otis Fuller

If you are a Christian, you are not a citizen of this world trying to get to heaven; you are a citizen of heaven making your way through this world.
Vance Havner

I reckon him a Christian indeed that is neither ashamed of the gospel nor a shame to it.
Matthew Henry

A Christian's life is a state of holy desire. *Jerome*

Christians are made, not born. *Jerome*

A Christ not in us is a Christ not ours.
William Law

There is one single fact that one may oppose to all the wit and argument of infidelity; namely, that no man ever repented of being a Christian on his death-bed. *Hannah More*

A saint is not merely a professing follower of Christ, but a professing follower presumed to be what he professes.
Handley C. G. Moule

They lose nothing who gain Christ. *Samuel Rutherford*

A Christian is a strange person. He is both dead and alive, he is miserable and glorious . . . He grows downwards and upwards at the same time; for as he dies in sin and misery, and natural death approaching, so he lives the life of grace, and grows more and more till he end in glory.
Richard Sibbes

To a man who lives unto God nothing is secular, everything is sacred.
C. H. Spurgeon

The Christian has been transplanted into a new soil and a new climate, and both soil and climate are Christ.

James S. Stewart

There is a sense in which the people of the Lord are a people apart, belonging to each other in a sense in which they don't belong to anyone else.

A. W. Tozer

The saints are the walking pictures of God.

Thomas Watson

CHRISTIANITY – Characteristics

If your Christianity is comfortable, it is compromised.

There is no such thing as an easy Christianity. If it is easy, it is not Christianity; if it is Christianity, it is not easy.

The Christian ideal has not been tried and found wanting. It has been found difficult and left untried.

G. K. Chesterton

There is no Christianity without the practice of it.

John R. De Witt

The proper temperature of Christianity is red-hot.

Alexander Duff

Christianity is the faith for men who are prepared to swim against the stream, the religion for radicals.

Michael Green

Christianity is not true because it works. It works because it is true.

Os Guinness

Authentic Christianity is not sophisticated but simple. *R. T. Kendall*

Christianity begins with the doctrine of sin.

Soren Kierkegaard

Christian living is not fighting for a position but from a position. *Paul O. Kroon*

Christianity, if false, is of no importance, and, if true, of infinite importance. The one thing it cannot be is moderately important.

C. S. Lewis

We must aim to have a Christianity which, like the sap of a tree, runs through twig and leaf of our character and sanctifies all.

J. C. Ryle

Nobody has understood Christianity who does not understand . . . the word 'justified'.
John R. W. Stott

Justification is the very hinge and pillar of Christianity. *Thomas Watson*

Christianity is not merely a programme of conduct; it is the power of a new life. *Benjamin B. Warfield*

CHRISTIANITY – Definition

Christianity is life under sealed orders. *Anon.*

Christianity is obedience.
Anon.

Christianity is not the religion of Jesus . . . but Christ religion. Christianity is now as dependent on him, moment by moment, as when he trod this earth.
Herman Bavinck

Christianity is the way of the cross . . . and your blood and sweat may mingle with Christ's before your life is finished.
Lionel Fletcher

Christ plus Christians equals Christianity. *Geoffrey King*

Christianity is a universal holiness in every part of life. *William Law*

'Crucified' is the only definitive adjective by which to describe the Christian life.
J. Furman Miller

Christianity is a religion about a cross. *Leon Morris*

Christianity is the power of God in the soul of man. *Robert B. Munger*

Christianity is not a system of doctrine but a new creature. *John Newton*

Christianity is very much greater than Christian doctrine . . . Theology can never take the place of faith. *Theodore Robinson*

Christianity is the total commitment of all I know of me to all I know of Jesus Christ.
William Temple

Christianity can be condensed into four words: admit, submit, commit and transmit.
Samuel Wilberforce

Christianity is not merely an assurance policy to take us to heaven; it is a bowing of the knee to the lordship of Christ. *Frederick P. Wood*

CHRISTIANITY – Uniqueness

The distinction between Christianity and all other systems of religion consists largely in this, that in these others men are found seeking after God, while Christianity is God seeking after men. *Thomas Arnold*

As you look into other faiths you will find an enormous amount that is true and worthy, that is moral and good, as well as much that is not. But you will not find anything that is good and true which cannot be found in Christ.
Michael Green

It is quite plain that, if treated fairly on its own premises, Christianity excludes the full truth and final validity of other religions. *Os Guinness*

All other religions are oblique: the founder stands aside and introduces another speaker . . . Christianity alone is direct speech. *Soren Kierkegaard*

We must never talk about the failure of Christianity. It is impossible for Christianity to fail. What fails is the shabby counterfeit of the real thing that we are willing to put up with. *Geoffrey King*

Christianity is essentially a religion of resurrection.
James S. Stewart

Christianity . . . is the revelation of God, not the research of man.
James S. Stewart

So Christianity is old, and is getting older every year. Yet it is also new, new every morning.
John R. W. Stott

Christianity is the one revealed religion.
Benjamin B. Warfield

CHRISTLIKENESS

(See also: Godliness; Holiness)

If you are in Christ, and Christ is in you, then the world should see nothing else. *Anon.*

The most deeply felt obligation on earth is that which the Christian feels to imitate the Redeemer.
Albert Barnes

The universal command of the gospel, that comprises all our duties, is to walk as Christ walked.
William Bates

A Christian's life should be nothing but a visible representation of Christ.
Thomas Brooks

The more the soul is conformed to Christ, the more confident it will be of its interest in Christ.
Thomas Brooks

None can know their election but by their conformity to Christ; for all that are chosen are chosen to sanctification.
Matthew Henry

The Christian's task is to make the Lord Jesus visible, intelligible and desirable.
Len Jones

God never gave man a thing to do concerning which it were irreverent to ponder how the Son of God would have done it. *George MacDonald*

It is not great talents that God blesses, so much as great likeness to Jesus.
Robert Murray M'Cheyne

Conformity to the world can be overcome by nothing but conformity to Jesus.
Andrew Murray

You and I were created to tell the truth about God by reflecting his likeness. That is normality. How many lies have you told about God today?
Ian Thomas

Our lives should be as many sermons upon Christ's life. *John Trapp*

When no mark of the cross appears in our discipleship, we may doubt the ownership. We should be branded for Christ. *Mary S. Wood*

CHURCH – Attendance and Membership

Don't stay away from church because there are so many hypocrites. There's always room for one more.
A. R. Adams

He cannot have God for his Father who refuses to have the church for his mother. *Augustine*

A person who says he believes in God but never goes to church is like one who says he believes in education but never goes to school.
Franklin Clark Fry

An avoidable absence from church is an infallible evidence of spiritual decay.
Frances Ridley Havergal

Church – Attendance and Membership

I believe in loyalty to the local church. I don't believe in that view of the invisible church that makes you invisible at church!
Vance Havner

Those that would enjoy the dignities and privileges of Christ's family must submit to the discipline of it. *Matthew Henry*

Those whom God leads, he leads to his holy hill, and to his tabernacles; those therefore who pretend to be led by the Spirit and yet turn their backs upon instituted ordinances, certainly deceive themselves. *Matthew Henry*

The New Testament knows nothing of free-lance Christianity. It is the corporate witness of the redeemed fellowship that is used by the Spirit of God.
Geoffrey King

The question whether or not to join the church or belong to the church is not one that is open for the Christian believer.
Donald MacLeod

A church membership does not make a Christian any more than owning a piano makes a musician.
Douglas Meador

You don't see the church on Sunday morning any more than you see the army when it's on dress parade. *Bill Popejoy*

We don't *go* to church; we *are* the church.
Ernest Southcott

Going to church doesn't make you a Christian any more than going to a garage makes you an automobile. *Billy Sunday*

We must meet with the Church Militant if ever we hope to meet with the Church Triumphant. Together in grace, God's people make ready for glory. *Malcolm Watts*

CHURCH – Blemishes

A church without the truth is not a true church, and a church without the Spirit is not a true church.
Anon.

A cold church, like cold butter, never spreads well.
Anon.

I looked for the church and I found it in the world; I looked for the world and I found it in the church.
Horatius Bonar

The church has halted somewhere between Calvary and Pentecost. *J. I. Brice*

Nothing will so avail to divide the church as love of power. *Chrysostom*

Too many church services begin at eleven o'clock sharp and end at twelve o'clock dull.
Vance Havner

Too many church members are starched and ironed but not washed.
Vance Havner

Never before have we had so many degrees in the church and yet so little temperature.
Vance Havner

When the night-club invades the sanctuary it ought not to be difficult for any Bible Christian to discern the time of day.
Vance Havner

I can think of some churches that would be even emptier if the gospel were preached in them.
William R. Inge

I know that the church has its stupidities and inanities and irrelevancies; but I love my mother in spite of her weaknesses and wrinkles.
E. Stanley Jones

To play little religious games in church with those of one's own kind may well be a prime index of man's fallenness.
Samuel J. Mikolaski

One of the main causes of present troubles in the church is the neglect of discipline. *Klaas Runia*

It would take a theologian with a fine-toothed comb to find the Holy Spirit recognizably present with power in much of our ecclesiastical routine.
Samuel M. Shoemaker

Much that passes for New Testament Christianity is little more than objective truth sweetened with song and made palatable by religious entertainment.
A. W. Tozer

There are churches so completely out of the hands of God that if the Holy Spirit withdrew from them they wouldn't find it out for many months. *A. W. Tozer*

CHURCH – and Christ

The church is Christ's body and the body of a man goes by the same name as the head. *Anon.*

The church is heir to the cross. *Thomas Adams*

The church is nothing but Christ displayed. *William Gurnall*

The church is in Christ as Eve was in Adam. *Richard Hooker*

If we accept the divine entry of God into human history through the man Jesus Christ, we cannot help accepting the unique nature of the fellowship which he founded. For in a true sense it is an extension of the actual visit, sustained by the living God. *J. B. Phillips*

Christ is the King of his church, and the church is the greatest queen in the world. *Richard Sibbes*

CHURCH – Duties

No church is obedient that is not evangelistic.

A church is a hospital for sinners, not a museum for saints. *Anon.*

The church is not a yachting club but a fleet of fishing boats. *Anon.*

The church exists by mission as a fire exists by burning. *Emil Brunner*

As the saving doctrine of Christ is the life of the church, so discipline is, as it were, its sinews. *John Calvin*

Wherever we see the Word of God purely preached and heard, there a church of God exists, even if it swarms with many faults. *John Calvin*

Only a virtuoso in exegetical evasion would dare to deny that the mission of the church is to make disciples. *Mariano di Gangi*

The church that ceases to be evangelistic will soon cease to be evangelical. *Alexander Duff*

The Christian church is not just a 'doctrine club'. *Paul Helm*

The Lord God hath given us three principal signs and marks by which we may know this his church, that is to say, the Word, the sacraments and discipline. *John Hooper*

Today's church . . . has no more solemn duty than to maintain purity of doctrine. *R. B. Kuiper*

The only valid consideration for the church to realize at all times must be what serves the gospel, its credibility, its deepening, its propagation. What forms, customs and ordinances must be removed, changed or avoided, lest the church itself be a burden to faith in the gospel? *Walter Kunneth*

Prayer meetings are the throbbing machinery of the church. *C. H. Spurgeon*

We shall never see much change for the better in our churches in general till the prayer meeting occupies a higher place in the esteem of Christians.
C. H. Spurgeon

If we ever forget our basic charter – 'My house is a house of prayer' – we might as well shut the church doors.
James S. Stewart

Every church should be engaged in continuous self-reformation.
John R. W. Stott

The church has nothing to do but to save souls; therefore spend and be spent in this work. It is not your business to speak so many times, but to save souls as you can; to bring as many sinners as you possibly can to repentance.
John Wesley

CHURCH – Fellowship

(See also: Fellowship)

The Christian church is a truly classless society.

The church should be a community of encouragement. *Fred Catherwood*

There is no place for any loose stone in God's edifice. *Joseph Hall*

Local churches are to be thought of not as churches of individuals but, primarily, *churches of families.* *Paul Helm*

We are not entitled to infer from the fact that a group of people are drawing nearer to each other that any of them is drawing nearer to the truth.
J. I. Packer

CHURCH – Security in God's Purposes

The church is not a democracy in which we have chosen God, but a theocracy in which he has chosen us.

Church – Security in God's purposes

The church is the only society in the world that never loses any of its members, even by death.

Never futile is the work of the church, for it is a product not of the mind of man but of the sovereign grace of God.
William Hendriksen

The church shall survive the world, and be in bliss when that is in ruins.
Matthew Henry

We may with the greatest assurance depend upon God for the safety of his church.
Matthew Henry

Ever since God had a church of redeemed sinners on earth the future of her destiny has been brighter than her past history.
William S. Plumer

God has twisted together his glory and our good.
Thomas Watson

CHURCH – Oneness

There is no doubt but that if there be one God, there is but one church; if there be but one Christ, there is but one church; if there be but one cross, there is but one church; if there be but one Holy Ghost, there is but one church.
A. A. Hodge

The real unity of the church must not be organized but exercised.
Johannes Lilje

The church is one body – you cannot touch a toe without affecting the whole body. *Friedrich Tholuck*

CHURCH – Power

The church has many critics but no rivals. *Anon.*

If it were not for the church, Satan would already have turned this world into hell.
Paul E. Billheimer

The church upon its knees would bring heaven upon the earth. *E. M. Bounds*

The church that does not work miracles is dead and ought to be buried.
Samuel Chadwick

The Christian church has the resurrection written all over it. *E. G. Robinson*

A holy church is an awful weapon in the hand of God.
C. H. Spurgeon

CHURCH UNITY

When the Bible speaks about church unity, it speaks of unity not at the expense of truth but on the basis of it.

Division is better than agreement in evil.
George Hutcheson

Unity must be ordered according to God's holy Word, or else it were better war than peace.
Hugh Latimer

Putting all the ecclesiastical corpses into one graveyard will not bring about a resurrection.
D. Martyn Lloyd-Jones

I am quite sure that the best way to promote union is to promote truth.
C. H. Spurgeon

The way to the union of Christendom does not lie through committee-rooms . . . It lies through personal union with the Lord so deep and real as to be comparable with his union with the Father.
William Temple

Unity without verity is not better than conspiracy.
John Trapp

COMMUNION WITH CHRIST

(See also: Love for Christ; Meditation; Prayer)

Let us use the world but enjoy the Lord.
Thomas Adams

Attachment to Christ is the secret of detachment from the world. *Anon.*

The more any man loves Christ, the more he delights to be with Christ alone. Lovers love to be alone.
Thomas Brooks

Unless you live in Christ, you are dead to God.
Rowland Hill

A dungeon with Christ is a throne, and a throne without Christ a hell.
Martin Luther

To please Christ is to live a life in such deep fellowship with him that our walk is characterized by an eagerness to explore his every wish.
W. Graham Scroggie

In forty years I have not spent fifteen waking minutes without thinking of Jesus. *C. H. Spurgeon*

COMMUNION WITH GOD

(See also: Love for God; Meditation; Prayer)

If you are a failure in your devotional life, you are a phoney in every other part.

You will never get far for God unless you get far with him.

God finds pleasure in us when we find pleasure in him. *Augustine*

Communion with God is the beginning of heaven.
William Bates

I have more to do with God than with all the world; yea, more and greater business with him in one day than with all the world in all my life.
Richard Baxter

Look into the Fountain, and the very looking will make you thirsty.
Andrew Bonar

No man who lives near to God lives in vain.
Horatius Bonar

To be little with God is to be little for God.
E. M. Bounds

A Christian may have as choice communion with God when his eyes are full of tears as he can have when his heart is full of joy. *Thomas Brooks*

Access to God lies open to none but his pure worshippers. *John Calvin*

I can afford to lose everything except the touch of God on my life.
Willard Cantelon

Fellowship with God means warfare with the world.
Charles E. Fuller

Though the gracious soul still desires more of God, it never desires more than God. *Matthew Henry*

To wait on God is to live a life of desire toward him, delight in him, dependence on him, and devotedness to him.
Matthew Henry

Adequate time for daily waiting on God . . . is the only way I can escape the tyranny of the urgent.
Charles Hummel

If we spend sixteen hours a day dealing with tangible things and only five minutes a day dealing with God, is it any wonder that tangible

things are 200 times more real to us than God?
William R. Inge

I am so busy at this present time I cannot do with less than four hours each day in the presence of God.
Martin Luther

I ought to spend the best hours of the day in communion with God. It is my noblest and most fruitful employment, and is not to be thrust into any corner.
Robert Murray M'Cheyne

Great eagles fly alone; great lions hunt alone; great souls walk alone – alone with God. *Leonard Ravenhill*

No man ever said, at the end of his days, 'I have read my Bible too much, I have thought of God too much, I have prayed too much, I have been too careful with my soul.'
J. C. Ryle

It is not sufficient to commune with the truth, for truth is impersonal. We must commune with the God of truth.
W. G. T. Shedd

My God and I are good company. *Richard Sibbes*

Water is not lost when it emptieth itself into the sea, for there it is in its proper element. A Christian is not lost when he loseth himself in his God, in his Saviour. *Richard Sibbes*

If we are weak in communion with God we are weak everywhere.
C. H. Spurgeon

Take away everything I have, but do not take away the sweetness of walking and talking with the King of glory! *John Stam*

God has not bowed to our nervous haste nor embraced the methods of our machine age. *The man who would know God must give time to him.*
A. W. Tozer

Only engrossment with God can maintain perpetual spiritual enthusiasm, because only God can supply everlasting novelty.
A. W. Tozer

At the profoundest depths in life, men talk not about God, but with him.
D. Elton Trueblood

COMMUNISM

The only difference between capitalism and Communism is that with capitalism man exploits man, but with Communism the reverse is the case! *Anon.*

What does it matter if 90% of the Russian people perish provided the surviving 10% be converted to the Communist faith?
Lenin

Everyone must be an atheist. We will never attain our goal until the myth of God has been removed from the thoughts of man.
Lenin

Communism is an enemy of God. It attacks and denies him who created heaven and earth.
Andrew Ben Loo

The greatest obstacle to evangelism today is the international conspiracy of Communism.
Andrew Ben Loo

We oppose Communism not because of politics but primarily because of faith in God, in Christ, in his Word the Bible and in his church.
Andrew Ben Loo

Communism is the devil's latest substitute for the Christian concept of the kingdom of God.
Frederick H. Olert

Communism levels men down; Christ levels men up. *Leonard Ravenhill*

Communism is the devil's enemy of Christianity.
A. W. Tozer

Who ever heard of a Marxist on his deathbed asking for *Das Kapital* to be read to him . . .?
Stephen Travis

COMPASSION

(See also Kindness; Love for Others; Mercy to Others)

The Christian should show the same concern for compassion as for creeds.

Compassion is what makes a person feel pain when somebody else hurts. *Anon.*

People will not care what you know until they know that you care. *Anon.*

There is no exercise better for the heart than reaching down and lifting people up.
John Andrew Holmer

As soon as we cease to bleed we cease to bless.
John Henry Jowett

Biblical orthodoxy without compassion is surely the ugliest thing in the world.
Francis Schaeffer

God cares, God is concerned. And since God is concerned his people have an obligation to be concerned too. *Foy Valentine*

COMPLACENCY

(See also: Apathy; Indifference)

No Christian should be complacent about his spiritual condition.

The fatal blow to progress is self-satisfaction. *Anon.*

When we are best at ease, when all things go with us according to our will and pleasure, then we are commonly furthest from God. *Hugh Latimer*

The calm which puts us to sleep may be more fatal than a storm which keeps us wide awake.
William S. Plumer

Complacency is the deadly enemy of spiritual progress.
A. W. Tozer

COMPROMISE

It is impossible to compromise with sin and conquer it at the same time.

It is perhaps the greatest sin of the greatest number of Christians that in so many details of life they put God second.

People who always bend backwards to please everybody soon weaken their spine. *Anon.*

The middle of the road is where most accidents happen. *Anon.*

Every lesser good has an essential element of sin.
Augustine

Lines of least resistance make crooked rivers and crooked men.
William H. Danforth

A soft and sheltered Christianity, afraid to be lean and lone, unwilling to face the storms and brave the heights, will end up fat and foul in the cages of conformity.
Vance Havner

We have been accustomed to the sacrifice of the ideal on the altar of the convenient and immediately profitable.
Stuart Holden

It is impossible at one and the same time to make earthly and heavenly

things the principal subject of your thoughts.
A. W. Pink

Compromise must always be impossible where the truth is essential and fundamental.
C. H. Spurgeon

May God save us from intermittent religion!
C. H. Spurgeon

There is no such cruelty to men's souls as clemency to their sins.
George Swinnock

We can tell when we have been influenced by the world. It is when we find ourselves neither hot nor cold, just compromised.
Malcolm Watts

Compromise is like dry rot in the fabric of the Christian church; sooner or later the structure will give way.
Mary S. Wood

CONCEIT

(See also: Egotism: Pride)

Every man is his own greatest dupe.
W. R. Alger

Conceit is the most incurable disease that is known to the human soul.
Henry Ward Beecher

Of all fools the conceited fool is the worst.
William Gurnall

Self-opinion is the bane of all virtue.
Edward Marbury

Ignorance and confidence are often twins.
George Swinnock

He is two fools that is wise in his own eyes.
John Trapp

CONFESSION

(See also Contrition; Conviction of Sin; Penitence; Repentance)

Acknowledging that one is a sinner is no more conviction of sin than believing the truth about Jesus is saving faith.

Sins concealed by man are never cancelled by God.

Confessing your sins is no substitute for forsaking them. *Anon.*

Confession of sin puts the soul under the blessing of God. *Anon.*

Before God can deliver us we must undeceive ourselves. *Augustine*

The confession of evil works is the first beginning of good works.
Augustine

Confessing sin is not informing God, it is agreeing with him.
Derek Cleave

A great part of our worthiness lies in an acknowledgement of our own unworthiness.
Matthew Henry

The way to cover our sin is to uncover it by confession.
Richard Sibbes

CONSCIENCE – and the Bible

My conscience is captive to the Word of God.
Martin Luther

Order my footsteps by
thy Word,
And make my heart sincere;
Let sin have no dominion,
Lord,
But keep my conscience
clear.
Isaac Watts

If conscience is to be directed by the Spirit of God it must be governed by the Word of God.
Mary S. Wood

CONSCIENCE – and God

Conscience is God's deputy, God's spy, God's notary, God's viceroy.
Thomas Brooks

Conscience is God's preacher in the bosom.
Thomas Brooks

Distinction between virtuous and vicious actions has been engraven by the Lord on the heart of every man. *John Calvin*

If there were no God, consciences were useless.
John Calvin

When men turn their back on God's revelation in Scripture he still sets the truth of it in their hearts.
Michael Green

Conscience is that candle of the Lord which was not quite put out.
Matthew Henry

Conscience hath somewhat divine in it.
Richard Sibbes

Conscience – and God

Conscience is God's vicar.
Richard Sibbes

Conscience is a mirror of God's holiness.
Augustus H. Strong

Conscience is the deputy-deity in the little world, man. *George Swinnock*

Conscience is God's spy and man's overseer.
John Trapp

If there were no Bible to tell us there is a God, yet conscience might.
Thomas Watson

A good conscience is the palace of Christ, the temple of the Holy Ghost, the paradise of delight, the standing sabbath of the saints. *Augustine*

A good conscience is the inseparable attendant of faith. *John Calvin*

Of all human experiences, the most universal is a bad conscience. *James Denney*

Most of us follow our conscience as we follow a wheelbarrow; we push it in front of us in the direction we want to go.
Billy Graham

CONSCIENCE–Importance

Conscience is to the soul as the stomach is to the body. *Thomas Adams*

Knowledge directs conscience; conscience perfects knowledge.
Thomas Adams

A good conscience is a soft pillow. *Anon.*

Conscience warns us as a friend before it punishes us as a judge. *Anon.*

Conscience is a man's judgement of himself, according to the judgement of God of him. *Thomas Aquinas*

Better to have a dog that will, by his barking, tell us a thief is in our yard, than one that will sit still and let us be robbed before we have any notice of our danger. *William Gurnall*

Peace of conscience is but a discharge under God's hand that the debt due to divine justice is fully paid. *William Gurnall*

Peace of conscience is nothing but the echo of pardoning mercy.
William Gurnall

Happy is that man who can be acquitted by himself

in private, by others in public and by God in both.
Joseph Hall

Conscience is a living thing, subject to growth and development.
Ole Hallesby

If we take care to keep a good conscience, we may leave it to God to take care of our good name.
Matthew Henry

Never was the voice of conscience silenced without retribution.
Anna Jameson

Cleanse your conscience and your faith will be out of danger. *William Jenkyn*

A good conscience is the best treasure ever held, the best pleasure ever tasted, the best honour ever conferred.
William S. Plumer

Cowardice asks, 'Is it safe?' Expediency asks, 'Is it politic?' Vanity asks, 'Is it popular?' Conscience asks, 'Is it *right*?'
William Morley Punshon

Money dishonestly acquired is never worth its cost, while a good conscience never costs as much as it is worth. *J. P. Senn*

We can do nothing well without joy, and a good conscience which is the ground of joy.
Richard Sibbes

Trust that man in nothing who has not a conscience in everything.
Lawrence Sterne

No flattery can heal a bad conscience, so no slander can hurt a good one. *Thomas Watson*

Preserve your conscience always soft and sensitive. If but one sin force its way into that tender part of the soul and is suffered to dwell there, the road is paved for a thousand iniquities. *Isaac Watts*

CONSCIENCE – Power

A guilty conscience is like a whirlpool, drawing in all to itself which would otherwise pass by.
Thomas Fuller

An evil conscience is like a raging sea, which can only be calmed by the sign of the cross of Christ. It is a gnawing worm in the bones, for the removal of which nothing less is required than the blood of the Son of God.
Friedrich Krummacher

A gnawing conscience keeps the memory terribly alert.
W. E. Sangster

Our consciences tell us that we might have done a great deal better than we have. *Richard Sibbes*

CONSCIENCE – and Sin

A guilty conscience is a hell on earth, and points to one beyond. *Anon.*

A guilty conscience needs no accuser. *Anon.*

Neglect of duty will never get guilt off the conscience.
Thomas Brooks

The torture of a bad conscience is the hell of a living soul. *John Calvin*

The greatest violation of conscience is the greatest of sins. *John Flavel*

All the floods of sin can never extinguish God's love to his people; but one single drop of sin upon the believer's conscience will extinguish his peace.
William Mason

Many a man has enough conscience to scare him in sin, but not enough to save him from sin. *C. H. Spurgeon*

Sin makes sad convulsions in the conscience.
Thomas Watson

CONSECRATION

(See also: Abandonment; Submission; Zeal)

Consecration is resolution that is not afraid of sacrifice. *Anon.*

Henceforth may no profane
delight
Divide this consecrated soul;
Possess it thou, who hast
the right,
As Lord and Master of the
whole.
Antoinette Bourignon

The body has two eyes, but the soul must have but one. *William Secker*

CONTENTMENT

The Bible teaches us to be content with what we have but never with what we are.

The Christian is called upon to make his material possessions immaterial.

A contented mind is a continual feast. *Anon.*

Let your riches consist, not in the largeness of your possessions, but in the fewness of your wants.
Anon.

It is the best riches not to desire riches.
Thomas Brooks

Content makes poor men rich; discontent makes rich men poor.
Benjamin Franklin

Contentment consisteth not in adding more fuel, but in taking away some fire; not in multiplying of wealth, but in subtracting men's desires. *Thomas Fuller*

The holy person is the only contented man in the world.
William Gurnall

He is much happier that is always content, though he has ever so little, than he that is always coveting, though he has ever so much. *Matthew Henry*

The wealthiest man is he who is contented with least.
Socrates

No chance is evil to him that is content.
Jeremy Taylor

There is no better antidote against coveting that which is another's than being content with that which is our own.
Thomas Watson

CONTRITION

(See also: Confession; Conviction of Sin; Penitence; Repentance)

God can do wonders with a broken heart if you give him all the pieces.
Victor Alfsen

Godly sorrow is a gift from God. No hand but a divine hand can make the heart soft and tender under the sight and sense of sin. *Thomas Brooks*

The broken heart is the only sound heart.
John Trapp

CONTROVERSY

Dissolution is the daughter of dissension.
Thomas Brooks

Christianity cannot flourish in a time of strife and contention among its professors. *Jonathan Edwards*

The worst thing we can bring to a religious controversy is anger.
Matthew Henry

Division has done more to hide Christ from the view of men than all the infidelity that has ever been spoken.

George MacDonald

The itch of disputing and zeal for an opinion, rather than religion in the main, are bad characters.

Thomas Manton

I have never yet known the Spirit of God to work where the Lord's people were divided.

D. L. Moody

I have other things to do than to be a contentious man. *John Penry*

Fractions always breed factions. *Richard Sibbes*

The devil loves to fish in troubled waters.

John Trapp

It is not controversy we have to dread so much as the spirit of controversy.

Richard Treffry

CONVERSION

(See also: Faith-Saving; Regeneration; Repentance)

Conversion is a deep work—a heart-work. It goes throughout the man, throughout the mind, throughout the members, throughout the entire life.

Joseph Alleine

Nature forms us; sin deforms us; school informs us; Christ transforms us.

Anon.

Man is not converted because he wills to be, but he wills to be because he is ordained to election.

Augustine

I remember this, that everything looked new to me . . . the fields, the cattle, the trees. I was like a new man in a new world.

Billy Bray

Conversion is not the smooth, easy-going process some men seem to think it, otherwise man's heart would never have been compared to fallow ground and God's Word to a plough. *John Bunyan*

Regeneration is a spiritual change; conversion is a spiritual motion.

Stephen Charnock

Conversion is but the first step in the divine life. As long as we live we should more and more be turning from all that is evil and to all that is good.

Tryon Edwards

Consideration is the first step towards conversion.
Matthew Henry

If no conversion, no salvation. *Matthew Henry*

Regeneration is a single act, complete in itself, and never repeated; conversion, as the beginning of holy living, is the commencement of a series, constant, endless and progressive.
A. A. Hodge

The almighty power of God in the conversion of a sinner is the most mysterious of all the works of God. *Thomas Hooker*

Conversions need to be weighed as well as counted.
Joseph Parker

I found that I was not only converted, but I was invaded. *Eugenia Price*

True conversion gives a man security, but it does not allow him to leave off being watchful.
C. H. Spurgeon

True conversion gives a man strength and holiness, but it never lets him boast.
C. H. Spurgeon

When the Word of God converts a man, it takes away from him his despair, but it does not take from him his repentance.
C. H. Spurgeon

CONVICTION OF SIN

(See also: Confession; Contrition; Penitence; Repentance)

It is a universal law of the higher life that the better a man becomes, the more sensitive he is to sin. *Anon.*

As the heart is more washed, we grow more sensible of its remaining defilement; just as we are more displeased with a single spot on a new coat than with a hundred stains on an old one.
John Berridge

No man begins to be good till he sees himself to be bad. *Thomas Brooks*

The greater the saint, the greater the sense of sinfulness. *G. B. Duncan*

Christ is not sweet till sin be made bitter to us.
John Flavel

Conviction of sin is conviction of sinnership . . . it is a conviction of a wrong relationship with God, of falling completely short of what man is meant to be. *Bryan Green*

When men begin to complain more of their sins than of their afflictions then there begins to be some hope of them.
Matthew Henry

I have no other name than sinner; sinner is my name, sinner is my surname. *Martin Luther*

The recognition of sin is the beginning of salvation.
Martin Luther

You cannot command convictions of sin to come when you like.
Robert Murray M'Cheyne

Conviction of sin is essentially an awareness of a wrong relationship with God. *J. I. Packer*

In review of God's manifold blessings, the thing I most seem to thank him for is the conviction of sin. *Friedrich Tholuck*

Until a man has got into trouble with his heart he is not likely to get out of trouble with God.
A. W. Tozer

No man can feel sin, but by grace. *Thomas Watson*

COURAGE

Courage is fear that has said its prayers. *Anon.*

Bravery is not the absence of fear, but the mastery of it. *Anon.*

Courage is absolutely necessary for goodness.
Richard Glover

I fear not the tyranny of man, neither yet what the devil can invent against me. *John Knox*

Courage consists not in hazarding without fear, but being resolutely minded in a just cause. *Plutarch*

COVENANT

Every breach of peace with God is not a breach of covenant with God.
Thomas Brooks

The covenant of grace is the saint's original title to heaven.
Thomas Brooks

The whole covenant is a bundle of promises.
Thomas Brooks

The bond of the covenant is able to bear the weight

of the believer's heaviest burden. *William S. Plumer*

COVETOUSNESS

(See also: Gluttony; Greed)

Charity gives itself rich; covetousness hoards itself poor. *Anon.*

Much trouble is caused by our yearnings getting ahead of our earnings. *Anon.*

Covetousness is the blight that is withering our church life in all directions.
Samuel Chadwick

He is much happier that is always content, though he has ever so little, than he that is always coveting, though he has ever so much. *Matthew Henry*

The soul of man is infinite in what it covets.
Ben Jonson

Beware . . . of the beginnings of covetousness, for you know not where it will end. *Thomas Manton*

One can be covetous when he has little, much, or anything between, for covetousness comes from the heart, not from the circumstances of life.
Charles Caldwell Ryrie

Covetousness is both the beginning and the end of the devil's alphabet – the first vice in corrupt nature that moves, and the last which dies. *Robert South*

Covetousness is dry drunkenness. *Thomas Watson*

There is no better antidote against coveting that which is another's than being content with that which is our own.
Thomas Watson

The itch of covetousness makes a man scratch what he can from another.
Thomas Watson

I have heard thousands of confessions, but never one of covetousness.
Francis Xavier

COWARDICE

There are times when silence is golden, but there are also times when it is just plain yellow.

A coward is one who in perilous emergency thinks with his legs.
Ambrose Bierce

A dog barks when his master is attacked. I would

be a coward if I saw that God's truth is attacked and yet would remain silent, without giving any sound.
John Calvin

Many that are swift-footed enough when there is no danger are cow-hearted when there is.
Matthew Henry

Some people deliberately avoid anything that may lead them to the divine encounter. *J. B. Phillips*

I can't abide cowardice. I refuse to make my God and Saviour a nonentity.
C. T. Studd

He is a base servant that is ashamed of his lord's livery. *George Swinnock*

CREATION

(See also: Evolution; Nature)

The solitary, sublime, simple reason the Bible gives for the existence of everything in all creation is that it came into being by God's will, because he chose that it should. For the unbeliever, no further explanation is possible; for the believer none is necessary.

The Himalayas are the raised letters upon which we blind children put our fingers to spell out the name of God.
J. H. Barrows

God is not a copyist – the devil is that because he can be no other: but everything God makes is original. *John Caiger*

The probability of life originating by accident is comparable to the probability of the complete dictionary resulting from an explosion in a printing factory. *Edwin Conklin*

If a universe could create itself, it would embody the powers of a creator, and we should be forced to conclude that the universe itself is a god.
George Davis

All I have seen teaches me to trust the Creator for all I have not seen.
Ralph Waldo Emerson

Every work of God serves to display his glory, and set off the greatness of his majesty. *John Gill*

There never was a theory of the universe that did not need a god to make it go.
James Clerk Maxwell

The argument from design is irresistible. Nature does testify to its Creator.
John Stuart Mill

Nobody can plead that he is ignorant of the existence of God. It can clearly be seen that there is an Unseen. *Stuart Olyott*

Posterity will some day laugh at the foolishness of modern materialistic philosophy. The more I study nature, the more I am amazed at the Creator.
Louis Pasteur

Every one of God's works is in its way *great.* All angels and all men united could not make one grasshopper. *William S. Plumer*

The supreme justification for all creation is that God has willed it to be.
Hans Rookmaaker

That the universe was formed by a fortuitous concourse of atoms, I will no more believe than that the accidental jumbling of the alphabet would fall into a most ingenious treatise of philosophy.
Jonathan Swift

What can be more foolish than to think that all this rare fabric of heaven and earth could come by chance, when all the skill of art is not able to make an oyster? *Jeremy Taylor*

The creation is both a monument of God's power and a looking-glass in which we may see his wisdom.
Thomas Watson

To create requires infinite power. All the world cannot make a fly.
Thomas Watson

CRITICISM BY OTHERS

(See also: Criticism of Others)

Never be afraid to test yourself by your critic's words.

If men speak ill of you, live so that no one will believe them. *Anon.*

It is just as much a Christian's duty to avoid taking offence as it is to avoid giving offence. *Anon.*

I had rather that true and faithful teachers should rebuke and condemn me, and reprove my ways, than that hypocrites should flatter me and applaud me as a saint. *Martin Luther*

Slander has a marvellous way of driving us into the arms of our heavenly Father.
Stuart Olyott

Criticism by Others

When people kick us, it is sometimes a sign that we are in front of them.
Percy Ray

If you were not strangers here the dogs of the world would not bark at you.
Samuel Rutherford

To be irritated by criticism is to acknowledge it was deserved. *Tacitus*

CRITICISM OF OTHERS

(See also: Criticism by Others; Fault-Finding)

Remember that whenever you throw mud at somebody you lose ground.

The man who seems unusually concerned with the demotion of others is usually concerned with the promotion of himself.

Blowing out the other fellow's candle doesn't make yours shine any brighter. *Anon.*

Never put your finger on someone's faults unless it is part of a helping hand.
Anon.

The best place to criticize your neighbour is in front of your own mirror. *Anon.*

The critic who starts with himself will have no time to take on outside contracts. *Anon.*

Christians would never dream of intentionally running down other people with their cars; then why do we do it with our tongues? *Doug Barnett*

It is much easier to be critical than to be correct.
Benjamin Disraeli

Clean your fingers before you point at my spots.
Benjamin Franklin

None are such critics of small faults as those guilty of grave ones.
Richard Glover

Unless we are willing to help a person overcome his faults, there is little value in pointing them out. *Robert J. Hastings*

Two things are very bad for the heart – running up stairs and running down people. *C. A. Joyce*

God has a habit of saving people in ways I especially dislike, therefore I have to be careful what I say.
C. S. Lewis

The man that is most busy in censuring others is always least employed in examining himself. *Thomas Lye*

Criticism is asserted superiority. *Henry E. Manning*

Censuring is a pleasing sin, extremely compliant with nature. *Thomas Manton*

I would rather play with the forked lightning, or take in my hands living wires with their fiery current, than speak a reckless word against any servant of Christ.
A. B. Simpson

Stoning prophets is poor work. *Harold St John*

A desire to disgrace others never sprang from grace.
George Swinnock

There is no readier way for a man to bring his own worth into question, than by endeavouring to detract from the worth of other men. *John Tillotson*

CROSS

(See also: Atonement; Jesus Christ—Death)

The cross of Christ will always be an offence to the natural man.

The cross is the cost of my forgiveness. *Anon.*

The righteous One upon the cross is the sinner's only point of contact with the saving power of God.
Lewis Sperry Chafer

Freed to draw by its own power, the cross remains the magnet of the souls of men. *Kenneth Cragg*

The wonder of the cross is not the blood, but *whose* blood, and to what purpose.
Donald English

There is not a word in the Bible which is *extra crucem,* which can be understood without reference to the cross.
Martin Luther

The cross is the centre of the world's history. The incarnation of Christ and the crucifixion of our Lord are the pivot round which all the events of the ages revolve.
Alexander MacLaren

Nobody who has truly seen the cross of Christ can ever again speak of hopeless cases.
G. Campbell Morgan

Christianity is a religion about a cross. *Leon Morris*

The saving power of the cross does not depend on faith being added to it; its saving power is such that faith flows from it. *J. I. Packer*

This one event of the cross of Christ is a final revelation both of the character and consequence of human sin and of the wonder and sacrifice of divine love. *Alan Stibbs*

The cross is the resting-place for sin, the tomb for self and the throne for our fears.
Harold St John

The cross of Christ is the most revolutionary thing ever to appear among men. *A. W. Tozer*

Calvary shows how far men will go in sin, and how far God will go for man's salvation.
H. C. Trumbull

DEATH – Anticipation

Lord, give me Simeon's dismissal: Christ in my arms. *Andrew Bonar*

Ah! Is this dying? How have I dreaded as an enemy this smiling friend!
Thomas Goodwin

He whose head is in heaven need not fear to put his feet into the grave.
Matthew Henry

When Christ calls me home I shall go with the gladness of a boy bounding away from school.
Adoniram Judson

This is my coronation day. I have been looking forward to it for years.
D. L. Moody

I am packed, sealed and waiting for the post.
John Newton

Through Christ death is become friendly to me.
Richard Sibbes

If I may die as I have seen some die, I court the grand occasion. I would not wish to escape death by some by-road if I may sing as they sang.
C. H. Spurgeon

Be sure to celebrate my funeral scripturally and send Hallelujahs all round. It is a better day than one's wedding day.
C. T. Studd

I lie down in comfort at night, not being anxious whether I awake in this world or another.
Isaac Watts

Lord, keep me from a sinful and too eager desire after death. I desire not to be impatient. I wish quietly to wait till my blessed change comes.

George Whitefield

My gems are falling away; but it is because God is making up his jewels.

Charles Wolfe

My happiest moment will be when God puts his hand on my heart and stops it beating.

Arthur S. Wood

DEATH – Blessings

Death for the Christian is an honourable discharge from the battles of life.

Anon.

Death is but a physical incident in an immortal career. *Anon.*

Death is not extinguishing the light; it is putting out the lamp because the dawn has come. *Anon.*

What is death but the burial of vices? *Ambrose*

When death becomes the property of the believer it receives a new name and is called sleep.

William Arnot

A believer's last day is his best day.

Thomas Brooks

Death is a blessing insomuch as it puts an end to all temptation.

François Fenelon

Dying saints may be justly envied, while living sinners are justly pitied.

Matthew Henry

Death is the foreshadowing of life. We die that we may die no more.

Thomas Hooker

By death I shall escape from death.

James Montgomery

Death is not so much something which happens to the Christian as something God works for him.

J. A. Motyer

Death mingles sceptres with spades. *William S. Plumer*

Satan may chase him to the gates of death, but he cannot pursue the Christian *through* the gates.

David C. Potter

A dying man is a balloon throwing down its ballast.

Petit Senn

Death is not now the death of me, but death will be the death of my misery, the death of my sins; it will be the death of my corruptions. But death will be my birthday in regard of happiness.
Richard Sibbes

To the Christian, death is an exodus, an unmooring, a home-coming. Here, we are as ships on the stocks; at death, we are launched into our true element.
Augustus H. Strong

Death is the funeral of all our sorrows.
Thomas Watson

At a funeral we bury something not someone; it is the house not the tenant that is lowered into the grave. *Verna Wright*

As many pores as there are in the skin, so many windows there are for death to enter at.
Thomas Brooks

Our death was bred when our life was first conceived.
William Gurnall

We can as soon run from ourselves as run from death.
William Gurnall

Righteousness delivers from the sting of death, but not from the stroke of it.
Matthew Henry

Every man must do two things alone: he must do his own believing, and his own dying. *Martin Luther*

One out of one dies.
George Bernard Shaw

DEATH – Certainty

Death is the greatest fact of life.

We are not here to stay; we are here to go.

All the world is a hospital and every person in it a terminal patient. *Anon.*

DEATH – and Heaven

Death does not put our relationship with God into the past tense.

When death strikes the Christian down, he falls into heaven.

Death for the Christian is not a miserable cul-de-sac, but a glorious open road into the presence of God.
Doug Barnett

Death to a saint is nothing but the taking of a sweet flower out of this wilderness, and planting of it in the garden of paradise.
Thomas Brooks

It is no credit to your heavenly Father for you to be loath to go home.
Thomas Brooks

Death is but a passage out of a prison into a palace.
John Bunyan

To the Christian death has redemptive significance. It is the portal through which we enter the presence of our Lord.
Hilys Jasper

The grave has a door on its inner side.
Alexander MacLaren

Some day you will read in the papers that D. L. Moody, of East Northfield, is dead. Don't you believe a word of it! At that moment I shall be more alive than I am now.
D. L. Moody

Shall I be afraid to die, when in death I commend my soul to such a sweet Lord, and go to my Husband and to my King?
Richard Sibbes

The belief that we shall never die is the foundation of our dying well.
François Turretin

The dust of a believer is part of Christ's mystic body. *Thomas Watson*

DEATH – Indiscriminate

Death takes away the difference between king and beggar, and tumbles both the knight and the pawn into one bag.
Thomas Adams

Death is oftentimes as near to the young man's back as it is to the old man's face.
Thomas Brooks

Death, which levels all men, is the most effective sermon for earthly rulers.
Friedrich Tholuck

DEATH – and Judgement

At death we leave behind all we have and take with us all we are. *Anon.*

As death leaves us, so judgement will find us.
Thomas Brooks

The character wherewith we sink into the grave at death is the very character

wherewith we shall reappear at the resurrection.
Thomas Chalmers

It is no miracle if he that lives like a beast dies like a beast. *Francis Cheynell*

If the second birth hath no place in you, the second death shall have power over you. *William Dyer*

Death . . . strips the soul of all the disguises wherein it appeared before men, that it may appear naked and open before God. Our grave-clothes are night-clothes. *Matthew Henry*

Death and what is beyond it will show who is wise and who is a fool.
William S. Plumer

Death brings with it the exposure of our entire life.
Basilea Schlink

Just as the tree cut down,
that falls
To north or southward,
there it lies;
So man departs to heav'n
or hell,
Fix'd in the state wherein
he dies.
Isaac Watts

One may live as a conqueror, a king or a magistrate; but he must die as a man.
Daniel Webster

DEATH – Meaning

The very existence of the fear of death, which is the root of practically all human fears, is a clear indication that death is unnatural even though its incidence is universal.
Akbar Abdul-Haqq

Were it not for sin, death had never had a beginning, and were it not for death sin would never have had an ending. *William Dyer*

Death is as due to a sinner as wages are to a servant.
Matthew Henry

Death is not part of the natural process, but is the judgement of God on sin.
Peter Misselbrook

Death is not extinction in any uses of the word. It is always separation.
Charles Caldwell Ryrie

DEATH – Preparation for

If men are prepared to die they are ready for anything.
Joseph Addison Alexander

There is nothing more certain than death, nothing more uncertain than the time of dying. I will therefore be prepared at all times for that which may come at any time. *Anon.*

Until you are free to die, you are not free to live.
Anon.

It is never too soon to begin to make friends with death.
Anon.

Look upon death as a thing you must meet with; look upon yourselves as a thing you must part with.
William Dyer

It ought to be the business of every day to prepare for our last day.
Matthew Henry

Where you die, when you die, or by what means, is scarcely worth a thought, if you do but die in Christ.
Rowland Hill

When death comes, have nothing to do, but just to die. *Henry Law*

Live mindful of death – it will have a mighty tendency to make you serious, discreet and industrious.
Cotton Mather

How many Christians live their lives packed up and ready to go? *J. I. Packer*

Above all things, let us every day think of our last day. *Pachomius*

Live so that when death comes you may embrace like friends, not encounter like enemies.
Francis Quarles

It is an easy matter for one to die that hath died in heart and affection before. *Richard Sibbes*

He who does not prepare for death is more than an ordinary fool. He is a madman. *C. H. Spurgeon*

If thou would'st die comfortably, live conscientiously. *George Swinnock*

He may look on death with joy who can look on forgiveness with faith.
Thomas Watson

Take care of your life and the Lord will take care of your death.
George Whitefield

DEATH – Triumph over

Death may be the king of terrors but Jesus is the King of kings. *Anon.*

Death – Triumph over

Christians out-die pagans and the resurrection of Christ is the reason.
T. R. Glover

Death stung himself to death when he stung Christ. *William Romaine*

No Christian has ever been known to recant on his deathbed. *C. M. Ward*

DEPRAVITY

(See also: Guilt; Man – a Sinner; Sin; Sinful Nature)

An unconverted person is deliberately off course.

We are born in sin and spend our lives coping with the consequences.

Since man is depraved, he will not ask ultimate questions until he is dislodged from his temporal illusion.
Anon.

We all come from the same mould – and some of us are mouldier than others!
Anon.

At the Fall, man's natural gifts were corrupted through sin, while his supernatural gifts were entirely lost. *Augustine*

There is the seed of all sins – of the vilest and worst of sins – in the best of men.
Thomas Brooks

Man naturally is apt to crown anything but Christ.
Thomas Brooks

Our corrupted hearts are the factories of the devil.
Thomas Browne

We owe our creation to God, our corruption to ourselves.
Stephen Charnock

When I look into my heart, and take a view of my wickedness, it looks like an abyss infinitely deeper than hell.
Jonathan Edwards

As we get to know ourselves better we always find ourselves to be more depraved than we thought.
François Fenelon

Man is not evolving upwards towards a knowledge of God. He was created with a knowledge of God and has been going the other way ever since.
Vance Havner

Grace does not run in the blood, but corruption does.

A sinner begets a sinner, but a saint does not beget a saint. *Matthew Henry*

Man was born and lives in sin. He cannot do anything for himself but can only do harm to himself.
Soren Kierkegaard

If it were left to sinners, totally depraved as they are, to respond of their own volition to the gospel in faith, not one would respond. *R. B. Kuiper*

So great is the depravity of unregenerate man that, although there is nothing that he needs more than the gospel, there is nothing that he desires less.
R. B. Kuiper

Original sin is in us, like the beard. We are shaved today and look clean, and have a smooth chin; tomorrow our beard has grown again, nor does it cease growing while we remain on earth. In like manner original sin cannot be extirpated from us; it springs up in us as long as we live. *Martin Luther*

Total depravity means . . . that conversion is beyond the capacity of the natural man. *Donald MacLeod*

We are born unrighteous; for each one tends to himself, and the bent toward self is the beginning of all disorder.
Blaise Pascal

Man's deepest problems lie within himself.
Clark Pinnock

If God were not omniscient (the human heart) would deceive *him*.
William S. Plumer

It is in our hearts that the evil lies, and it is from our hearts that it must be plucked out.
Bertrand Russell

There never yet was a mother who taught her child to be an infidel.
Henry W. Shaw

Alas! Our heart is our greatest enemy.
C. H. Spurgeon

Man is a double-dyed villain. He is corrupted by nature and afterwards by practice.
Augustus H. Strong

Depravity is the great hindrance to faith, but . . . grace is God's way of overcoming the hindrance. *Malcolm Watts*

DEPRESSION

(See also: Despair)

Our feelings of depression and despair tell more about ourselves than about the way things really are.

Anon.

The Christian's chief occupational hazards are depression and discouragement. *John R. W. Stott*

DESIRES

(See also: Lust)

A wise man will desire no more than he may get justly, use soberly, distribute cheerfully and leave contentedly. *Anon.*

We often desire most what we ought not to have.

Anon.

A Christian's life is a state of holy desire. *Jerome*

The habitual inclination of heart in believers is unto good, unto God, unto holiness, unto obedience.

John Owen

If all our wishes were gratified, most of our pleasures would be destroyed.

Richard Whateley

DESPAIR

(See also: Depression)

Despair is hope stark dead, as presumption is hope stark mad.

Thomas Adams

Despair is Satan's masterpiece; it carries men headlong to hell as the devils did the herd of swine into the deep.

Thomas Brooks

Despair is the damp of hell, as joy is the serenity of heaven. *John Donne*

He that despairs degrades the Deity. *Owen Feltham*

I will never despair, because I have a God; I will never presume, because I am but a man.

Owen Feltham

You may despair of yourself as much as you like, but never of God.

François Fenelon

God does not despair of you, therefore you ought not to despair of yourself.

C. C. Grafton

Hopeless and lifeless go together.

William Gurnall

It is impossible for that man to despair who remembers that his Helper is omnipotent.
Jeremy Taylor

Despair is Satan's masterpiece. *John Trapp*

Despair cuts the sinews of endeavour.
Thomas Watson

Let us never despair while we have Christ as our leader! *George Whitefield*

DETERMINATION

(See also: Perseverance)

It is not theology that makes a man of valour what he is, but 'plodology'! *Leslie Carter*

Christ wants not nibblers at the possible, but grabbers of the impossible.
C. T. Studd

DIFFICULTIES

When problems get Christians praying they do more good than harm.

Difficulties are God's errands; and when we are sent upon them we should esteem it a proof of God's confidence – as a compliment from God.
Henry Ward Beecher

There are no difficulties with God. Difficulties wholly exist in our own unbelieving minds.
Thomas Charles

It is difficulties which show what men are. *Epictetus*

Difficulties prove men.
Johannes Von Goethe

DISAPPOINTMENTS

We mount to heaven mostly on the ruins of our cherished schemes, finding our failures were successes.
A. B. Alcott

Disappointments are *his* appointments. *Anon.*

There are no disappointments to those whose wills are buried in the will of God. *Frederick W. Faber*

In the light of eternity we shall see that what we desired would have been fatal to us, and that what we would have avoided was essential to our well-being. *François Fenelon*

There is many a thing which the world calls disappointment, but there is no such a word in the dictionary of faith. What to others are disappointments are to believers intimations of the way of God.
John Newton

Disappointment is often the salt of life.
Theodore Parker

DISCIPLESHIP

It costs to follow Jesus Christ, but it costs more not to. *Anon.*

Salvation without discipleship is 'cheap grace'.
Dietrich Bonhoeffer

To leave all and follow Christ is the biggest thing that a living soul on this earth can do.
A. Lindsay Glegg

Jesus promised his disciples three things – that they would be completely fearless, absurdly happy and in constant trouble.
F. R. Maltby

A disciple is a person who learns to live the life his teacher lives.
Juan Carlos Ortiz

Discipleship is more than getting to know what the teacher knows. It is getting to be what he is.
Juan Carlos Ortiz

The making of a disciple means the creating of a duplicate.
Juan Carlos Ortiz

The new Christian is like a man who has learned to drive in a country where the traffic moves on the left side of the highway and suddenly finds himself in another country and forced to drive on the right. He must unlearn his old habit and learn a new one and, more serious than all, he must learn in heavy traffic. *A. W. Tozer*

DISHONESTY

(See also: Lying)

One of the marks of spiritual rebellion is deviousness.
Ian Barclay

Nothing is more offensive to God than deceit in commerce. *Matthew Henry*

That which is won ill will never wear well.
Matthew Henry

No wickedness on earth is more common than the

various forms of deceit.
William S. Plumer

To depart from the truth affords a testimony that one first despises God and then fears man. *Plutarch*

If there were no law against thieving most of us would be thieves.
Bertrand Russell

Every time a Christian cheats on his Income Tax he perverts and obscures the gospel.
John Sanderson

Oh! what a tangled web we weave
When first we practise to deceive!
Walter Scott

Money dishonestly acquired is never worth its cost, while a good conscience never costs as much as it is worth. *J. P. Senn*

An honest death is better than a dishonest life.
Socrates

DOCTRINE

(See also: Theology)

Doctrinal indifference is no solution to the problem of doctrinal differences.

The question is not whether a doctrine is beautiful, but whether it is true. *Anon.*

The doctrines of Christianity have just as much right to be believed as its duties have to be practised.
M. Arnaud

If you believe what you like in the gospel, and reject what you like, it is not the gospel you believe, but yourself. *Augustine*

Doctrine is practical, for it is that that stirs up the heart. *Andrew Bonar*

Doctrine is not an affair of the tongue but of the life . . . It is received only when it possesses the whole soul. *John Calvin*

How humbling it is to all learning when a man is made to know that his doctrine has outrun his experiences!
Thomas Chalmers

Doctrine without duty is a tree without fruits; duty without doctrine is a tree without roots.
Talbot W. Chambers

Some things we trust God with, some things God trusts us with . . . That

which God trusts us chiefly with is his truth.
William Gurnall

The plainest truths are sometimes the strongest arguments for the hardest duties. *Matthew Henry*

The doctrines of the Bible are not isolated but interlaced; and the view of one doctrine must necessarily affect the view taken of another. *A. A. Hodge*

Let us embrace the whole truth, or renounce Christianity altogether.
Joseph Irons

You cannot drop the big themes and create great saints. *John Henry Jowett*

Today's church . . . has no more solemn duty than to maintain purity of doctrine. *R. B. Kuiper*

To say, 'Never mind doctrine, let's get on with evangelism' is as ridiculous as a football team saying, 'Never mind about a ball, let's get on with the game.'
Peter Lewis

Any teaching which does not square with the Scriptures is to be rejected even if it snows miracles every day. *Martin Luther*

The end for which God instructs the mind is that he might transform the life. *Al Martin*

Weak doctrines will not be a match for powerful temptations.
William S. Plumer

If we do not make clear by word and by practice our position *for* truth and *against* false doctrine we are building a wall between the next generation and the gospel.
Francis Schaeffer

He that believes ill can never live well, for he hath no foundation.
Richard Sibbes

Men to be truly won must be won by truth.
C. H. Spurgeon

The purpose behind all doctrine is to secure moral action. *A. W. Tozer*

DOUBT

(See also: Uncertainty)

For too many Christians, vagueness is the vogue; all they have is the courage of their confusions.
Anon.

All doubts are not honest.
Victor Budgen

The doubter can't find God for the same reason that a thief can't find a policeman. *Robert Cleath*

Believe your beliefs and doubt your doubts; do not make the mistake of doubting your beliefs and believing your doubts.
Charles F. Deems

Never doubt in the dark what God told you in the light.
V. Raymond Edman

Doubters invert the metaphor and insist that they need faith as big as a mountain in order to move a mustard seed.
Webb B. Garrison

Give me the benefit of your convictions, if you have any. Keep your doubts to yourself; I have enough of my own.
Johannes Von Goethe

Doubt indulged soon becomes doubt realized.
Frances Ridley Havergal

The art of doubting is easy, for it is an ability that is born with us.
Martin Luther

Doubt is brother devil to despair.
John Boyle O'Reilly

Satan loves to fish in muddy water.
William S. Plumer

Men who wrap themselves in question marks cannot crusade.
David K. Wachtel

Man is not made to question, but adore.
Edward Young

DRUNKENNESS

(See also: Alcohol)

Drunkenness unmans the man. *Thomas Brooks*

The sight of a drunkard is a better sermon against that vice than the best sermon that was ever preached on that subject.
Sarah E. Saville

Drunkenness is nothing else but a voluntary madness.
Seneca

Drunkenness places man as much below the level of the brutes, as reason elevates him above them.
John Sinclair

Drunken porters keep open gates. *Henry Smith*

DUTY

(See also: Responsibility; Service)

Duties delayed are the devil's delight. *Anon.*

If God gives himself to us in promises, we must give ourselves to him in duties. *Anon.*

The Christian's privileges lie in pronouns; but his duty in adverbs. *Anon.*

Duty makes us do things well, but love makes us do them beautifully.
Phillips Brooks

It is your duty and glory to do that every day that you would willingly do on a dying day.
Thomas Brooks

Neglect of duty will never get guilt off the conscience.
Thomas Brooks

Doctrine without duty is a tree without fruits; duty without doctrine is a tree without roots.
Talbot W. Chambers

Eternity cannot free us from duty.
Stephen Charnock

If we once become listless to duty, we shall quickly become lifeless in it. *Stephen Charnock*

The reward of one duty done is the power to do another. *George Eliot*

Those who give to God only the shadow of duty can never expect from him a real reward.
John Flavel

He that leaves a duty may soon be left to commit a crime. *William Gurnall*

Never did the holy God give a privilege where he did not expect a duty.
Joseph Hall

No pretence of humility must make us decline our duty. *Matthew Henry*

When the law of God is written in our hearts, our duty will be our delight.
Matthew Henry

Let us not run out of the path of duty lest we run into the way of danger.
Rowland Hill

You would not think any duty small if you yourself were great.
George MacDonald

Ability involves responsibility. Power to its last participle is duty.
Alexander MacLaren

Who escapes a duty, avoids a gain. *Theodore Parker*

Duty fits the heart for duty. *George Swinnock*

EARNESTNESS

(See also: Enthusiasm; Zeal)

Execute every act of thy life as if it were thy last.
Marcus Aurelius

Earnestness is the devotion of all the faculties.
C. N. Bovee

It is your duty and glory to do that every day that you would willingly do on a dying day.
Thomas Brooks

The kingdom of God is not for the well meaning, but for the desperate.
James Denney

Don't touch Christianity unless you mean business. I promise you a miserable existence if you do.
Henry Drummond

Earnestness is the salt of eloquence. *Victor Hugo*

Earnestness is enthusiasm tempered by reason.
Blaise Pascal

EDUCATION

(See also: Knowledge; Mind; Reason)

Education without religion, as useful as it is, seems rather to make man a more clever devil. *C. S. Lewis*

When you educate a man in mind and not in morals you educate a menace to society.
Franklin D. Roosevelt

EGOTISM

(See also: Conceit; Pride)

An egotist is a person who is his own best friend.
Anon.

Egotism is obesity of the head. *Anon.*

ELECTION – and Calling

As Christians we ought always to remember that the Lord called us to himself not because of our virtues, but in spite of our vices.

Christians are a select minority – and God has made the selection.

In whatever dunghill God's jewels be hid, election will both find them out there and fetch them out from hence. *John Arrowsmith*

Thou didst seek us when we sought thee not; didst seek us indeed that we might seek thee.
Augustine

Amiable agnostics will talk cheerfully about man's search for God. For me, they might as well talk about the mouse's search for a cat . . . God closed in on me. *C. S. Lewis*

Election is the cause of our vocation and vocation is the sign of our election.
Thomas Watson

It is only as God seeks us that we can be found of him. God is seeker rather than sought.
Arthur Skevington Wood

ELECTION – and Conversion

(See also: Predestination)

You begin at the wrong end if you first dispute about your election. Prove your conversion, and then never doubt your election.
Joseph Alleine

Man is not converted because he wills to be, but he wills to be because he is ordained to election.
Augustine

Election kills at the roots salvation by merits and works. *George S. Bishop*

Every departure from the doctrine of election in any degree has been a departure from the gospel, for such departure always involves the introduction of some obligation on man's part to make a contribution towards his own salvation, a contribution he simply cannot make.
Arthur C. Custance

Oh, happy day, that fixed my choice
On thee, my Saviour and my God!
Well may this glowing heart rejoice,
And tell its raptures all abroad.
Philip Doddridge

The saved are singled out not by their own merits, but by the grace of the Mediator. *Martin Luther*

Let a man go to the grammar school of faith and repentance before he goes to the university of election and predestination.
George Whitefield

ELECTION – and Eternal Security

(See also: Eternal Security)

The Christian's eternal security is rooted not in what he has done, but in where he has been placed.

We do despite to the doctrines of election and predestination when we use them as a kind of theological hand grenade to throw at each other. They are not given to us for that purpose; they are given as mighty stabilizers.

Eric Alexander

As God did not at first choose you because you were high, so he will not forsake you because you are low. *John Flavel*

God's plans reach from an eternity past to an eternity to come. Let him take his own time.

William S. Plumer

God will never cast away his jewels, but gather them into his cabinet of just men made perfect.

William S. Plumer

Salvation is no precarious half-measure but a foundation laid in heaven.

E. K. Simpson

God never repents of his electing love.

Thomas Watson

God's call is founded upon his decree, and his decree is immutable.

Thomas Watson

If once God's electing love rises upon the soul, it never sets.

Thomas Watson

ELECTION – and Faith

If God did not choose some men without any conditions, no man would ever choose God under any conditions.

God chooses us, not because we believe, but that we may believe.

Augustine

Election is not in consequence of faith, but faith is in consequence of election. *C. J. Ellicott*

God does not choose us *for* faith but *to* faith.

Thomas Watson

ELECTION – and Forgiveness

Those who deny election deny that God can have mercy.
Robert Murray M'Cheyne

Who shall the Lord's elect
 condemn?
'Tis God that justifies their
 souls,
And mercy like a mighty
 stream
O'er all their sins divinely
 rolls.
Isaac Watts

ELECTION – and Holiness

No man can prove that he is a child of God without showing the family likeness.

Thou mayest know thou art elect as surely by a work of grace in thee as if thou hadst stood by God's elbow when he writ thy name in the book of life. *William Gurnall*

The calling of God never leaves men where it finds them. *Joseph Hall*

None can know their election but by their conformity to Christ; for all that are chosen are chosen to sanctification.
Matthew Henry

Holiness is the only evidence of election.
Charles Hodge

The doctrines of grace humble a man without degrading him and exalt a man without inflating him. *Charles Hodge*

The Holy Spirit does *something more* in each of God's elect than he does in the non-elect. He works in them 'both to will and to do of God's good pleasure'. *A. W. Pink*

The proof of our election is always and only to be found in a holy life.
William S. Plumer

The Bible speaks of election through sanctification, and predestination to be conformed to the image of the Son of God. If these are lacking, it is a waste of time to speak of election. *J. C. Ryle*

The names and number of the elect are a secret thing, no doubt . . . But if there is one thing clearly and plainly laid down about election, it is this – that elect men and women may

be known and distinguished by holy lives.
J. C. Ryle

It is idle to seek assurance of election outside of holiness of life.
Benjamin B. Warfield

We can never know that we are elected of God to eternal life except by manifesting in our lives the fruits of election.
Benjamin B. Warfield

Sanctification is the earmark of Christ's elect sheep.
Thomas Watson

ELECTION – Mystery of

God's sovereign election is the mould into which the whole universe is poured.

Take away the glorious truth of God's unconditional election and not only would every Christian fall out of the church, but every star would fall out of the sky and every page out of the Bible!

The ground of the discrimination that exists among men is the sovereign will of God and that alone; but the ground of damnation to which the reprobate are consigned is sin and sin alone.
John Calvin

Either God is sovereign and election is an expression of God's will, or man is sovereign and election is an expression of God's foreknowledge.
Arthur C. Custance

God graciously elected some to salvation, and he decreed justly to leave others to their deserts.
R. B. Kuiper

Eternal love devised the plan; eternal wisdom drew the model; eternal grace comes down to build it.
Henry Law

The doctrine of election does not . . . exist in a vacuum. It must be seen in the context of the divine sovereignty, the depravity of man and the givenness of faith.
Donald MacLeod

The Son cannot die for them whom the Father never elected, and the Spirit will never sanctify them whom the Father hath not elected nor the Son redeemed. *Thomas Manton*

Election – Mystery of

We had a Saviour before we were born.

Richard Sibbes

I believe the doctrine of election, because I am quite sure that if God had not chosen me I would never have chosen him; and I am sure he chose me before I was born, or else he never would have chosen me afterward.

C. H. Spurgeon

We may better praise God that he saves any than charge him with injustice because he saves so few.

Augustus H. Strong

The marvel of marvels is not that God, in his infinite love, has not elected all of this guilty race to be saved, but that he has elected any.

Benjamin B. Warfield

ELOQUENCE

(See also: Speech)

Eloquence and ignorance sometimes go together.

True eloquence is vehement simplicity.

Richard Cecil

Eloquence is the transference of thought and emotion from one heart to another, no matter how it is done.

John B. Gough

EMOTIONS

It is certainly true that our faith is not to be based on our feelings – but equally true that if our faith is not accompanied by feelings it is suspect.

If you resolve to make sense and feeling the judge of your conditions, you must resolve to live in fears and lie down in tears. *Thomas Brooks*

When Christ comes in, the wonder is not that one has emotion, but the wonder is that one can be so restrained! *E. Stanley Jones*

Emotion arises out of the truth; emotionalism is poured on to it.

W. R. Maltby

The man who screams at a football game, but is distressed when he hears of a sinner weeping at the cross, and murmurs about the dangers of emotionalism, hardly merits intelligent respect. *W. E. Sangster*

ENCOURAGEMENT

Encouragement is oxygen to the soul.
George M. Adams

If you wish to be disappointed look at others; if you wish to be disheartened, look at yourself; if you wish to be encouraged, look to Jesus. *Anon.*

The church should be a community of encouragement. *Fred Catherwood*

ENTHUSIASM

(See also: Earnestness; Zeal)

Most great men and women are not perfectly rounded in their personalities, but are instead people whose one driving enthusiasm is so great it makes their faults seem insignificant.
Charles A. Cerami

Nothing great was ever achieved without enthusiasm.
Ralph Waldo Emerson

Enthusiasm is easier than obedience.
Michael Griffiths

Enthusiasm, like fire, must not only burn, but must be controlled.
Augustus H. Strong

Only engrossment with God can maintain perpetual spiritual enthusiasm, because only God can supply everlasting novelty.
A. W. Tozer

ENVY

(See also: Jealousy)

Envy provides the mud that failure throws at success. *Anon.*

Every time you turn green with envy you are ripe for trouble. *Anon.*

If envy were a fever, all the world would be ill.
Anon.

Envy, it tortures the affections, it vexes the mind, it inflames the blood, it corrupts the heart, it wastes the spirits; and so it becomes man's tormentor and man's executioner at once.
Thomas Brooks

Envy is a denial of providence. *Stephen Charnock*

As a moth gnaws a garment, so doth envy consume a man. *Chrysostom*

It is as hard to keep our hearts and envy asunder as

it is to hinder two lovers from meeting together.
William Gurnall

Envy of another man's calling can work havoc in our own.
Watchman Nee

There is no worse passion than envy.
William S. Plumer

Envy and malice are quick-sighted. *Richard Sibbes*

ETERNAL LIFE

(See also: Heaven – The Christian's Eternal Home)

Everlasting life is a jewel of too great a value to be purchased by the wealth of this world.
Matthew Henry

Eternal life does not begin with death; it begins with faith. *Samuel Shoemaker*

All who die in faith are firmly grasped by Christ's love, and will not be conscious of any passage of time until the moment when Christ returns – any more than we are conscious of time passing between our going to sleep and waking up in the morning.
Stephen Travis

ETERNAL SECURITY

(See also: Election – and Eternal Security; Eternal Life; Heaven – The Christian's Eternal Home)

Glory for the Christian is more certain than the grave.

God has never torn up a Christian's birth certificate.

The Christian can be as certain of arriving in heaven as he is that Christ has already ascended there.

The fact that a Christian is uncertain does not mean that he is insecure.

The reason no Christian can be snatched out of the Father's hand is that it was the Father who placed him there.

Christ is to be answerable for all those that are given to him, at the last day, and therefore we need not doubt but that he will certainly employ all the powers of his Godhead to secure and save all those that he must be accountable for. *Thomas Brooks*

Earthly jewels sometimes get separated from their owner, Christ's jewels, never . . . Earthly jewels are sometimes lost, Christ's jewels, never . . . Earthly jewels are sometimes stolen, Christ's jewels, never!

Thomas Brooks

According to Scripture, there is no salvation purposed, offered, or undertaken under grace which is not infinitely perfect and that does not abide for ever.

Lewis Sperry Chafer

It may be that we are sinful; but God did not love us for our goodness, neither will he cast us off for our wickedness.

John Cotton

Did Christ finish his work *for* us? Then there can be no doubt but he will also finish his work *in* us.

John Flavel

The life of Christ's own glory is bound up in the eternal life of his saints.

William Gurnall

If the elect should perish then Jesus Christ should be very unfaithful to his Father, because God the Father hath given this charge to Christ, that whomsoever he elected Christ should preserve them safe, to bring them to heaven.

Christopher Love

God never finally forsakes his people.

Martin Luther

God's seed will come to God's harvest.

Samuel Rutherford

No soldiers of Christ are ever lost, missing or left dead on the battlefield.

J. C. Ryle

The perseverance of the saints is only possible because of the perseverance of God.

J. Oswald Sanders

Christianity is the world's monumental fraud if there be no future life.

Martin J. Scott

As God numbers the hairs of his people, he must needs preserve their heads.

William Secker

Though Christians be not kept altogether from falling, yet they are kept from falling altogether.

William Secker

An inheritance is not only kept for us, but we are kept for it.

Richard Sibbes

When we die, we have not a place to seek. Our

house is provided beforehand . . . We had a place in heaven before we were born. *Richard Sibbes*

The Lord's trees are all evergreen. *C. H. Spurgeon*

My name from the palms
  of his hands
Eternity will not erase;
Impressed on his heart it
  remains,
In marks of indelible grace;
Yes, I to the end shall
  endure,
As sure as the earnest is
  given;
More happy, but not more
  secure,
The glorified spirits in
  heaven.
Augustus M. Toplady

Payment God cannot twice
  demand;
First at my bleeding
  Saviour's hand,
And then again at mine
Augustus M. Toplady

The work which his good-
  ness began,
The arm of his strength
  will complete;
His promise is Yea and
  Amen
And never was forfeited
  yet;
Things future, nor things
  that are now,
Not all things below nor
  above,
Can make him his purpose
  forgo,
Or sever my soul from his
  love.
Augustus M. Toplady

Never did a believer in Jesus die or drown in his voyage to heaven.
Robert Traill

God may for a time desert his children, but he will not disinherit them.
Thomas Watson

If one justified person may fall away from Christ, all may; and so Christ would be a head without a body.
Thomas Watson

ETERNITY

(See also: Heaven; Hell)

Alas! that the farthest end of all our thoughts should be thought of our ends.
Thomas Adams

The thought of eternity particularly delights those assured of grace, while it terrifies others.
J. A. Bengel

The great weight of eternity hangs upon the small wire of time. *Thomas Brooks*

We do all for eternity.
Thomas Brooks

We treat sensible and present things as realities, and future and eternal things as fables: whereas the reverse should be our habit. *Richard Cecil*

All the world's ends, arrangements, changes, disappointments, hopes and fears are without meaning if not seen and estimated by eternity.
Tryon Edwards

Eternity shall be at one and the same time a great eye-opener and a great mouth-shutter.
Jim Elliot

If you look past the world, you put your head up into eternity.
Thomas Goodwin

Any philosophy which deals only with the here and now is not adequate for man. *Billy Graham*

Eternity will be too short to exhaust our learning of God or to end our enjoyment of him.
Peter Green

As meditation on this word, 'eternity', has been so beneficial to my own soul, I would advise others to make the same experiment.
Thomas Jones

In our sad condition, our only consolation is the expectancy of another life. Here below all is incomprehensible. *Martin Luther*

After our death a gate will open; it could be called 'the gate of reality'.
Basilea Schlink

This word 'eternal', it is a *heavy* word.
Richard Sibbes

Those who hope for no other life are dead even for this.
Johannes Von Goethe

An eternity past puzzles all human comprehension.
Daniel Waterland

Eternity to the godly is a day that has no sunset: eternity to the godless is a night that has no sunrise.
Thomas Watson

The wicked have a never-dying worm and the godly a never-fading crown.
Thomas Watson

I desire to have both heaven and hell ever in my eye, while I stand on this isthmus of life, between two boundless oceans.
John Wesley

ETHICS

(See also: Goodness; Morality)

There are no pastel shades in the Christian ethic.

Arnold H. Lowe

Christian ethics are eschatological ethics, that is to say that they derive strength from what God will do in Christ at the last day.

J. A. Motyer

Christian ethics do not contain a particle of chaff – all is pure wheat.

E. G. Robinson

EVANGELISM – Cost

The church is not a yachting club but a fleet of fishing boats. *Anon.*

When a Christian presents the good news about Jesus he is preaching treason in the devil's kingdom.

Doug Barnett

Anyone who witnesses to the grace of God revealed in Christ is undertaking a direct assault against Satan's dominion.

Thomas Cosmades

The gospel is for lifeboats not showboats, and a man must make up his mind which he is going to operate. *Vance Havner*

When Christians evangelize, they are not engaging in some harmless and pleasant pastime. They are engaging in a fearful struggle, the issues of which are eternal.

Leon Morris

There is a tremendous price to be paid for winning men and women to Jesus Christ. After all, the price to God . . . was a cross on a hill. *Alan Walker*

It is impossible to save a life from burning and avoid the heat of the fire.

Mary S. Wood

EVANGELISM – Definition and Aim

Evangelism is truth demanding a verdict.

Lionel Fletcher

Evangelism's highest and ultimate end is not the welfare of men, not even their eternal bliss, but the glorification of God.

R. B. Kuiper

Evangelism is one beggar telling another beggar where to get bread.

D. T. Niles

EVANGELISM – Divine Initiative

The gospel does not fall from the clouds like rain, by accident, but is brought by the hands of men to where God has sent it.
John Calvin

When our Lord sends us out to witness for him, he does not send us out against a wall. Rather, he gives us an open door for personal evangelism, an open door that no man can shut. *Josip Horak*

The Spirit of Christ is the spirit of missions, and the nearer we get to him the more intensely missionary we must become.
Henry Martyn

There is not a better evangelist in the world than the Holy Spirit.
D. L. Moody

Evangelism is still God's Word for this hour.
Alan Walker

Our God is a missionary God. *William J. C. White*

Evangelism is not a human enterprise; it is a divine operation.
Arthur Skevington Wood

EVANGELISM – and Doctrine

You cannot evangelize in a doctrinal vacuum.
Anon.

I have not the slightest interest in a theology which doesn't evangelize.
James Denney

Evangelism must be trinitarian if it is to be biblical.
Harold J. Ockenga

In the last analysis . . . there is only one means of evangelism: namely, the gospel of Christ, explained and applied. *J. I. Packer*

In all evangelism, the primacy of the Bible is essential. *Douglas Webster*

Evangelism is not primarily a matter of method. It is a channel of the Word.
Arthur Skevington Wood

No refinements of technique can make up for any failure to recognize that the Word of God itself is the true method of evangelism.
Arthur Skevington Wood

EVANGELISM – and Election

In the Bible, election and

evangelism meet with joined hands, not clenched fists.

Election *demands* evangelism. All of God's elect must be saved. Not one of them may perish. And the gospel is the means by which God bestows saving faith upon them.

R. B. Kuiper

EVANGELISM – Message

The evangel is not denunciatory of sin. It is not pronunciatory of judgement. It is annunciatory of salvation.

G. Campbell Morgan

What is the first hypothesis for evangelism? That God is there, and is the kind of God that the Bible says he is, and that he has not been silent but has given us propositional truth. *Francis Schaeffer*

The driving force of the early Christian mission was not propaganda of beautiful ideals of the brotherhood of man. It was proclamation of the mighty acts of God.

James S. Stewart

When social action is mistaken for evangelism the church has ceased to manufacture its own blood cells and is dying of leukemia.

Sherwood Wirt

EVANGELISM – Principles

You cannot evangelize and entertain at the same time.

The incarnation is the pattern for all evangelism. Jesus Christ was totally in the world yet wholly uncontaminated by it.

Everett L. Cattell

The skill of the evangelist, or the pastor who would do the work of an evangelist, is seen in the ability to present the limited body of redemptive truth repeatedly, yet with freshness and variety.

Lewis Sperry Chafer

Sinners are not pelted into Christ with stones of hard provoking language, but wooed into Christ by heart-melting exhortations.

William Gurnall

Christian labourers disconnected from the church are like sowing and reaping without having any barn in which to store the fruits of the harvest; they are useful but incomplete.

C. H. Spurgeon

The only New Testament precedents for spreading the gospel are godly living, praying and bold speaking.
Geoffrey Thomas

EVANGELISM – Responsibility for

(See also: Witnessing; Soul-Winning)

No church is obedient that is not evangelistic.

To refuse to evangelize is as sinful as to commit adultery or murder.

Evangelism in the New Testament sense is the vocation of every believer and there is therefore something radically wrong when we imply that personal evangelism is the province of those who have the time and/or inclination to take special courses and learn special techniques.
Roland Allen

In making a person a Christian, God takes a burden off the heart and places another on the shoulders. *Anon.*

No church has the right to send out missionaries. God alone sends missionaries. The church's part is simply to release them as soon as God's plan is revealed. *Derek Bigg*

The whole world is assigned to be reduced under the obedience of Christ.
John Calvin

Evangelism is the perpetual task of the whole church, and not the peculiar hobby of certain of its members.
E. Wilson Carlisle

The church that ceases to be evangelistic will soon cease to be evangelical.
Alexander Duff

Evangelism is the disinterested interest of the comparative few.
James Denney

We are to evangelize not because it is pleasant, not because it is easy, not because we may be successful, but because Christ has called us. He is our Lord. We have no other choice but to obey him.
Leighton Ford

The Word of God is not just for domestic consumption; it is also for export. *William Freel*

There is but one question of the hour: how to bring the truth of God's Word

into vital contact with the minds and hearts of all classes of people.
William E. Gladstone

No Christian is outside our Lord's last command.
A. W. Goodwin Hudson

Every single believer is a God-ordained agent of evangelism. *R. B. Kuiper*

What above all else makes Christian evangelism urgent is its contribution to the hastening of the day when God shall receive all the glory due to his great and holy name. *R. B. Kuiper*

We must consider it an honour that the gospel of salvation has been committed to the church.
Shuichi Matsumura

Christian mission is the only reason for our being on earth.
Andrew Murray

Always and everywhere the servants of Christ are under order to evangelize.
J. I. Packer

The command to evangelize is a part of God's law. It belongs to God's revealed will for his people.
J. I. Packer

The gospel is nothing but a frozen asset unless it is communicated.
J. B. Phillips

Vision is not enough, or even resolution; it is action that is required in the work of evangelism.
W. T. H. Richards

Every age is an age for evangelism. God has no grandchildren.
Eugene L. Smith

No man is truly awake today who has not developed a supra-national horizon to his thinking. No church is anything more than a pathetic pietistic backwater unless it is first and fundamentally and all the time a world missionary church.
James S. Stewart

In the last resort, we engage in evangelism today not because we want to or because we choose to or because we like to, but because we have been told to. *John R. W. Stott*

Evangelism is always dangerous, though it is not so dangerous as the lack of evangelism.
George Sweazey

The church has nothing to do but to save souls; therefore spend and be spent in this work. It is not your business to speak so many times, but to save souls as you can; to bring as many sinners as you possibly can to repentance.

John Wesley

EVANGELISM – Scope

We cannot bring the whole world to Christ, but we must bring Christ to the whole world.

Evangelism is not a spare-time activity.

Thomas Cosmades

Our task is a world task. It cannot longer be divided into the artificial and geographical compartments of home and foreign.

John W. Decker

Evangelism, like charity, begins at home.

Arthur Skevington Wood

EVANGELISM – Spontaneity

The great need in the church is for a spirit of evangelism, not just a spurt of evangelism.

What we read in the New Testament is not anxious appeal to Christians to spread the gospel, but a note here and there which suggests how the gospel was being spread abroad . . . for centuries the Christian church continued to expand by its own inherent grace and threw up an unceasing supply of missionaries without any direct exhortation.

Roland Allen

When our hearts are filled with Christ's presence, evangelism is as inevitable as it is contagious.

Robert E. Coleman

Evangelism should be an attitude permeating all the activities of the Christian.

Bryan Green

Evangelism never seemed to be an 'issue' in the New Testament. That is to say, one does not find the apostles urging, exhorting, scolding, planning and organizing for evangelistic programmes . . . Evangelism happened! Issuing effortlessly from the community of believers as light from the sun, it was automatic, spontaneous, continuous, contagious.

Richard C. Halverson

Evangelism for the early Christians was not something they isolated from other aspects of Christian living in order to specialize, analyse, theorize and organize. They just did it!
Roy Joslin

EVOLUTION

(See also: Creation; Nature)

The evolutionists seem to know everything about the missing link except the fact that it is missing.
G. K. Chesterton

The doctrine of evolution, if consistently accepted, makes it impossible to believe the Bible.
T. H. Huxley

Evolution is the greatest hoax ever foisted on human minds.
Malcolm Muggeridge

EXAMPLE

(See also: Influence)

No man is so insignificant as to be sure his example can do no hurt. *Anon.*

Be such a man and live such a life that if every man were such as you and every life a life like yours, this earth would be a paradise.
Phillips Brooks

Example is the most powerful rhetoric.
Thomas Brooks

The light of a holy example is the gospel's main argument. *R. L. Dabney*

Of all commentaries upon the Scriptures, good examples are the best and the liveliest. *John Donne*

Example is not the main thing in influencing others; it is the only thing.
Albert Schweitzer

Our lives should be such as men may safely copy.
C. H. Spurgeon

Man is a creature that is led more by patterns than by precepts.
George Swinnock

EXPERIENCE

Unused experience is a dead loss. *Anon.*

A man with an experience is never at the mercy of a man with an argument.
Anon.

How humbling it is to all learning when a man is made to know that his doctrine has outrun his experiences! *Thomas Chalmers*

All experience must be subservient to the discipline of Scripture.
Erroll Hulse

FAITH – and Deeds
(See also: Good Deeds)

Idle faith is as useless as idle words.

It is faith alone that justifies, but the faith that justifies is not alone.
John Calvin

Faith is the starting-post of obedience.
Thomas Chalmers

He does not believe that does not live according to his belief. *Thomas Fuller*

The only saving faith is following faith.
Richard Glover

Faith that saves has one distinguishing quality; saving faith is a faith that produces obedience, it is a faith that brings about a way of life.
Billy Graham

The true, living faith, which the Holy Spirit instils into the heart, simply cannot be idle. *Martin Luther*

Believing and obeying always run side by side.
C. H. Spurgeon

Faith and obedience are bound up in the same bundle. He that obeys God, trusts God; and he that trusts God, obeys God.
C. H. Spurgeon

If God gives you St Paul's faith, you will soon have St James's works.
Augustus M. Toplady

FAITH – Definition
(See also: Faith – Saving)

At the end of the day, faith means letting God be God.

Faith is the means by which the infirmity of man lays hold on the infinity of God.

Walking by faith means being prepared to trust where we are not permitted to see.

Faith is in the spiritual realm what money is in the commercial realm.
Anon.

Trusting means drawing on the inexhaustible resources of God. *Anon.*

Faith is the soul's ear.
John Boys

Faith is like the hand of the beggar that takes the gift while adding nothing to it. *Thomas Chalmers*

Belief is not faith without evidence but commitment without reservation.
Leighton Ford

Faith is to the Christian what Nehemiah was to Artaxerxes. Of all the graces this is the Christian's cup-bearer. *William Gurnall*

Faith is an activity of the whole soul bringing into movement the intellect, the emotions and the will, and anything less than this is not biblical faith.
Iain Inglis

Faith is the sight of the inward eye.
Alexander MacLaren

Faith is the power of putting self aside that God may work unhindered.
F. B. Meyer

Faith is our seal; assurance of faith is God's seal.
Christopher Nesse

Faith is the soul riding at anchor. *H. W. Shaw*

Faith is the marriage of the soul to Christ.
Richard Sibbes

Faith is reason at rest in God. *C. H. Spurgeon*

Faith is the grip which connects us with the moving energy of God.
Augustus H. Strong

FAITH – Essence

Grace is not a reward for faith; faith is the result of grace.

Repentance and faith are graces we have received, not goals we have achieved.

When Abraham went out, he was not sure of his destiny, but he was sure of his company.

Faith follows God implicitly, albeit with trembling on occasion; while sight calculates, considers, cautions and cringes.
Anon.

Faith is dead to doubt, dumb to discouragement, blind to impossibilities.
Anon.

Faith never fears that it will overdraw its account at the bank of heaven. *Anon.*

Some people think they need faith as big as a mountain to remove a mustard seed. *Anon.*

Faith is to believe what we do not see, and the reward of this faith is to see what we believe.
Augustine

Faith forces its way to Christ through every obstacle. *J. A. Bengel*

Faith is the daring of the soul to go farther than it can see.
William N. Clarke

Believe your beliefs and doubt your doubts; do not make the mistake of doubting your beliefs and believing your doubts.
Charles F. Deems

There are three acts of faith; assent, acceptance and assurance.
John Flavel

Faith is the trunk of the tree whose roots represent grace and whose fruit symbolizes good works.
William Hendriksen

There is no merit in believing. It is only the act of receiving a proffered favour. *Charles Hodge*

Saving faith is not creative, but receptive. It does not make our salvation, it accepts it gratefully.
Robert Horn

Faith is a refusal to panic.
D. Martyn Lloyd-Jones

The property of faith is not to be proud of what the eye sees, but to rely on what the Word reveals.
Martin Luther

Faith has no back door.
Poul Madsen

Some people are always telegraphing to heaven for God to send a cargo of blessings to them; but they are not at the wharfside to unload the cargo when it comes. *F. B. Meyer*

Seeing is not believing. Seeing is seeing. Believing is being confident without seeing.
G. Campbell Morgan

Faith does not operate in the realm of the possible. There is no glory for God in that which is humanly possible. Faith begins where man's power ends. *George Muller*

In faith two characteristics are inherent: it is worked by God and willed by man.
Adolf Schlatter

The walk of faith is not getting a series of jerks from God.

David Shepherd

A believer sees invisible things. *Richard Sibbes*

The essence of faith lies in the heart's choice of Christ. *C. H. Spurgeon*

It is the peculiar business of faith's eye to see in the dark.

Augustus M. Toplady

Faith tries God and God tries the faith he gives.

Mary Winslow

FAITH – Ground

You will never understand why God does what he does, but if you believe him, that is all that is necessary. Let us learn to trust him for who he is.

Elisabeth Elliot

Faith which is built on emotion is resting on a very changeable foundation.

François Fenelon

The authority for faith is the revelation of God.

G. B. Foster

Why are we so slow to trust an infinite God?

William S. Plumer

If our faith were as strong as our security is good, we need fear no combination of enemies, no revolutions in kingdoms, and no convulsions in nature.

Thomas Scott

FAITH – Importance

You can do a great deal without faith, but nothing that is pleasing to God.

If you do not believe you will not understand.

Augustine

Strike from mankind the principle of faith and men would have no more history than a flock of sheep.

John Bulwer

Where there is no hope, there is no faith.

William Gouge

However little we see or feel, let us believe.

Andrew Murray

Faith is God's measure of a man.

Augustus H. Strong

Faith is the vital artery of the soul. *Thomas Watson*

FAITH – Increase

So many Christians badly need a faith lift!

Let faith have elbow room.
Thomas Brooks

Faith does not grow by being pulled up by the roots time and again to see how it is getting on. Faith grows when we look steadily towards God for the supply of all our needs and concentrate on him. There is little point in becoming engrossed with our faith as if that were the thing we believed in!
J. C. P. Cockerton

We live by faith and faith lives by exercise.
William Gurnall

Labour to have large faith, answerable to our large riches. *Richard Sibbes*

Faith is fostered by prayer, is fortified by the study of the Word, and is fulfilled by our yielding moment by moment to the Lord Jesus himself.
J. Charles Stern

FAITH – and Knowledge

Faith that goes no farther than the head can never bring peace to the heart.

Where reason fails, faith can rest.

God does not expect us to submit our faith to him without reason, but the very limits of our reason make faith a necessity. *Augustine*

It is not a very robust faith which in order to survive must distort or ignore the facts.
Elisabeth Elliot

All I have seen teaches me to trust the Creator for all I have not seen.
Ralph Waldo Emerson

One grain of faith is more precious than a pound of knowledge. *Joseph Hall*

Faith must have adequate evidence, else it is mere superstition. *A. A. Hodge*

The more we know of God, the more unreservedly we will trust him; the greater our progress in theology, the simpler and more childlike will be our faith. *J. Gresham Machen*

The faith that does not come from reason is to be doubted, and the reason that does not lead to faith is to be feared.
G. Campbell Morgan

Belief is a truth held in the mind. Faith is a fire in the heart.
Joseph Fort Newton

True faith and saving knowledge go together.
George Swinnock

Faith is seated in the understanding as well as in the will. It has an eye to see Christ as well as a wing to fly to Christ.
Thomas Watson

A man at his wit's end is not at his faith's end.
Matthew Henry

Nothing but faith will ever rectify the mistakes of reason on divine things.
William S. Plumer

Faith can place a candle in the darkest night.
Margaret E. Sangster

Faith enables us so to rejoice in the Lord that our infirmities become platforms for the display of his grace. *C. H. Spurgeon*

Faith in Jesus laughs at impossibilities.
C. T. Studd

All God's giants have been weak men who did great things for God because they reckoned on God being with them.
J. Hudson Taylor

The poor man's hand is Christ's bank. *John Trapp*

A little faith is faith as a spark of fire is fire.
Thomas Watson

FAITH – Power

Life asks no questions that faith cannot answer.
Anon.

Faith keeps us, but God keeps our faith.
Andrew Bonar

Faith deadens a man's heart to the things of this world. *Thomas Brooks*

Faith makes invisible things visible, absent things present, and things that are very far off to be very near to the soul.
Thomas Brooks

Faith is a plant that can grow in the shade, a grace that can find the way to heaven in a dark night.
William Gurnall

FAITH – and Prayer

(See also: Prayer – and Faith)

The door is closed to prayer unless it is opened with the key of trust.
John Calvin

Faith cannot grow outside of the environment of prayer. Prayer is its natural habitat. *J. C. P. Cockerton*

Faith is to prayer what the feather is to the arrow.
Thomas Watson

Prayer is the key of heaven; faith is the hand that turns it. *Thomas Watson*

FAITH – Rewards

Faith is to believe what we do not see, and the reward of this faith is to see what we believe.
Augustine

Hope is never ill when faith is well.
John Bunyan

Faith makes the uplook good, the outlook bright, the inlook favourable and the future glorious.
V. Raymond Edman

Faith sucks peace from the promise.
William Gurnall

How blest thy saints! how safely led!
How surely kept! how richly fed!
Saviour of all in earth and sea,
How happy they who rest in thee!
Henry Francis Lyte

Take any class of society, the highest or the lowest, and there is not an instance of one who trusted in the Lord and was confounded.
William Pennefather

It is because God has promised certain things that we can ask for them with the full assurance of faith.
A. W. Pink

Faith in God will always be crowned.
William S. Plumer

The larger faith we bring, the larger measure we carry from Christ.
Richard Sibbes

The outlook may be dark, but if we know the secret of the uplook . . . we shall find our God is able to deliver. *J. Charles Stern*

FAITH – Saving

(See also: Conversion; Regeneration; Repentance)

Saving faith is not consent to a proposition, but commitment to a person.

Saving faith is grasping God with the heart.
Anon.

Saving faith is repentant faith. *Anon.*

Upon a life I did not live,
Upon a death I did not die;
Another's life, another's
death,
I stake my whole eternity.

Horatius Bonar

Faith is nothing else but the soul's venture. It ventures *to* Christ, in opposition to all legal terrors. It ventures *upon* Christ, in opposition to our guiltiness. It ventures *for* Christ, in opposition to all difficulties and discouragements.

W. Bridge

Faith wraps itself in the righteousness of Christ.

Thomas Brooks

Saving faith is not *offered* to man by God: it is *conferred* upon him.

Arthur C. Custance

Saving faith is not the human contribution of a sinner seeking salvation, but the divine contribution of the gracious God seeking a sinner.

Arthur C. Custance

I am not skilled to understand
What God hath willed, what God hath planned;
I only know at his right hand
Stands one who is my Saviour.

Dorothy Greenwell

Faith hath two hands; with one it pulls off its own righteousness and throws it away . . . with the other it puts on Christ's.

William Gurnall

The very act of faith by which we receive Christ is an act of utter renunciation of self and all its works, as a ground of salvation. *Mark Hopkins*

Before faith and obedience become acts of man they are gifts of God.

R. B. Kuiper

Saving faith is a gift of the electing God to his elect by which their election is realized. Instead of being the *ground* of election, it is one of its consequences. *R. B. Kuiper*

We cannot *force* ourselves to have faith. We are as much in need of this as everything. Faith can only originate in the soul of man by the gift of God.

Marcus Loane

Faith lays hold of Christ and grasps him as a present possession, just as the ring holds the jewel.

Martin Luther

Let us conclude that faith alone justifies and that

faith alone fulfils the law.
Martin Luther

We must not close with Christ because we *feel* him, but because God has *said* it, and we must take God's word *even in the dark.*
Robert Murray M'Cheyne

In the Bible, faith . . . involves both credence and commitment. *J. I. Packer*

It is not the strength of our faith that saves but the truth of our faith.
John Rogers

Saving faith is the hand of the soul . . . the eye of the soul . . . the mouth of the soul . . . the foot of the soul. *J. C. Ryle*

It requires not only a power, but an almighty power, to raise the heart of man to believe.
Richard Sibbes

We are not saved *for* believing but *by* believing.
Thomas Taylor

Nothing in my hand I bring,
Simply to thy cross I cling;
Naked, come to thee for
  dress;
Helpless, look to thee for
  grace;
Foul, I to the fountain fly;
Wash me, Saviour, or I die.
Augustus M. Toplady

No man's salvation depends on his *believing that he believes*; but it does depend on his seeing and receiving Jesus Christ as his Saviour.
M. R. Vincent

A weak faith may receive a strong Christ.
Thomas Watson

Simple faith honours God and God honours simple faith. *Mary Winslow*

FAITH – Supremacy

Faith is the grace of graces.
Thomas Brooks

All other graces, like birds in the nest, depend on what faith brings in to them. *John Flavel*

Men and brethren, a simple trust in God is the most essential ingredient in moral sublimity of character.
Richard Fuller

No one can occupy higher spiritual ground than that of simply being a believer.
Frank Gabelein

The errors of faith are better than the best thoughts of unbelief.
Thomas Russell

Love is the crowning grace in heaven, but faith is the conquering grace upon earth. *Thomas Watson*

Where reason cannot wade, there faith may swim.
Thomas Watson

FAITH – Testing

Faith is demonstrated by Christians who refuse to accept failure as final.
Anon.

If our faith is not in the present tense it will never be able to stand the test of the days in which we live. *Anon.*

That faith which is never assaulted with doubting is but a fancy. Assuredly that assurance which is ever secure is but a dream.
Robert Bolton

Our faith is really and truly, tested only when we are brought into very severe conflicts, and when even hell itself seems opened to swallow us up.
John Calvin

God . . . often reveals himself to the souls of the elect only in the deep night of pure faith.
François Fenelon

The Christian must trust in a withdrawing God.
William Gurnall

When God's way is in the sea, so that he cannot be traced, yet we are sure his way is in the sanctuary, so that he may be trusted. *Matthew Henry*

When I cannot live by the faith of assurance I live by the faith of adherence. *Matthew Henry*

Trust God even when the pieces don't seem to fit.
John Hercus

There may be a time when God will not be found, but no time wherein he must not be trusted.
Thomas Lye

Faith, like a muscle, grows by stretching. *A. W. Tozer*

Faith tries God and God tries the faith he gives.
Mary Winslow

FAITHFULNESS

(See also: God – Faithfulness)

When faithfulness is most difficult it is most necessary. *Anon.*

Without consistency there is no moral strength.
Anon.

Faithfulness in little things is a big thing.
Chrysostom

God requires no more than faithfulness in our place.
William Gurnall

Faithfulness to God is our *first* obligation in all that we are called to do in the service of the gospel.
Iain H. Murray

Consistency is a jewel.
William S. Plumer

Reverent fear of God is the key to faithfulness in any situation.
Alan Redpath

FAMILY LIFE – Importance

Holy families must be the chief preservers of the interest of religion in the world. *Richard Baxter*

A happy family is but an earlier heaven.
John Bowring

Home is the seminary of all other institutions.
E. H. Chapin

The family circle is the supreme conductor of Christianity.
Henry Drummond

If Christ is in your house your neighbours will soon know it. *D. L. Moody*

A home is not a building; it is a relational structure.
Stephen Olford

FAMILY LIFE – Influence on children

Our children need our presence more than our presents.

A pat on the back is all right provided it is administered early enough, hard enough and low enough.
Anon.

Many parents give their children everything except themselves. *Anon.*

The best time to tackle a minor problem is before he grows up. *Anon.*

For parents to see a child grow up without Christ is a far greater dereliction of duty than for parents to have children who grow up without learning to read or write.
Donald Grey Barnhouse

There is little hope of children who are educated

wickedly. If the dye have been in the wool, it is hard to get it out of the cloth. *Jeremiah Burroughs*

A permissive home is a home where you don't love enough to exercise the authority that Christ gave you. *Ben Haden*

No man or woman ever had a nobler challenge or a higher privilege than to bring up a child for God, and whenever we slight that privilege or neglect that ministry for anything else, we live to mourn it in heartache and grief.
Vance Havner

It is emphatically not a Christian duty to let a child 'make up its own mind' without first informing, guiding and encouraging him. *Paul Helm*

Godly parents do not inflict upon their children the cruelty of telling them that they should do 'just as they please'.
William Hendriksen

The most important thing a father can do for his children is to love their mother.
Theodore M. Hesburgh

The cure of crime is not the electric chair, but the high chair.
J. Edgar Hoover

Children need love, especially when they do not deserve it.
Harold S. Hulbert

It is common sense to put the seal to the wax while it is soft.
Arthur Jackson

Children have more need of models than of critics.
Joseph Joubert

Parents wonder why the streams are bitter, when they themselves have poisoned the fountain.
John Locke

One of the greatest means of grace in the life of a child is the biblical implementation of discipline.
Al Martin

How many careless parents does God's pure eye see among you who will one day, if you turn not, meet your neglected children in an eternal hell!
Robert Murray M'Cheyne

The parent's life is the child's copybook.
John Partridge

The best way to beat the devil is to hit him over the head with a cradle.
Billy Sunday

The most influential of all educational factors is the conversation in a child's home. *William Temple*

I learned more about Christianity from my mother than from all the theologians of England.
John Wesley

FAMILY LIFE – Love

(See also: Marriage)

Love is the master key to a happy home. *Anon.*

Money can build a house, but it takes love to make it a home. *Anon.*

When hugging and kissing end in any home, trouble is on the way.
Stephen Olford

FAMILY LIFE – a Test of Character

A Christian should so live that he would not be afraid to sell the family parrot to the town gossip.
Anon.

Holiness begins at home and sanctification at the sink. *W. F. Batt*

A severe test of a man's essential nature is how he appears to the members of his own family.
Maldwyn Edwards

Can he be a good Christian that spends all his religion abroad and leaves none for his nearest relations at home . . .?
William Gurnall

I would give nothing for that man's religion whose very dog and cat are not the better for it.
Rowland Hill

It is the mark of a hypocrite to be a Christian everywhere except at home.
Robert Murray M'Cheyne

No service for God is of any value which is contradicted by the life at home.
G. Campbell Morgan

A man has no right to stand and preach if his home is not in alignment with the Word of God.
Stephen Olford

If we serve the church or serve the Lord at the expense of our duty to our loved ones and the responsibilities of our home, there is something wrong with the balance of our Christian lives.

Alan Redpath

The best test of a sanctified man is to ask his family about him.

C. T. Studd

Home is a mighty test of character. What you are at home you are everywhere, whether you demonstrate it or not.

Thomas Dewitt Talmadge

FAMILY LIFE – Worship

Families that pray together stay together. *Anon.*

The family altar would alter many a family.

Anon.

If family religion were duly attended to and properly discharged, I think the preaching of the Word would not be the common instrument of conversion.

Richard Baxter

Let family worship be short, savoury, simple, plain, tender, heavenly.

Richard Cecil

Where we have a tent God must have an altar.

Matthew Henry

A house without family worship has neither foundation nor covering.

J. M. Mason

FAULTFINDING

(See also: Criticism of Others)

Faultfinding is a trade that can be carried on with very little capital. *Anon.*

Faultfinding is one talent that ought to be buried.

Anon.

People who are out to find fault seldom find anything else. *Anon.*

The easiest thing to find is fault. *Anon.*

When you are looking for faults to correct, look in the mirror. *Anon.*

FEAR

(See also: Anxiety; Worry)

Fear is the beginning of defeat. *Anon.*

Let none but the servants of sin be the slaves of fear.

John Flavel

The chains of love are stronger than the chains of fear. *William Gurnall*

We fear men so much because we fear God so little. *William Gurnall*

We are so afraid of being offensive that we are not effective. *Vance Havner*

If you stood alone, it would be presumption to hope. Because you are not alone, it is offence to tremble. *Henry Law*

Fear is the tax that conscience pays to guilt.
George Sewell

It is only the fear of God that can deliver us from the fear of man.
John Witherspoon

FEAR OF GOD

(See also: Awe; Worship)

He who knows what it is to enjoy God will dread his loss. He who has seen his face will fear to see his back.
Richard Alleine

I fear God, yet am not afraid of him.
Thomas Browne

The learning of the Christian man ought to begin with the fear of God.
Thomas Cranmer

True piety is never separate from the fear of God.
William S. Plumer

Reverent fear of God is the key to faithfulness in any situation.
Alan Redpath

No one can know the true grace of God who has not first known the fear of God. *A. W. Tozer*

It is only the fear of God that can deliver us from the fear of man.
John Witherspoon

FELLOWSHIP

(See also: Church—Fellowship; Friendship)

Man is made for society and Christians for the communion of saints.
Matthew Henry

We ought not to make any conditions of our brethren's acceptance with us but such as God has made the conditions of their acceptance with him.
Matthew Henry

For the early Christians *koinonia* was not the frilly 'fellowship' of church-sponsored bi-weekly outings. It was not tea, biscuits and sophisticated small talk in the Fellowship Hall after the sermon. It was an unconditional sharing of their lives with the other members of Christ's body.

Ronald J. Sider

FLATTERY

Flattery has turned more heads than garlic. *Anon.*

You would not fear reproof if you did not love flattery.

Augustine

Flattery is the devil's invisible net.

Thomas Brooks

Whilst an ass is stroked under the belly you may lay on his back what burden you please.

Thomas Brooks

Flatterers look like friends as wolves look like dogs.

George Chapman

Talk to a man about himself and he will listen for hours. *Benjamin Disraeli*

It is a dangerous crisis when a proud heart meets with flattering lips.

John Flavel

Flatterers are the worst of tame beasts.

Thomas Fuller

As pressing irons can smooth the greatest wrinkles in cloth, so can flattering tongues do as to the most deformed actions. *Thomas Goodwin*

All other flattery would be harmless if we did not flatter ourselves.

William S. Plumer

Flatterers are the worst kind of enemies.

Tacitus

FORGIVENESS BY GOD

(See also: Atonement; Cross; Jesus Christ – Death)

God has never promised to forgive a single sin that man is not willing to forsake.

What man uncovers, God will cover; what man covers, God will uncover.

Sins are so remitted as if they had never been committed. *Thomas Adams*

I will not glory because I am righteous, but because I am redeemed; not because

I am clear of sin, but because my sins are forgiven. *Ambrose*

Christ comes with a blessing in each hand – forgiveness in one and holiness in the other; and never gives either to any who will not take both. *Anon.*

Sin forsaken is the best evidence of sin forgiven. *Anon.*

The cross is the cost of my forgiveness. *Anon.*

It is shallow nonsense to say God forgives us because he is love. The only ground upon which God can forgive us is the cross. *Oswald Chambers*

In these days of guilt complexes, perhaps the most glorious word in the English language is 'forgiveness'. *Billy Graham*

When is your life more fragrant than when the kiss of forgiveness is most fresh upon your cheek? *Al Martin*

Nothing will make you want to give up sinning more than knowing that Christ has actually taken and remitted all your sin, past, present and future. *John Metcalfe*

Forgiveness is to be set loose from sins. *G. Campbell Morgan*

God never forgives sin without at the same time changing the nature of the sinner. *Iain H. Murray*

Sinners need nothing more than pardon. *William S. Plumer*

God is as sternly and inflexibly just towards sin as if he never forgave iniquity, and yet he forgives sinners through Christ Jesus as freely and fully as if he never punished a transgression. *C. H. Spurgeon*

Release! Signed in tears, sealed in blood, written on heavenly parchment, recorded in eternal archives. The black ink of the indictment is written all over with the red ink of the cross: 'The blood of Jesus Christ cleanseth us from all sin.' *T. De Witt Talmage*

Our guilty spirits dread
To meet the wrath of heaven;
But in his righteousness arrayed,
We see our sins forgiven.
Isaac Watts

Forgiveness by God

Ours is the religion of the forgiven.
Theodore Williams

The Bible knows nothing of mere pardon. There can be no pardon except on the ground of satisfaction of justice.
Geoffrey Wilson

FORGIVENESS OF OTHERS

We are most like beasts when we kill. We are most like men when we judge. We are most like God when we forgive.
Anon.

It is the person who most knows himself liable to fall that will be most ready to overlook any offences from his fellow men.
Alexander Auld

You should forgive many things in others, but nothing in yourself.
Ausonius

Every man should have a fair-sized cemetery in which to bury the faults of his friends.
Henry Ward Beecher

Nothing in this low and ruined world bears the meek impress of the Son of God so surely as forgiveness. *Alice Clay*

The unforgiving spirit as a pride form is the number one killer of spiritual life. *James Coulter*

We are not finished with the need of forgiveness when we become Christians.
G. B. Duncan

Everyone says forgiveness is a lovely idea until he has something to forgive.
C. S. Lewis

If we really know Christ as our Saviour our hearts are broken and cannot be hard, and we cannot refuse forgiveness.
D. Martyn Lloyd-Jones

Those who say they will forgive but can't forget, simply bury the hatchet but leave the handle out for immediate use.
D. L. Moody

If you have a thing to pardon, pardon it quickly. Slow forgiveness is little better than no forgiveness.
Arthur W. Pinero

To err is human, to forgive divine. *Alexander Pope*

Humanity is never so beautiful as when praying for

forgiveness, or else when forgiving another.
Jean Paul Richter

Forgive and forget. When you bury a mad dog, don't leave his tail above the ground. *C. H. Spurgeon*

You never so touch the ocean of God's love as when you forgive and love your enemies.
Corrie Ten Boom

A man may as well go to hell for not forgiving as for not believing.
Thomas Watson

FORMALISM

(See also: Ritualism)

The house of a formalist is as empty of religion as the white of an egg is of savour.
John Bunyan

Our heads are travelling by fast express these days, and our hearts follow by slow freight.
Vance Havner

Using Christian terminology means nothing if one is not a Christian. Having a case of athlete's foot doesn't make you an athlete! *Vance Havner*

Formal religion always makes fertile soil for false religion. *Gilbert W. Kirby*

Men may hasten to perdition with the name of Jesus upon their lips.
Friedrich W. Krummacher

Painted fire needs no fuel; a dead, formal profession is easily kept up.
Thomas Manton

I would sooner risk the dangers of a tornado of religious excitement than see the air grow stagnant with a deadly formality.
C. H. Spurgeon

FREE WILL

(See also: Will)

If a man could will himself to be saved, he could just as easily change his mind and will himself to become unsaved.

The myth of man's free will is exploded by the simple statistic that all men by nature decide against God.

If Christ came to save that which is lost, free will has no place.
J. N. Darby

The will is not free . . . the affections love as they do and the will chooses as it does because of the state of the heart, and . . . the heart is deceitful above all things and desperately wicked. *A. W. Pink*

The will is not sovereign; it is a servant, because influenced and controlled by the other faculties of man's being. The will is not free because *the man* is the slave of sin.
A. W. Pink

The friends of free will are the enemies of free grace. *John Trapp*

FRIENDSHIP

(See also: Fellowship)

A friend is one who comes in when the world goes out. *Anon.*

Christians may not see eye to eye, but they can walk arm in arm. *Anon.*

Nothing is more dangerous than associating with the ungodly. *John Calvin*

The only way to have a friend is to be one.
Ralph Waldo Emerson

Nothing is more stimulating than friends who speak the truth in love.
Os Guinness

There may be those with whom we cannot fall in and yet with whom we need not fall out.
Matthew Henry

Counterfeiting friendship is worse than counterfeiting money. *Thomas Watson*

FRUITFULNESS

A fruitless person is not a failed Christian, but a false one – in other words, not a Christian at all.

Fruit is evidence of the root.

Have you ever noticed the difference in the Christian life between work and fruit? A machine can do work; only life can bear fruit.
Andrew Murray

FULNESS OF LIFE

We will never crave to be filled until we are convinced that we are empty.

The whole secret of abundant living can be summed

up in this sentence: 'Not your responsibility but your response to God's ability.' *Carl F. H. Henry*

Christians should have . . . such abundant life that in poverty they are rich, in sickness they are in spiritual health, in contempt they are full of triumph and in death full of glory.
C. H. Spurgeon

FUTURE

(See also: Hope)

The future belongs to those who belong to God. This is hope. *W. T. Purkiser*

We know not what the future holds, but we do know who holds the future.
Willis J. Ray

God assures us of a future that is better than all our past. *J. Charles Stern*

GAMBLING

Gambling is stealing by mutual consent. *Anon.*

The specific indictment of betting, gambling and lotteries is that they are a means, or device, or stratagem for attempting to appropriate other people's money . . . a person can only win if others lose. Success in gambling depends entirely on the failure of others . . . this is that which makes the practice so sordid and contemptible. *Fred Caddick*

In essence, gambling is a sin against charity; for the gambler hopes to gain at the expense of the total loss of the other competitors.
Kenneth F. W. Prior

GENEROSITY

(See also: Charity; Giving; Kindness)

The quickest generosity is the best. *Anon.*

When it comes to generosity, some people stop at nothing. *Anon.*

Liberality was formerly called honesty, as if to imply that unless we are liberal we are not honest, either toward God or man.
Tryon Edwards

He who is not liberal with what he has, does but deceive himself when he thinks he would be liberal if he had more.
William S. Plumer

A generous action is its own reward.

William Walsh

GIVING

(See also Charity; Generosity; Kindness; Tithing)

Your money can make you an overseas missionary without ever leaving your home town, an evangelist without ever mounting a platform, a broadcaster without ever entering a studio, a Bible teacher without ever writing a book.

Are you giving God what is right, or what is left?

Anon.

If you don't give away anything God wants you to give, you don't own it – it owns you. *Anon.*

Let us give according to our incomes lest God make our incomes match our gifts. *Anon.*

Give to all, lest the one you pass over should be Christ himself. *Augustine*

In this world it is not what we take up but what we give up that makes us rich.

Henry Ward Beecher

It is possible to give without loving, but it is impossible to love without giving.

Richard Braunstein

From what curses and degradations should we be delivered if Christian people gave as the Scriptures direct! *Samuel Chadwick*

I am persuaded that there is nothing upon which the Christian conscience is so ill-informed as the subject of Christian giving.

Samuel Chadwick

What we spend in piety and charity is not tribute paid to a tyrant, but the response of gratitude to our Redeemer. *James Denney*

Labour hard, consume little, give much – and all to Christ.

Anthony Norris Groves

Whatever we part with for God's sake shall be made up to us in kind or kindness. *Matthew Henry*

We make a living by what we get. We make a life by what we give.

Duane Hulse

He gives twice who gives quickly. *Publius Mimus*

If we would have God open his treasury, we must open ours.
Thomas V. Moore

We ask how much a man *gives*; Christ asks how much he *keeps*.
Andrew Murray

I shall not value his prayers at all, be he never so earnest and frequent in them, who gives not alms according to his ability.
John Owen

When we have given God all we have and are, we have simply given him his own. *William S. Plumer*

There are three kinds of giving: grudge giving, duty giving and thanksgiving. Grudge giving says, 'I have to'; duty giving says, 'I ought to'; thanksgiving says, 'I want to'.
Robert Rodenmayer

Grace does not make giving optional.
Charles Caldwell Ryrie

The only way to have more than enough to spare is to give God more than you can spare.
Oswald J. Smith

Many a man becomes empty-handed because he does not know the art of distribution.
C. H. Spurgeon

If I leave more than £10, you and all mankind bear witness that I lived and died a thief and a robber.
John Wesley

GLUTTONY

(See also: Covetousness; Greed)

Gluttons dig their graves with their teeth. *Anon.*

Bridle the appetite of gluttony and thou wilt with less difficulty restrain all other inordinate desires of animal nature.
Thomas à Kempis

Those who eat too much are just as guilty of sin as those who drink too much.
Joseph Caryl

Meat kills as many as the musket; the board as the sword. *Chrysostom*

GOD – Condescension

God never plays philosopher with a washerwoman.
C. S. Lewis

God's condescension is nowhere more conspicuous than in his hearing of prayer. *Austin Phelps*

God's condescension is equal to his majesty.
Henry Scott

GOD – Eternity

God can as well and as soon cease to be, as he can cease to be holy.
Thomas Brooks

God can neither die nor lie. *Thomas Brooks*

God is his own eternity.
Stephen Charnock

The eternity of God is nothing else but the duration of God, and the duration of God is nothing else but his existence enduring. *Stephen Charnock*

There is no higher mystery than God's eternity.
William S. Plumer

It is not for us to set an hour-glass to the Creator of time.
Samuel Rutherford

GOD – Existence

Not one word in the Bible seeks to explain God; God is assumed.

God is his own best evidence. *Anon.*

He who leaves God out of his reasoning does not know how to count.
Anon.

The existence of God is the foundation of all religion.
Stephen Charnock

I could prove God statistically. Take the human body alone – the chance that all the functions of the individual would just happen is a statistical monstrosity. *George Gallup*

God's existence not only *cannot* be proved, it *should not* be attempted.
Os Guinness

God is not for proof but proclamation; not for argument but acceptance.
Robert Horn

One of the great needs of today is a profound conviction that God *is*.
W. Holloway Main

If God did not exist, it would be necessary to invent him.
François M. Voltaire

Until a man has found God he begins at no beginning and ends at no end.
H. G. Wells

GOD – Faithfulness

A man were better to say there is no God than say that God is unfaithful.
Thomas Brooks

God is always like himself.
John Calvin

What more powerful consideration can be thought on to make us true to God, than the faithfulness and truth of God to us?
William Gurnall

Though men are false, God is faithful.
Matthew Henry

What God is to one saint he is to all saints.
William S. Plumer

You can never understand the faithfulness of God by taking the short view.
Paul S. Rees

GOD – Glory

As no place can be without God, so no place can compass and contain him.
Stephen Charnock

The most perfect idea of God that we can form in this life is that of an independent, unique, infinite, eternal, omnipotent, immutable, intelligent and free First Cause, whose power extends over all things.
E. B. De Condillac

Perish each thought of human pride,
Let God alone be magnified;
His glory let the heavens resound,
Shouted from earth's remotest bound.
Philip Doddridge

The Lord's presence is infinite, his brightness insupportable, his majesty awful, his dominion boundless and his sovereignty incontestable. *Matthew Henry*

A man can no more diminish God's glory by refusing to worship him than a lunatic can put out the sun by scribbling the word 'darkness' on the walls of his cell. *C. S. Lewis*

God is as incomparable as he is immutable. He is infinitely farther above the tallest archangel than that archangel is above a worm.
William S. Plumer

What is the glory of God? It is the manifestation of any

or all of his attributes. In other words, it is the displaying of God to the world. Thus, things which glorify God are things which show the characteristics of his being to the world.
Charles Caldwell Ryrie

There is nothing little in God. *C. H. Spurgeon*

Creation can add nothing to the essential wealth or worthiness of God.
Augustus H. Strong

GOD – Goodness

God gives not only generously but genuinely, not only with an open hand but with a full heart.

God is never less than generous, even when we are less than grateful.

His love has no limit, his
grace has no measure,
His power has no boundary
known unto men;
For out of his infinite
riches in Jesus
He giveth, and giveth, and
giveth again!
Annie Johnson Flint

If I could write as I would about the goodness of God to me, the ink would boil in my pen!
Frances Ridley Havergal

God is just, and he is good, and he is solvent.
Matthew Henry

We cannot look for too little from the creature nor too much from the Creator. *Matthew Henry*

The goodness of God is as curious as his disappointments. *J. A. Motyer*

God's goodness is the root of all goodness; and our goodness, if we have any, springs out of his goodness.
William Tyndale

GOD – Holiness

God's holiness and his nature are not two things, they are but one. God's holiness is his nature, and God's nature is his holiness.
Thomas Brooks

Holiness in angels and saints is but a quality, but in God it is his essence.
Thomas Brooks

The holiness of God is his glory, as his grace is his riches. *Stephen Charnock*

No attribute of God is more dreadful to sinners than his holiness.
Matthew Henry

We only learn to behave ourselves in the presence of God, and if the sense of that presence weakens, humanity tends to lark about. *C. S. Lewis*

No attribute of God is more rejoiced in by unfallen angels and redeemed men than his holiness.
William S. Plumer

God cannot have more holiness, because he is perfectly holy; so he cannot have less holiness, because he is unchangeably holy.
Thomas Watson

GOD – Immutability

The unchangeableness of the divine purposes is a necessary consequence of the unchangeableness of the divine nature.
Johann Keil

God cannot change for the better, for he is perfect; and being perfect, he cannot change for the worse.
A. W. Pink

With God the only difference between the future and the past is that certain truths which are as eternal as God himself have not yet become part of human history. *W. Ian Thomas*

All God's reasons come from within his uncreated being. Nothing has entered the being of God from eternity, nothing has been removed and nothing has been changed.
A. W. Tozer

Since God is self-existent, he is not composed. There are in him no parts to be altered. *A. W. Tozer*

GOD – Independence

God is not in need of anything, but all things are in need of God.
Marcianus Aristides

Even if God did have needs we could not supply them, for we have only what he has first given us.
Robert Horn

God is the cause of causes.
Christopher Nesse

He who is over all and in all is yet distinct from all.
G. D. B. Pepper

God is; if he were not, nothing could be.
Richard Sibbes

God is the cause of all causes, the soul of all souls.
Augustus H. Strong

GOD – Inscrutability

Man can find God but never fathom him.

No Christian is truly spiritual who does not revel as much in his ignorance of God as in his knowledge of him.

The utmost that we know of God is nothing in respect of that which he is.
Thomas Aquinas

God is more truly imagined than expressed, and he exists more truly than he is imagined. *Augustine*

There is infinitely more in God than the tongues of men or angels can express. *Thomas Brooks*

God knows the way that you take; you don't know his. *Elisabeth Elliot*

We must believe God great without quantity, everlasting without time, and containing all things without extent; and when our thoughts are come to their highest, let us stop, wonder and adore. *Joseph Hall*

Whenever God is at work there is the inexplicable.
Ralph P. Martin

We must never imagine that the existence of love and wrath in the same nature is evidence of a split personality, but only evidence that God is greater than can be grasped in our finite logic. *J. A. Motyer*

Exposition fails to fathom that before which sanctified understanding is affixed with amazement.
John Murray

We must not judge the Lord by any rules we would apply to men, or even to angels. *William S. Plumer*

A comprehended God is no God at all.
Gerhard Tersteegen

GOD – Love

God loved us when there was nothing good to be seen in us and nothing good to be said for us.

God loves each one of his people as if there was only one of them to love.

God's love is not lazy good nature, as a great many

think it to be and so drag it in the mud; it is rigidly righteous, and therefore Christ died.
Donald Grey Barnhouse

Our great matters are little to God's infinite power, and our little matters are great to his Father love.
Donald Grey Barnhouse

God loves to smile most upon his people when the world frowns most.
Thomas Brooks

The only ground of God's love is his love.
Thomas Brooks

God would not be holy if he were not love, and could not be love if he were not holy.
William Newton Clarke

God in his love pitcheth upon persons . . . Christ died not for propositions only, but for persons . . . He loved *us*, not ours.
Thomas Goodwin

How good is the God we adore,
Our faithful, unchangeable Friend!
His love is as great as his power,
And knows neither measure nor end!
Joseph Hart

God's love is always supernatural, always a miracle, always the last thing we deserve. *Robert Horn*

God did not make us because he stood to gain for the making. He made us out of sheer love.
T. G. Jalland

There is no human wreckage, lying in the ooze of the deepest sea of iniquity, that God's deep love cannot reach and redeem.
John Henry Jowett

Divine love, unlike human love, is not dependent on its object. *R. B. Kuiper*

Rather than find fault with God for his altogether righteous dealings with certain hell-deserving sinners, let us adore him for his eternal, gracious, saving love for others just as deserving of damnation. *R. B. Kuiper*

God is love, and law is the way he loves us. But it is also true that God is law, and love is the way he rules us. *G. S. Lee*

God's love is not drawn out by our lovableness, but wells up, like an artesian spring, from the depths of his nature.
Alexander MacLaren

Eternal love means that the redeemed were never objects of divine hatred, but it does not mean that they were never objects of God's anger. *Donald MacLeod*

That God should pity the world I understand, because when I walk down a hospital and see a sick child, I pity the child . . . but that God should *love* the world – the more I think about it, the more staggered I am. *F. B. Meyer*

It is the love of God that makes him the sworn enemy of sin.
G. Campbell Morgan

The love of God does not measure you by eyesight.
Frederick Sampson

'God so loved that he gave . . .'! And the giving – with Calvary at its heart, was not a trickle but a torrent. *Paul S. Rees*

God soon turns from his wrath, but he never turns from his love.
C. H. Spurgeon

There are no changes in Jehovah's love, though there may be changes in the ways of showing it.
C. H. Spurgeon

It is God's love which, all unseen outwardly, supplies our life inwardly.
J. Charles Stern

God chose us for his love, and now loves us for his choice. *John Trapp*

Thy providence is kind and large,
Both man and beast thy bounty share;
The whole creation is thy charge,
But saints are thy peculiar care.
Isaac Watts

God has never been casual about the condition of the lost. *Thomas Zimmerman*

GOD – Name

God's name is his revealed character.

God's name is God himself in his revealed holiness.
F. J. Delitzsch

GOD – Omnipotence

God can do more in a moment than man in a millennium.

If God is against us, who can be for us?

Man's requirements are not a drain on God's resources.
Anon.

Water is stronger than earth, fire stronger than water, angels stronger than men, and God stronger than them all. *Thomas Brooks*

One with God is a majority.
William Carey

God's power is the best guard, the safest convoy and surest castle that any can have. *William Gouge*

One Almighty is more than all mighties.
William Gurnall

God cannot be withstood by man's incompetence or by Satan's enmity.
Watchman Nee

You will never need more than God can supply.
J. I. Packer

Our theology is never right till in our hearts we invest God with infinite power and perfections.
William S. Plumer

My faith has no bed to sleep upon but omnipotency.
Samuel Rutherford

It is the glory of Omnipotence to work by improbabilities.
C. H. Spurgeon

God has all the power that is consistent with infinite perfection.
Augustus H. Strong

GOD – Omnipresence

From every point of earth we are equally near to heaven and the infinite.
Henri Amiel

God is an infinite circle whose centre is everywhere and whose circumference is nowhere. *Augustine*

Though heaven be God's palace, yet it is not his prison. *Thomas Brooks*

If God is not everywhere, he is not true God anywhere.
William Newton Clarke

There is a God in science, a God in history, and a God in conscience, and these three are one.
Joseph Cook

This is the fundamental thing, the most serious thing of all, that we are always in the presence of God.
D. Martyn Lloyd-Jones

A man may hide God from himself, and yet he cannot hide himself from God.
William Secker

God is neither shut up in nor shut out of any place. *George Swinnock*

He that fills all must needs see and know all.
Richard Sibbes

There is nothing round the corner which is beyond God's view.
J. Charles Stern

God knows us altogether and cares for us in spite of that knowledge.
J. Charles Stern

GOD – Omniscience

Anyone can count the seeds in one apple, but only God can count the apples in one seed.
Anon.

You cannot too often think there is a never-sleeping eye which reads the heart and registers our thoughts. *Francis Bacon*

As a Christian is never out of the reach of God's hand, so he is never out of the view of God's eye.
Thomas Brooks

There is comfort in the fact that God can never be taken by surprise.
Frank Gabelein

God not only sees men, he sees through them.
Matthew Henry

Omniscience cannot be separated from omnipotence. *Matthew Henry*

GOD – Patience

God is patient because he is eternal. *Augustine*

God's love for sinners is very wonderful, but God's patience with ill-natured saints is a deeper mystery.
Henry Drummond

GOD – Perfection

God writes with a pen that never blots, speaks with a tongue that never skips, and acts with a hand that never fails.
Anon.

The character of God is a perfect and glorious whole.
William S. Plumer

The harmony of God's being is the result not of a perfect balance of parts but of the absence of parts.
A. W. Tozer

God can neither deceive, nor be deceived; he cannot deceive because he is truth, nor be deceived because he is wisdom.
Thomas Watson

GOD – Purposes

God's purposes always have God's provision.

God is in control of every atom in his universe, and even those things which seem a direct contradiction of his love will one day be seen to be a dynamic confirmation of his power.

All a believer's present happiness, and all his future happiness springs from the eternal purposes of God.
Thomas Brooks

God knows what he is doing and he is not under any obligation to make us any explanation.
Elisabeth Elliot

God never needs to change his counsels.
Matthew Henry

The purposes of God are his concealed promises; the promises – his revealed purposes! *Philip Henry*

The whole world is ordered and arranged to match and meet the needs of the people of God.
J. A. Motyer

All the events that take place in the world carry on the same work – the glory of the Father and the salvation of his children. *Daniel Rowlands*

God watches and weeds us, and continues his labour upon us, till he brings us to the end of his promise.
Richard Sibbes

What God does, he always purposed to do.
Augustus H. Strong

God's cause is never in danger; what he has begun in the soul or in the world he will complete unto the end. *B. B. Warfield*

GOD – Sovereignty

To speak of the sovereignty of God is nothing less than to speak of his Godhood.

Man proposes, God disposes. *Ludovic Ariosto*

The sovereignty of God is that golden sceptre in his

hand by which he will make all bow, either by his word or by his works, by his mercies or by his judgements.

Thomas Brooks

To be God and sovereign are inseparable.

Stephen Charnock

The Lord is King! Who then shall dare
Resist his will, distrust his care,
Or murmur at his wise decrees,
Or doubt his royal promises?

Josiah Conder

Whatever you do, begin with God. *Matthew Henry*

To admit universal providence and deny special is nonsense. You might as well talk of a chain without any links.

A. A. Hodge

God does all that he does because he is who he is.

R. B. Kuiper

God does not stop to consult us.

D. Martyn Lloyd-Jones

The fixed point in the universe, the unalterable fact, is the throne of God.

G. Campbell Morgan

The world dwarfs us all, but God dwarfs the world.

J. I. Packer

God is a law unto himself, and . . . he is under no obligation to give an account of his matters to any.

A. W. Pink

Whether you shall live to reach home today or not, depends absolutely upon God's will.

C. H. Spurgeon

God can make a straight stroke with a crooked stick.

Thomas Watson

There's not a plant or flower below
But makes his glories known;
And clouds arise, and tempests blow
By order from his throne.

Isaac Watts

God's sovereignty is not arbitrariness, as some misunderstand it, for God has his reasons, based on his infinite wisdom, which he does not always choose to reveal to us.

Spiros Zodhiates

GOD – Wisdom

If God would concede me his omnipotence for twenty-four hours, you would see how many changes I would make in the world. But if he gave me his wisdom, too, I would leave things as they are. *J. M. L. Monsabre*

He formed the stars, those heavenly flames,
He counts their numbers, calls their names;
His wisdom's vast, and knows no bound,
A deep where all our thoughts are drowned.
Isaac Watts

GOD – Wrath

If sin is man's contradiction of God and his expressed will, God cannot be complacent about sin and still be God.
Saphir P. Athyal

The reality of God's wrath is as much a part of the biblical message as is God's grace. *Leighton Ford*

At every door where sin sets its foot, there the wrath of God meets us.
William Gurnall

As God's mercies are new every morning toward his people, so his anger is new every morning against the wicked. *Matthew Henry*

Just as sin belongs to persons, so the wrath rests upon the persons who are the agents of sin.
John Murray

God's wrath is his righteousness reacting against unrighteousness. *J. I. Packer*

Wrath . . . is the expression of God's holy, loving displeasure with sin.
Arthur Skevington Wood

GODHEAD

(See also: God)

If asked to define the Trinity, we can only say that it is not this or that.
Augustine

No wonder that the doctrine of the Trinity is inexplicable, seeing that the nature of God is incomprehensible. Our faith must assent to what our reason cannot comprehend, otherwise we can never be Christians.
Francis Burkitt

Thousands of the ablest minds of the centuries have pondered this problem and no man has been able to explain it; who then invented it? What man can invent, man can explain: what man cannot explain, man cannot have. It must be a revelation.
G. H. Lang

The Trinity is the basis of the gospel, and the gospel is a declaration of the Trinity in action.
J. I. Packer

Nothing will so enlarge the intellect and magnify the whole soul of man as a devout, earnest, continued investigation of the whole subject of the Trinity.
C. H. Spurgeon

Love and faith are at home in the mystery of the Godhead. Let reason kneel in reverence outside.
A. W. Tozer

Our narrow thoughts can no more comprehend the Trinity in Unity than a nutshell will hold all the water in the sea.
Thomas Watson

Tell me how it is that in this room there are three candles and but one light, and I will explain to you the mode of the divine existence. *John Wesley*

GODLINESS

(See also: Christlikeness; Holiness)

God is never more properly thanked for his goodness than by our godliness.

Godliness is the child of truth, and it must be nursed . . . with no other milk than that of its own mother. *William Gurnall*

Godliness is nothing but God-likeness.
George Swinnock

GOOD DEEDS

(See also: Faith – and Deeds; Fruitfulness; Holiness – and Justification)

We are saved not by our deeds but by Christ's sacrifice for our misdeeds.
Fred Catherwood

When we take least notice of our good deeds ourselves, God takes most notice of them.
Matthew Henry

Although . . . disciples are to be seen doing good works, they must not do good works in order to be seen. *Paul B. Levertoff*

We no more earn heaven by good works than babies earn their food and drink by crying and howling.
Martin Luther

No amount of good deeds can make us good persons. We must be good before we can do good.
Chester A. Pennington

Do all the good you can, in all the ways you can, to all the people you can, as long as ever you can.
John Wesley

GOODNESS

(See also: Ethics; Morality)

Good in the heart works its way up into the face and prints its own beauty there. *Anon.*

We can do more good by being good than in any other way. *Rowland Hill*

Goodness is the only investment that never fails.
Henry D. Thoreau

God's goodness is the root of all goodness; and our goodness, if we have any, springs out of his goodness.
William Tyndale

GOSPEL

(See also: Evangelism; Soul-Winning)

The law gives menaces, the gospel gives promises.
Thomas Adams

The Christian message is for those who have done their best *and failed*!
Anon.

The law sends us to the gospel, that we may be justified, and the gospel sends us to the law again to enquire what is our duty, being justified.
Samuel Bolton

The gospel is an anvil that has broken many a hammer, and will break many hammers yet.
John Calvin

The gospel is the clear manifestation of the mystery of Christ.
John Calvin

The gospel is the chariot wherein the Spirit rides victoriously when he makes his entrance into the hearts of men. *William Gurnall*

The gospel reminds all men of an inescapable personal destiny in eternity, based on a conclusive decision in time. *Carl F. H. Henry*

The gospel begins and ends with what God is, not with what we want or think we need.
Tom Houston

The gospel makes husbands better husbands, wives better wives, parents better parents, masters better masters and servants better servants; in a word, I would not give a farthing for that man's religion whose cat

and dog were not the better for it.
Rowland Hill

The law is what we must do; the gospel is what God will give. *Martin Luther*

The Trinity is the basis of the gospel, and the gospel is a declaration of the Trinity in action.
J. I. Packer

The gospel is neither a discussion nor a debate. It is an announcement.
Paul S. Rees

I bless my Lord and Master he has given me a gospel which I can take to *dead* sinners, a gospel which is available for the vilest of the vile. *C. H. Spurgeon*

The gospel has the hallmark of heaven upon it.
William J. C. White

GOSSIP

(See also: Rumour; Slander; Speech)

Gossip is halitosis of the brain. *Anon.*

Gossip is something that goes in the ear and comes out of the mouth greatly enlarged. *Anon.*

No one can have a gossiping tongue unless he has gossiping ears. *Anon.*

Whoever gossips to you will gossip of you. *Anon.*

I hold it to be a fact, that if all persons knew what each said of the other, there would not be four friends in the world.
Blaise Pascal

GRACE – The Christian's Indebtedness to

A man may find out many ways to hide his sin, but he will never find out any way to subdue his sin, but by the exercise of grace.
Thomas Brooks

The more grace thrives in the soul, the more sin dies in the soul.
Thomas Brooks

As by the grace of God we are what we are, so by his grace it is we are not what we are not.
Francis Burkitt

The marvel of God's grace is that he will not take 'No' for an answer from some men. *Walter Chantry*

A Christian never lacks what he needs when he

possesses in Christ the unsearchable riches of God's grace. *G. B. Duncan*

All grace comes from the God of grace.
William Gurnall

All the Christian's rights are his by grace.
William Hendriksen

It takes grace to accept grace. *Robert Horn*

Everything is of grace in the Christian life from the very beginning to the very end.
D. Martyn Lloyd-Jones

The saved are singled out not by their own merits, but by the grace of the Mediator. *Martin Luther*

When I stand before the throne,
Dressed in beauty not my own,
When I see thee as thou art,
Love thee with unsinning heart,
Then, Lord, shall I fully know,
Not till then, how much I owe.
Robert Murray M'Cheyne

I am not what I might be, I am not what I ought to be, I am not what I wish to be, I am not what I hope to be; but I thank God I am not what I once was, and I can say with the great apostle, 'By the grace of God I am what I am.' *John Newton*

Oh, to grace how great a debtor
Daily I'm constrained to be!
Let that grace, Lord, like a fetter,
Bind my wandering heart to thee.
Prone to wander, Lord, I feel it,
Prone to leave the God I love;
Take my heart, Oh, take and seal it,
Seal it from thy courts above!
Robert Robinson

I know Christ and I shall never be even; I shall die in his debt.
Samuel Rutherford

Our salvation is a pure gratuity from God.
Benjamin B. Warfield

GRACE – Common Grace

Grace is a universal principle.
William Gurnall

We need to thank God that there is such a thing as common grace; were it not so, we would have a taste of what hell would be like here and now. *Al Martin*

There is nothing but God's grace. We walk upon it; we breathe it; we live and die by it; it makes the nails and axles of the universe.
Robert Louis Stevenson

GRACE – Daily

Grace is something more than 'unmerited favour' . . . grace is favour shown where there is positive *demerit* in the one receiving it.
Anon.

Temptations are everywhere, *and so is the grace of God.* *Anon.*

Grace grows by exercise and decays by disuse.
Thomas Brooks

As grace is first from God, so it is continually from him, as much as light is all day long from the sun, as well at first dawn or at sun-rising.
Jonathan Edwards

He giveth more grace when
the burdens grow greater,
He sendeth more strength
when the labours increase;
To added affliction he
addeth his mercy,
To multiplied trials, his
multiplied peace.
Annie Johnson Flint

GRACE – Essence

Sin and grace are like two buckets at a well; when one is up the other is down. *Thomas Brooks*

Grace . . . turns lions into lambs, wolves into sheep, monsters into men and men into angels.
Thomas Brooks

Grace . . . turns counters into gold, pebbles into pearls, sickness into health, weakness into strength and wants into abundance.
Thomas Brooks

Grace is the freeness of love. *Thomas Goodwin*

The doctrines of grace humble a man without degrading him, and exalt him without inflating him.
Charles Hodge

From what the Bible says it seems to me that we shall not know the full explanation of grace even in heaven. *Robert Horn*

Grace is not native but donative. *William Jenkyn*

The essence of the doctrine of grace is that God is *for us.* *T. H. L. Parker*

No one can know the true grace of God who has not first known the fear of God. *A. W. Tozer*

There is no reason to be given for grace but grace.
Ralph Venning

GRACE – and Heaven

Grace is glory militant and glory is grace triumphant.
Thomas Brooks

Grace is glory begun, and glory is grace consummated. Grace is glory in the bud, and glory is grace in the fruits. Grace is the lowest degree of glory, and glory the highest degree of grace.
Francis Burkitt

Grace in the soul is heaven in that soul.
Matthew Henry

Grace and glory are one and the same thing in a different print, in a smaller and greater letter. Glory lies couched and compacted in grace, as the beauty of a flower lies couched and eclipsed in the seed.
Thomas Hopkins

Grace is young glory.
Alexander Peden

Glory must begin in grace.
Richard Sibbes

GRACE – and Salvation

Grace is especially associated with men in their sins: mercy is usually associated with men in their misery. *Anon.*

The grace of God does not find men fit for salvation, but makes them so.
Augustine

God's grace can save souls without preaching; but all the preaching in the world cannot save souls without God's grace.
Benjamin Beddome

Nothing is sure for sinners that is not gratuitous . . . Unless we are saved by grace, we cannot be saved at all. *Charles Hodge*

Man does not 'secure' the grace of God: the grace of God 'secures' the activities of man.
Benjamin B. Warfield

GRACE – Supremacy

It is only by the grace of God that man can

obey the law of God.

Grace is richer than prayer, for God always gives more than is asked of him.
Ambrose

Grace is a ring of gold, and Christ is the sparkling diamond in that ring.
Thomas Brooks

Great God of wonders! All
thy ways
Are matchless, Godlike, and
divine;
But the fair glories of thy
grace,
More Godlike and unrivalled
shine.
Samuel Davies

With the doctrine of prevenient grace the evangelical doctrine stands or falls.
John Foster

Knowledge is but folly unless it is guided by grace.
George Herbert

A drop of grace is worth a sea of gifts.
William Jenkyn

The religion of the Bible is a religion of grace or it is nothing. *James Moffatt*

GRACES

A man's true spiritual quality is to be judged by his graces, not his gifts.

Jewels are to wear, not hide; so are our graces.
Thomas Brooks

Gifts are but as dead graces, but graces are living gifts. *Christopher Nesse*

Love is the queen of all the Christian graces.
A. W. Pink

Gifts are what a man has but graces are what a man is. *F. W. Robertson*

There are some of your graces which would never be discovered if it were not for your trials.
C. H. Spurgeon

It is better to grow in grace than gifts.
Thomas Watson

GRATITUDE

(See also: Thanksgiving)

God is never more properly thanked for his goodness than by our godliness.

The greatest sufferer that lives in this world of redeeming love, and who has the offer of heaven before him, has cause of gratitude. *Albert Barnes*

How strange that the Lord must plead with those whom he has saved from the pit to show gratitude to him!
Donald Grey Barnhouse

Christians should have a gratitude attitude.
Stuart Briscoe

He who receives a benefit should never forget it; he who bestows should never remember it.
Pierre Charron

The finest test of character is seen in the amount and the power of gratitude we have. *Milo H. Gates*

Where God becomes a donor man becomes a debtor. *William Secker*

It ought to be as habitual to us to thank as to ask.
C. H. Spurgeon

He who forgets the language of gratitude can never be on speaking terms with happiness. *C. Neil Strait*

GREED

(See also: Covetousness; Gluttony)

Greed of gain is nothing less than the deification of self, and if our minds are set on hoarding wealth we are being idolatrous.

The world provides enough for every man's need but not for every man's greed.
Mohandas Gandhi

Whereas other vices grow old as a man advances in life, avarice alone grows young. *Jerome*

Avarice increases with the increasing pile of gold.
Juvenal

GROWTH

Moving in the right circles is not the same as making progress.

The Christian who has stopped repenting has stopped growing.

There is a world of difference between activity and progress.

A sculptor can leave his work and come back to it another day, and take it up where he left off. But it is

not so with the growth of the soul. The work of grace in us either waxes or wanes, flows or ebbs.
Andrew Anderson

The biggest room in the world is the room for improvement. *Anon.*

Everywhere, everything in apostolic times was on the stretch . . . No premium was given to dwarfs, no encouragement to an old babyhood. *E. M. Bounds*

Spiritual growth consists most in the growth of the root, which is out of sight.
Matthew Henry

Some people's religion reminds me of a rocking-horse, which has motion without progress.
Rowland Hill

Happy is he who makes daily progress and who considers not what he did yesterday but what advance he can make today.
Jerome

The perfect Christian is the one who, having a sense of his own failure, is minded to press towards the mark.
Ernest F. Kevan

I am persuaded that nothing is thriving in my soul unless it is growing.
Robert Murray M'Cheyne

The progressing Christian must cultivate the concentrated gaze of a person living in the future.
J. A. Motyer

Just as the sinner's despair of any help from himself is the first prerequisite of a sound conversion, so the loss of all confidence in himself is the first essential in the believer's growth in grace. *A. W. Pink*

Sanctification is always a progressive work.
J. C. Ryle

Growth is not the product of effort, but of life.
Augustus H. Strong

Refuse to be average.
A. W. Tozer

A good Christian is not like Hezekiah's sun that went backwards, nor Joshua's sun that stood still, but is always advancing in holiness, and increasing with the increase of God.
Thomas Watson

It is better to grow in grace than gifts. *Thomas Watson*

The right manner of growth is to grow less in one's own eyes. *Thomas Watson*

When we stop growing we stop living and start existing. *Warren Wiersbe*

GUIDANCE

(See also: Will of God)

God always provides a light through every one of his tunnels. *Anon.*

I can say from experience that 95% of knowing the will of God consists in being prepared to do it before you know what it is.
Donald Grey Barnhouse

The Lord does not shine upon us, except when we take his Word as our light.
John Calvin

Take God into thy counsel. Heaven overlooks hell. God at any time can tell thee what plots are hatching there against thee.
William Gurnall

The devil can give you remarkable guidance . . . There are powers that can counterfeit almost anything in the Christian life.
D. Martyn Lloyd-Jones

I know not the way God leads me, but well do I know my guide.
Martin Luther

The life of the believer is a conducted tour, and the skilful guide is Abraham's guide and ours. He knows the end of the journey which is in view, and he knows the best way to arrive there.
Fred Mitchell

Where God's glory rests we need not ask the way.
Watchman Nee

God's promises of guidance are not given to save us the bother of thinking.
John R. W. Stott

The Bible is not a kind of horoscope by which to tell your fortune . . . I do not deny that God sometimes reveals his particular will by lighting up a verse of Scripture. But this is not his usual method, and it is highly dangerous to follow such supposed guidance without checking and confirming it.
John R. W. Stott

It is my deliberate conviction that the only way of arriving at a knowledge of the divine will, in regard to us, is by simplicity of

purpose and earnest prayer.
J. H. Thornwell

GUILT

(See also: Depravity; Man; Sin; Sinful Nature)

Guilt is the very nerve of sorrow. *Horace Bushnell*

Man falls according as God's providence ordains, but he falls by his own fault.
John Calvin

The terrors of God are the effects of guilt.
Stephen Charnock

Guilt is to danger what fire is to gunpowder.
John Flavel

Nothing is more personal than guilt.
Donald MacLeod

Guilt is related to sin as the burnt spot to the blaze.
Augustus H. Strong

It is guilt which makes us shy of God.
George Swinnock

Guilt is present universally in the human soul, and we cannot deal with guilt without dealing with the religious questions it poses.
Paul Tournier

HABIT

Habits that begin as cobwebs sometimes end as cables.

Habit, if not resisted, soon becomes necessity.
Augustine

All acts strengthen habits.
Thomas Brooks

An old dog can't alter his way of barking.
Thomas Fuller

Habit is overcome by habit.
Thomas à Kempis

I never knew a man to overcome a bad habit gradually. *John R. Mott*

The best way to stop a bad habit is never to begin it. *J. C. Penney*

Habit is stronger than reason. *George Santayana*

Custom in sin takes away all conscience of sin.
George Swinnock

Powerful indeed is the empire of habit.
Publilius Syrus

HAPPINESS

(See also: Joy)

A man may be satisfied but not sanctified, contented but not converted, happy but not holy.

Superficial happiness without spiritual holiness is one of hell's major exports.

Man wishes to be happy even when he lives so as to make happiness impossible. *Augustine*

Happiness is not the end of life; character is.
Henry Ward Beecher

The way of holiness that leads to happiness is a narrow way; there is but just room enough for a holy God and a holy soul to walk together.
Thomas Brooks

The secret of happiness is renunciation.
Andrew Carnegie

A happy man is he that knows the world and cares not for it. *Joseph Hall*

God cannot give us happiness and peace apart from himself, because it is not there. There is no such thing. *C. S. Lewis*

If you're not allowed to laugh in heaven, I don't want to go there.
Martin Luther

My true happiness is to go and sin no more.
Robert Murray M'Cheyne

Happiness is neither within us only, or without us; it is the union of ourselves with God. *Blaise Pascal*

Searching for true happiness in the context of a godless life is like looking for a needle in a haystack that doesn't have any.
W. T. Purkiser

He who forgets the language of gratitude can never be on speaking terms with happiness. *C. Neil Strait*

Sow holiness and reap happiness.
George Swinnock

There is no happiness out of God. *John Wesley*

HATRED

(See also: Anger; Revenge)

Hate no one; hate their vices, not themselves.
John Gardiner Brainard

Hatred is blind as well as love. *Thomas Fuller*

Hate, like love, picks up every shred of evidence to justify itself.
Os Guinness

Hate is too great a burden to bear.
Martin Luther King

HEART

I am more afraid of my own heart than of the pope and all his cardinals.
Martin Luther

God alone sees the heart; the heart alone sees God.
Thomas Manton

The heart is a triangle which only the Trinity can fill. *Thomas Watson*

HEAVEN – The Christian's Eternal Home

(See also: Eternal Life; Eternal Security)

Heaven is a reality, not seen by eyes of flesh, but made known by revelation and received by faith.
Archibald Alexander

Heaven is a prepared place for prepared people.
Anon.

Those who live in the Lord never see each other for the last time. *Anon.*

In our first paradise in Eden there was a way to go out but no way to go in again. But as for the heavenly paradise, there is a way to go in, but no way to go out again.
Richard Baxter

A dog is at home in this world because this is the only one a dog will ever live in. We are not at home in this world because we are made for a better one. *Vance Havner*

Those that are acquainted with God and Christ are already in the suburbs of life eternal.
Matthew Henry

My whole outlook upon everything that happens to me should be governed by these three things: my realization of who I am, my consciousness of where I am going, and my knowledge of what awaits me when I get there.
D. Martyn Lloyd-Jones

We shall not rest from our work but from our labours. There will be no toil, no pain in our work.
Robert Murray M'Cheyne

When I get to heaven, I shall see three wonders there – the first wonder will be to see many people there whom I did not expect to see; the second wonder will be to miss many people whom I did expect to see; and the third and greatest wonder of all will be to find myself there. *John Newton*

Heaven is not all rest. On the door is inscribed: 'No admission except on business.' *Augustus H. Strong*

HEAVEN – Glory

Heaven is not a conditional reward, but a consummated relationship.

Heaven will pay for any loss we may suffer to gain it; but nothing can pay for the loss of heaven.
Richard Baxter

There is nothing but heaven worth setting our hearts upon. *Richard Baxter*

If one man should suffer all the sorrows of all the saints in the world, yet they are not worth one hour's glory in heaven.
Chrysostom

Joy is the serious business of heaven. *C. S. Lewis*

It is not death to close
The eye long dimmed by tears,
And wake in glorious repose
To spend eternal years.
Henri Abraham Cesar Malan

If it be sweet to be the growing corn of the Lord here, how much better to be gathered into his barn!
Robert Murray M'Cheyne

Earth has no sorrow that heaven cannot heal.
Thomas Moore

One breath of paradise will extinguish all the adverse winds of earth.
A. W. Pink

HEAVEN – God's Presence

Christ is the centre of attraction in heaven.
Archibald Alexander

It is God alone who makes heaven to be heaven.
Thomas Brooks

The heavenly state is so organized as to express visibly what God thinks of the cross of Christ.
J. A. Motyer

Heaven – God's Presence

Heaven will chiefly consist in the enjoyment of God.
William S. Plumer

The humble heart is God's throne in regard to his gracious presence; and heaven is his throne as to his glorious presence.
Thomas Watson

If you're not allowed to laugh in heaven, I don't want to go there.
Martin Luther

It will be one of the felicities of heaven that saints shall no longer misunderstand each other.
Isaac Milner

HEAVEN – Perfection

There are no furrowed brows in heaven.

There are no regrets in heaven, no remorseful tears, no second thoughts, no lost causes.

Heaven begins where sin ends. *Thomas Adams*

Heaven would be a very hell to an unholy person.
Thomas Brooks

In the streets of that new Jerusalem above, none shall ever complain that others have too much, or that themselves have too little. *Thomas Brooks*

There is no misbelief in heaven. *Andrew Gray*

If an unholy man were to get to heaven he would feel like a hog in a flower garden. *Rowland Hill*

Christ and his cross are not separable in this life; howbeit, they part at heaven's door. There is no storage place for crosses in heaven.
Samuel Rutherford

When an eagle is happy in an iron cage, when a sheep is happy in water, when an owl is happy in the blaze of the noonday sun, when a fish is happy on dry land – then, and not till then, will I admit that the unsanctified man could be happy in heaven.
J. C. Ryle

If a thief should get into heaven unchanged, he would begin by picking the angels' pockets.
C. H. Spurgeon

HEAVEN – Preparation for

The more of heaven we cherish, the less of earth we covet. *Anon.*

Grace is glory begun, and glory is grace consummated. Grace is glory in the bud, and glory is grace in the fruits. Grace is the lowest degree of glory, and glory the highest degree of grace.
Francis Burkitt

It is certain that all that will go to heaven hereafter begin their heaven now, and have their hearts there. *Matthew Henry*

Our duty as Christians is always to keep heaven in our eye and earth under our feet. *Matthew Henry*

Grace and glory are one and the same thing in a different print, in a smaller and greater letter. Glory lies couched and compacted in grace, as the beauty of a flower lies couched and eclipsed in the seed.
Thomas Hopkins

The Lord Christ leads none to heaven but whom he sanctifies on earth. This living Head will not admit of dead members.
John Owen

Holiness indeed is perfected in heaven: but the beginning of it is invariably confined to this world.
John Owen

Grace is young glory.
Alexander Peden

Glory must begin in grace.
Richard Sibbes

No man may go to heaven who hath not sent his heart thither before.
Thomas Wilson

HELL

(See also: Eternity; Judgement; Satan)

All the roads that lead to hell are one-way streets.

Those who demand nothing more than a God of justice get precisely what they ask; the Bible calls it hell.

Hell is truth seen too late.
H. G. Adams

Each man's sin is the instrument of his punishment, and his iniquity is turned into his torment.
Augustine

Could every damned sinner weep a whole ocean, yet all those oceans together would never extinguish one spark of eternal fire.
Thomas Brooks

The damned shall live as long in hell as God

himself shall live in heaven.
Thomas Brooks

The wicked have the seeds of hell in their own hearts.
John Calvin

If there is no belief in hell the concept of judgement also becomes meaningless; and then all that is left of Christianity is a system of ethics. *Geoffrey Gorer*

Christ needs take no other revenge on a soul for refusing him . . . than to condemn such a one to have its own desire.
William Gurnall

A man who realizes in any measure the awful force of the words *eternal hell* won't shout about it, but will speak with all tenderness. *A. A. Hodge*

Men may hasten to perdition with the name of Jesus on their lips.
Friedrich W. Krummacher

There are no personal relationships in hell.
C. S. Lewis

The lost will eternally suffer in the satisfaction of justice, but they will never satisfy it.
John Murray

The second death is the continuance of spiritual death in another and timeless existence.
E. G. Robinson

There are two ways of going to hell; one is to walk into it with your eyes open . . . the other is to go down by the steps of little sins.
J. C. Ryle

Suffering that is penal can never come to an end, because guilt is the reason for its infliction, and guilt once incurred never ceases to be . . . One sin makes guilt, and guilt makes hell.
W. G. T. Shedd

It will be hell to a man to have his own voluntary choice confirmed, and made unchangeable.
C. H. Spurgeon

If you in any way abate the doctrine of hell it will abate your zeal.
R. A. Torrey

The breath of the Lord kindles the infernal lake, and where shall we have engines or buckets to quench that fire?
Thomas Watson

HERESY

An error no wider than a hair will lead a hundred miles away from the goal.
Anon.

The passion for ruling is the mother of heresy.
Chrysostom

When Bible believers take a stand against false doctrine, they are accused of 'rocking the boat'. It is better that belief should rock the boat than that unbelief should wreck the boat. *Vance Havner*

Heresy is the school of pride. *George Herbert*

Heresy is picking out what you want to believe and rejecting, or at least ignoring, the rest. *A. W. Tozer*

Heresy is the leprosy of the head. *John Trapp*

A man may go to hell as well for heresy as for adultery.
Thomas Watson

HISTORY

What history does is to uncover man's universal sin.
Herbert Butterfield

To test the present you must appeal to history.
Winston Churchill

Human history is the sad result of everyone looking out for himself.
Jullo Cortazar

What are all histories but God manifesting himself?
Oliver Cromwell

History is just the accumulated stories of how God is working in the lives of all the individual people on earth. *John Hercus*

The key to the history of the world is the kingdom of God.
D. Martyn Lloyd-Jones

The whole of Bible history exists to tell us that history turns upon the hinge of sinfulness, not upon the hinge of politics.
J. A. Motyer

Blessed is he who sees God in history and in nature as well as in revelation. *William S. Plumer*

All history is incomprehensible without Christ.
Ernest Renan

The hinge of history is on the door of a Bethlehem stable. *Ralph W. Sockman*

HOLINESS – Definition

(See also: Christlikeness)

Holiness is the habit of being of one mind with God. *Anon.*

Do you know what holiness is? It is pure love.

Samuel Logan Brengle

A holy life is not an ascetic, or gloomy, or solitary life, but a life regulated by divine truth and faithful in Christian duty. It is living above the world while we are still in it.

Tryon Edwards

Holiness is an unselfing of ourselves.

Frederick W. Faber

What health is to the heart, that holiness is to the soul.

John Flavel

A holy life is the life of God.

William Gurnall

Holiness is the symmetry of the soul.

Philip Henry

To know what holiness is you have to be holy.

Donald Nicholl

Holiness is not an optional extra to the process of creation, but rather the whole point of it.

Donald Nicholl

Sanctification is the progressive restoration of a man's rationality so that he becomes a man.

J. I. Packer

Holiness in man is the image of God's.

E. G. Robinson

Holiness is the visible side of salvation.

C. H. Spurgeon

HOLINESS – Essence

Morally, a Christian is called to holiness; dynamically, he is called to service.

Holiness is a constellation of graces.

Thomas Boston

A holy person looks upon his sins as the crucifiers of his Saviour.

Thomas Brooks

The most holy men are always the most humble men. *Thomas Brooks*

Holiness can no more approve of sin than it can commit it.

Stephen Charnock

Holiness can only be attained by living by the revealed Word of God.

C. Tom Fincher

There is no true holiness without humility.

Thomas Fuller

The secret of Christian holiness is heart occupation with Christ himself.

H. A. Ironside

My mind is the central control area of my personality, and sanctification is the mind coming more and more under the Holy Spirit's control.

David Jackman

The greatest wisdom on this earth is holiness.

William S. Plumer

Unless grace has radically altered my behaviour it cannot possibly alter my destiny. *Alan Redpath*

The trouble with too many Christians is that they are more concerned about their doctrine of holiness than they are about being clothed with the beauty of Christ's purity.

Paul S. Rees

We must aim to have a Christianity which, like the sap of a tree, runs through twig and leaf of our character and sanctifies all.

J. C. Ryle

The secret of holy living is in the mind.

John R. W. Stott

There is a beauty in holiness as well as a beauty of holiness.

George Swinnock

Sanctification is progressive; if it does not grow it is because it does not live.

Thomas Watson

HOLINESS – God's Work

Holiness is to be measured not in terms of man's ecstasy but of God's energy.

He who gave his image to us must of necessity wish to see his image in us.

Anon.

I am one of those who do not think that the beauty of holiness consists in beauty but rather in holiness, in that holiness which is God and which comes from God and in which alone there is strength to live and work and pray.

John R. De Witt

So in love is Christ with holiness that he will buy it with his blood for us.
John Flavel

A holiness which is the device of our heart is not the holiness after God's heart. *William Gurnall*

God loves purity so well that he had rather see a hole than a spot in his child's garments.
William Gurnall

God saved us to make us holy, not happy. Some experiences may not contribute to our happiness, but all can be made to contribute to our holiness.
Vance Havner

God useth many a moving persuasion to draw us to holiness, not a hint to encourage us to sin.
Thomas Manton

I often pray, 'Lord make me as holy as a pardoned sinner can be.'
Robert Murray M'Cheyne

God works in us and with us, not against us or without us. *John Owen*

There is no way that we by ourselves can generate sanctification. Our sanctification is Christ. There is no way we can be good. Our goodness is Christ. There is no way we can be holy. Our holiness is Christ.
A. W. Pink

Holiness is not only commanded by God's law, but it is made available to men by his grace.
Kenneth F. W. Prior

The greatest miracle that God can do today is to take an unholy man out of an unholy world, and make that man holy and put him back into that unholy world and keep him holy in it.
Leonard Ravenhill

Holiness is not the way to Christ; Christ is the way to holiness. *Adrian Rogers*

Holiness is not the laborious acquisition of virtue from without, but the expression of the Christ-life from within.
J. W. C. Wand

HOLINESS – Importance

An unholy Christian is a contradiction of everything the Bible teaches.

Christ comes with a blessing in each hand – forgiveness in one and holiness in the other; and never gives either to any who will not take both. *Anon.*

Holiness is to be the touchstone of the Christian life.
Donald Grey Barnhouse

No subject which ever engages the thought of Christian believers can be more sacredly commanding than that of personal holiness. *J. Sidlow Baxter*

Regeneration is the fountain; sanctification is the river. *J. Sidlow Baxter*

Prayer and a holy life are one. They mutually act and react. Neither can survive alone. The absence of the one is the absence of the other. *E. M. Bounds*

The destined end of man is not happiness, nor health, but holiness. God's one aim is the production of saints.
Oswald Chambers

'Be ye holy' is the great and fundamental law of our religion.
Matthew Henry

Holiness is necessary to present peace and future glory. *William Jay*

Christianity is a universal holiness in every part of life. *William Law*

'Holiness' is the most intimately divine word the Bible possesses.
J. A. Motyer

Nothing can set aside the evidence of a holy life. It is better than a revelation from heaven.
William S. Plumer

It is better to be innocent than penitent.
William Secker

The serene, silent beauty of a holy life is the most powerful influence in the world, next to the might of the Spirit of God.
C. H. Spurgeon

Heaven must be in thee before thou canst be in heaven. *George Swinnock*

The important point is where you are *today* in terms of holiness.
George Verwer

HOLINESS – and Justification

Justification never results from good works; justification always results in good works.

Any attempt to make justification dependent upon sanctification is to rob grace of its freeness and to add works to saving grace.

Donald Grey Barnhouse

Justification and sanctification are inseparable companions; distinguished they must be, but divided they can never be.

Thomas Brooks

Any man who thinks that he is a Christian, and that he has accepted Christ for justification, when he did not at the same time accept him for sanctification, is miserably deluded in that very experience.

A. A. Hodge

We must first be made good before we can do good; we must first be made just before our works can please God – for when we are justified by faith in Christ, then come good works. *Hugh Latimer*

If Christ justifies you he will sanctify you! He will not save you and leave you in your sins.

Robert Murray M'Cheyne

According to Scripture it is quite impossible to be justified by faith and not to experience the commencement of true sanctification, because the spiritual life communicated by the Spirit in the act of regeneration (which introduces the new power to believe) is morally akin to the character of God and contains within it the germ of all holiness.

Iain H. Murray

Justification and sanctification are distinguishable but not separable.

William S. Plumer

I fear it is sometimes forgotten that God has married together justification and sanctification. *J. C. Ryle*

In the court of justification merits are nothing worth, insufficient; but in the court of sanctification . . . they are jewels and ornaments. *Richard Sibbes*

Sanctification is so involved in justification that the justification can never be real unless it be followed by sanctification.

Benjamin B. Warfield

If God should justify a people and not sanctify them, he would justify a people whom he could not glorify. *Thomas Watson*

HOLINESS – Man's Part

The holiness which can only be accomplished by the power of God will only be accomplished by the care of man.

We do not suddenly become holy in one moment by making Christ Lord; we are to be holy moment by moment because he is Lord.

The way of holiness that leads to happiness is a narrow way; there is but just room enough for a holy God and a holy soul to walk together.

Thomas Brooks

I went on with my eager pursuit after more holiness and conformity to Christ. The heaven I desired was a heaven of holiness.

Jonathan Edwards

We ought to behave ourselves every day as though we had no dependence on any other.

Jonathan Edwards

It is not enough to wish to be good unless we *hunger* after it. *Jerome*

The trouble with much holiness teaching is that it leaves out the Sermon on the Mount and asks us to experience sanctification. That is not the biblical method.

D. Martyn Lloyd-Jones

The sanctifying grace of God is appropriated by the obedient and unrelenting activity of the regenerate man.

J. A. Motyer

Sanctification is always a progressive work.

J. C. Ryle

There is no holiness without a warfare.

J. C. Ryle

There is no short cut to sanctity.

A. W. Tozer

HOLINESS – Rewards

Holiness is its own reward.

Thomas Brooks

Man's holiness is now his greatest happiness, and in heaven man's greatest happiness will be his perfect holiness.

Thomas Brooks

The holy person is the only contented man in the world.

William Gurnall

The Christian who has the smile of God needs no status symbols.

Leonard Ravenhill

Sow holiness and reap happiness.

George Swinnock

HOLY SPIRIT

(See also: Godhead)

A Christian may not always be conscious of the Holy Spirit's presence, but he would not even be a Christian in his absence.

It is the Spirit's ministry to bring the sinner to the Saviour and to make the sinner like the Saviour.

No one may ask a believer whether he has been baptized with the Spirit. The very fact that a man is in the body of Christ demonstrates that he has been baptized with the Spirit, for there is no other way of entering the body.

Donald Grey Barnhouse

To be filled with the Spirit is to have the Spirit fulfilling in us all that God intended him to do when he placed him there.

Lewis Sperry Chafer

A great part of your prayer work should be imploring the Almighty for a greater measure of his Spirit.

Walter Chantry

Spirit of God, descend upon my heart;
Wean it from earth; through all its pulses move;
Stoop to my weakness, mighty as thou art,
And make me love thee as I ought to love.

George Croly

The fruit of the Spirit is not excitement or orthodoxy: it is *character*.

G. B. Duncan

The Christian's birthright is the power of the Holy Ghost. *Lionel Fletcher*

We may take it as a rule of the Christian life that the more we are filled with the Holy Spirit, the more we shall glorify the Lord Jesus.

Frank Gabelein

Before Pentecost the disciples found it hard to do easy things; after Pentecost they found it easy to do hard things.

A. J. Gordon

The Holy Spirit is the heavenly Lover's engage-

ment ring given to us.
Michael Green

All the Holy Spirit's influences are heaven begun, glory in the seed and bud.
Matthew Henry

If it were possible to put the Holy Spirit into a textbook of pharmacology I would put him under the stimulants, for that is where he belongs.
D. Martyn Lloyd-Jones

Proper understanding of the Scriptures comes only through the Holy Spirit.
Martin Luther

He who has the Holy Spirit in his heart and the Scriptures in his hands has all he needs.
Alexander MacLaren

There is not a better evangelist in the world than the Holy Spirit.
D. L. Moody

If the Holy Spirit guides us at all, he will do it according to the Scriptures, and never contrary to them.
George Muller

As all the Word of God is given by the Spirit of God, so each word must be interpreted to us by that same Spirit.
Andrew Murray

If Pentecost is not repeated, neither is it retracted . . . This is the era of the Holy Spirit.
John Murray

With a perversity as pathetic as it is impoverishing we have become preoccupied today with the sporadic extraordinary and non-universal ministries of the Spirit to the neglect of . . . the more general ones.
J. I. Packer

Before Christ sent the church into the world, he sent the Spirit into the church. The same order must be observed today.
John R. W. Stott

The Holy Spirit is God's imperative of life.
A. W. Tozer

Without the Spirit of God we can do nothing but add sin to sin.
John Wesley

The Holy Spirit loves so to arrange men's circumstances that they are brought within the sphere of God's influence.
Maurice A. P. Wood

HONESTY

(See also: Integrity; Truth)

For the Christian, honesty

is not the best policy – it is the only one.

Honesty is a question of right and wrong, not a matter of policy. *Anon.*

One thing you can give and still keep is your word. *Anon.*

There are no degrees of honesty. *Anon.*

Honesty is a fine jewel, but much out of fashion. *Thomas Fuller*

The life of an honest man is an oath. *Richard Sibbes*

One's mere word should be as trustworthy as a signed agreement attested by legal witnesses. *Curtis Vaughan*

HOPE

(See also: Eternal Life; Eternal Security; Future; Heaven)

'Hope' is biblical shorthand for unconditional certainty.

The Christian's hope of glory is not the fact that Christ is in him, but the Christ who is in him as a fact.

Hope is faith in the future tense. *Peter Anderson*

Bless God that there is *in* us resurrection life, and that there *awaits* us a resurrection morn! *J. J. Bonar*

Hope can see heaven through the thickest clouds. *Thomas Brooks*

Hope is never ill when faith is well. *John Bunyan*

Where there is no hope, there is no faith. *William Gouge*

Hope is the saint's covering wherein he wraps himself when he lays his body down to sleep in the grave. *William Gurnall*

He that was our help from our birth ought to be our hope from our youth. *Matthew Henry*

Our fear must save our hope from swelling into presumption, and our hope must save our fear from sinking into despair. *Matthew Henry*

Hoping is disciplined waiting. *E. Hoffmann*

Hope is the mother of patience. *William Jenkyn*

My future is as bright as the promises of God.
Adoniram Judson

I am walking toward a bright light and the nearer I get the brighter it is.
D. L. Moody

The future belongs to those who belong to God. This is hope. *W. T. Purkiser*

The nature of hope is to expect that which faith believes. *Richard Sibbes*

The Christian hope is not a matter for tickling our minds but for changing our lives and for influencing society. *Stephen Travis*

HUMANISM

The strange thing is that while on the one hand man cries for help in his desperate sickness, on the other hand he refuses to consider even the possibility of a panacea beyond the range of his ability.
Akbar Abdul-Haqq

Christians need to recognize the solemn fact that humanism is not an ally in making the world a better place in which to live. It is a deadly enemy, for it is a religion without God and without hope in this world or the next.
L. Nelson Bell

Human doctrines have no humbling power in them.
Thomas Brooks

He builds too low who builds below the skies.
Richard Cecil

Humanism cannot, in any fair sense, apply to one who still believes in God.
Paul Kurtz

The humanist counsellor cannot give the assurance of sin forgiven, guilt assuaged, life beyond death, a loving God, or a caring Jesus. *Gerald Larue*

So long as we cling to the idea that we live in a closed-world system, the most we can do is to adjust and rearrange existing forces. *J. B. Phillips*

Humanism is not wrong in its cry for sociological healing, but humanism is not producing it.
Francis Schaeffer

HUMILITY – Blessings

God thinks most of the man who thinks himself least.

He that will be knighted must kneel for it.
Thomas Adams

Swallowing of pride seldom leads to indigestion. *Anon.*

It was pride that changed angels into devils; it is humility that makes men as angels. *Augustine*

The proud hilltops let the rain run off; the lowly valleys are richly watered.
Augustine

If you lay yourself at Christ's feet he will take you into his arms.
William Bridge

The most holy men are always the most humble men. *Thomas Brooks*

Humility is the root, mother, nurse, foundation and bond of all virtue.
Chrysostom

Humility is the hallmark of wisdom. *Jeremy Collier*

It is with men as with wheat; the light heads are erect even in the presence of Omnipotence, but the full heads bow in reverence before him. *Joseph Cook*

As rivers flow through valleys and low countries, so the root of all holy actions is nourished by humility.
Thomas De Villanova

If we learned humility it might spare us humiliation.
Vance Havner

When we take least notice of our good deeds ourselves, God takes most notice of them.
Matthew Henry

If you want to see the height of the hill of God's eternal love you must go down into the valley of humility. *Rowland Hill*

God's choice acquaintances are humble men.
Robert Leighton

All God's thrones are reached by going downstairs.
G. Campbell Morgan

Not until we have become humble and teachable, standing in awe of God's holiness and sovereignty . . . acknowledging our own littleness, distrusting our own thoughts, and willing to have our minds turned upside down, can divine wisdom become ours.
J. I. Packer

Just as the sinner's despair of any help from himself is the first prerequisite of a sound conversion, so the loss of all confidence in himself is the first essential in the believer's growth in grace. *A. W. Pink*

The best way to see divine light is to put out thine own candle.
Francis Quarles

The right manner of growth is to grow less in one's own eyes.
Thomas Watson

The lowest parts of the land are warm and fertile; the lofty mountains are cold and barren.
Spiros Zodhiates

HUMILITY – Characteristics

If you know Hebrew, Greek and Latin, do not put them where Pilate did, at the head of Christ; put them at his feet. *Anon.*

The sufficiency of my merit is to know that my merit is not sufficient.
Augustine

If there is one thing I would like to have said of me by those who are left behind when I have gone into the glory land, it would be just this – that the overflow hid the vessel!
A. Lindsay Glegg

Humility is a necessary veil to all other graces.
William Gurnall

Better be a humble worm than a proud angel.
William Jenkyn

I sometimes think that the very essence of the whole Christian position and the secret of a successful spiritual life is just to realize two things . . . I must have complete, absolute confidence in God and no confidence in myself.
D. Martyn Lloyd-Jones

Oh for true, unfeigned humility! I know I have cause to be humble; and yet I do not know one half of that cause. I know I am proud; and yet I do not know the half of that pride.
Robert Murray M'Cheyne

The higher a man is in grace, the lower he will be in his own esteem.
C. H. Spurgeon

Let my name be forgotten, let me be trodden under the feet of all men, if Jesus may thereby be glorified.
George Whitefield

HUMILITY – Essence

Humility is the knees of the soul. *Thomas Adams*

Humility is to have a just estimate of oneself.
Anon.

It is one of the hardest matters under the sun to become nothing in ourselves. *Elisha Coles*

Humility is the ornament of angels and the deformity of devils.
William Jenkyn

Humility is pure honesty.
Jack McAlister

Humility . . . is simply the sense of entire nothingness. *Andrew Murray*

Humility is that grace that, when you know you have it, you have lost it.
Andrew Murray

Humility is the repentance of pride.
Nehemiah Rogers

Humility is not a Sunday frock, but a workaday smock. *J. Oswald Sanders*

The humble heart is God's throne in regard to his gracious presence; and heaven is his throne as to his glorious presence.
Thomas Watson

HUMILITY – False

No pretence of humility must make us decline our duty. *Matthew Henry*

False humility is really a lie, and cannot be acceptable to a God of truth.
William S. Plumer

Our humility serves us falsely when it leads us to shrink from any duty. The plea of unfitness or inability is utterly insufficient to excuse us.
Spiros Zodhiates

HUMILITY – Importance

There is no limit to the good a man can do if he doesn't care who gets the credit. *Anon.*

He who has other graces without humility is like one who carries a box of precious powder without a cover on a windy day. *Anon.*

Many would be scantily clad if clothed in their humility. *Anon.*

As pride was the beginning of sin, so humility must be the beginning of the Christian discipline.
Augustine

For those who would learn God's ways, humility is the first thing, humility is the second, humility is the third. *Augustine*

Life is a long lesson in humility. *James M. Barrie*

God will never come to his right unless we are totally reduced to nothing, so that it may be clearly seen that all that is laudable in us comes from elsewhere. *John Calvin*

They that know God will be humble; they that know themselves cannot be proud. *John Flavel*

There is no true holiness without humility.
Thomas Fuller

The richest pearl in the Christian's crown of graces is humility.
John Mason Good

Humility is one of the chief of all the Christian virtues; it is the hallmark of the child of God.
D. Martyn Lloyd-Jones

In order to make us trust him, God works hard to make us lose trust in ourselves. *Dick Lucas*

There is no need for us to devise means to draw attention to our work. God in his sovereign providence can well bear that responsibility.
Watchman Nee

No grace is stronger than humility. *Richard Sibbes*

Esteem thyself not to have profited by religion unless thou thinkest well of others and meanly of thyself. *Jeremy Taylor*

They are quite mistaken that faith and humility are inconsistent; they not only agree well together, but they cannot be parted.
Robert Traill

HURRY

Rush is destructive of rest, and pace of peace.
Thomas Adams

The hurrier I go, the behinder I get! *Anon.*

There are no deadlines against which God must work. Only to know this

is to quiet our spirits and relax our nerves.
A. W. Tozer

Though I am always in haste, I am never in a hurry. *John Wesley*

HYPOCRISY

(See also: Formalism)

Hypocrisy is nothing better than skin-deep holiness.

It is possible to be back-slapping and backsliding at the same time.

A hypocrite is a man who lets his light so shine before men that they can't tell what is going on behind! *Anon.*

To profess to love God while leading an unholy life is the worst of false-hoods. *Augustine*

God will not be put off with the shell while we give the devil the kernel.
Thomas Brooks

Self-ends are the operative ingredients in all a hyp-ocrite does.
Thomas Brooks

The hypocrite is only con-stant in inconstancy.
Thomas Brooks

A running sore may lie under a purple robe.
Stephen Charnock

A man may have the tongue of an angel and the heart of a devil. *John Flavel*

There is nothing worse than being something on the outside that you are not on the inside.
Mohandas Gandhi

There are three things I don't like – they are liver, kidneys and hypoc-risy. *A. Lindsay Glegg*

Hypocrisy not only covers faults, but swiftly eats out of the soul every remnant of truth and honour left in it. *Richard Glover*

Piety outside and corrup-tion inside is a revolting mixture. *Michael Green*

Hypocrisy is a sin that offers violence to the very light of nature.
William Gurnall

Piety from the teeth out-ward is an easy thing.
Matthew Henry

A rotten apple discovers itself in a windy day.
William Jenkyn

It is the mark of a hyp-ocrite to be a Christian

everywhere except at home.
Robert Murray M'Cheyne

Whitewashing the pump won't make the water pure.
D. L. Moody

A painted harlot is less dangerous than a painted hypocrite. *William Secker*

Nothing is more to be despised than a mere painted fire, the simulation of earnestness. Sooner let us have an honest death than a counterfeit life.
C. H. Spurgeon

Religion which is begun in hypocrisy will certainly end in apostasy.
William Spurstowe

Hypocrisy is the loudest lie. *George Swinnock*

I cannot believe that a man is on the road to heaven when he is habitually performing the kind of deeds that would logically indicate that he ought to be on his way to hell.
A. W. Tozer

The righteous man hath grace beyond expression; the hypocrite hath expression beyond grace.
Ralph Venning

The hypocrite hath a squint eye, for he looks more to his own glory than God's.
Thomas Watson

IDOLATRY

We are all born idolators.
Thomas Adams

Man's mind is like a store of idolatry and superstition; so much so that if a man believes his own mind it is certain that he will forsake God and forge some idol in his own brain.
John Calvin

Idolatry is anything which cooleth thy desires after Christ. *Oliver Cromwell*

Idols are called lies because they belie God, as if he had a body, whereas he is a spirit. *Matthew Henry*

A made God is no God.
Matthew Henry

When we invent our own ideas of God, we simply create him in our own image. *Kenneth F. W. Prior*

Anything above God is idolatry. *Richard Sibbes*

An idol of the mind is as offensive to God as an idol of the hand.
A. W. Tozer

The essence of idolatry is the entertainment of thoughts about God that are unworthy of him.
A. W. Tozer

God made man of the dust of the earth and man makes a god of the dust of the earth.
Thomas Watson

IGNORANCE

To be aware that you are ignorant is a great step to knowledge. *Anon.*

Ignorance is your disease; knowledge must be your cure. *Richard Baxter*

By comparison with God's perfect understanding, we are like a man inside a barrel looking through a bunghole. *R. R. Brown*

It is a common fault, that ignorance is closely followed by obstinacy.
John Calvin

We do not know a millionth part of one per cent about anything.
Thomas Edison

I feel like a man chained. I get a glimpse of reality and then it flees. If only I could be free from the shackles of my intellectual smallness, then I could understand the universe in which I live.
Albert Einstein

You cannot find knowledge by rearranging your ignorance. *Ronald Eyre*

I am still searching for the truth. *Buddha Siddhartha Gautama*

There is nothing so frightful as an active ignorance.
Johannes Von Goethe

Every natural man is a fool.
Thomas Granger

Ignorance is the mother of mischief. *Thomas Hall*

The more we know, the more we see of our own ignorance. *Matthew Henry*

Ignorance is the beaten path to hell.
William Jenkyn

Can we not be persuaded to believe that specks of consciousness on this little planet cannot, in all reasonableness, be thought of as accurate critics of the total purpose behind creation?
J. B. Phillips

The only thing I know certainly is that I am ignorant. *Socrates*

Conviction of ignorance is the doorstep to the temple of wisdom.
C. H. Spurgeon

Ignorance is the mother of superstition, not of devotion.
Augustus H. Strong

Ignorance and confidence are often twins.
George Swinnock

To be proud of learning is the greatest ignorance.
Jeremy Taylor

Not ignorance, but the ignorance of ignorance, is the death of knowledge.
Alfred North Whitehead

IMAGINATION
(See also: Mind; Thoughts)

The devil would have us continually crossing streams that do not exist. *Anon.*

You should no more allow sinful imaginations to accumulate in your mind and soul than you would allow garbage to collect in your living-room. *Anon.*

The soul without imagination is what an observatory would be without a telescope.
Henry Ward Beecher

Modern psychologists tell us that in any battle between the imagination and the will, the imagination always wins.
E. Stanley Jones

IMPENITENCE

Hardening of the heart ages people more quickly than hardening of the arteries. *Anon.*

To those whom God finds impenitent sinners he will be found to be an implacable Judge.
Matthew Henry

A stone in the heart is worse than in the kidneys.
Thomas Watson

IMPIETY
(See also: Atheism; Unbelief)

How many are there like children, who play till their candle be out, and then they go to bed in the dark!
Thomas Brooks

There is no stupidity more brutish than forgetfulness of God. *John Calvin*

Forgetfulness of God is at the bottom of all the wickedness of the wicked.
Matthew Henry

Impiety

The carnal mind sees God in nothing, not even in spiritual things. The spiritual mind sees him in everything, even in natural things. *Robert Leighton*

Mocking God is life's great impossibility.
W. T. Purkiser

INCARNATION – Jesus Christ

(See also: Virgin Birth)

The Son of God became the Son of Man in order that the sons of men might become the sons of God.

When Jesus came to earth, it was not his Godhood he laid aside, but his glory.

Christ veiled his deity but he did not void it. *Anon.*

The Son came out from the Father to help us to come out from the world; he descended to us to enable us to ascend to him. *Anthony of Padua*

Christ became what we are that he might make us what he is.
Athanasius

The incarnation is the pattern for all evangelism. Jesus Christ was totally in the world yet wholly uncontaminated by it.
Everett L. Cattell

Rejoice that the immortal God is born that mortal men may live in eternity.
Jan Hus

God became man to turn creatures into sons; not simply to produce better men of the old kind but to produce a new kind of man. *C. S. Lewis*

The mystery of the humanity of Christ, that he sunk himself into our flesh, is beyond all human understanding. *Martin Luther*

The Incarnation is not an event; but an institution. What Jesus once took up he never laid down.
Vincent McNabb

The divine Son became a Jew; the Almighty appeared on earth as a helpless human baby, unable to do more than lie and stare and wriggle and make noises, needing to be fed and changed and taught to talk like any other child . . . The more you think about it, the more staggering it gets. *J. I. Packer*

Before Christ could marry us he must be born in our nature, for the husband and the wife must be of one nature.
Richard Sibbes

The hinge of history is on the door of a Bethlehem stable. *Ralph W. Sockman*

The awful majesty of the Godhead was mercifully sheathed in the soft envelope of human nature to protect mankind.
A. W. Tozer

Christ took our flesh upon him that he might take our sins upon him.
Thomas Watson

Let earth and heaven combine,
Angels and men agree,
To praise in songs divine
The incarnate Deity,
Our God contracted to a span,
Incomprehensibly made man.
Charles Wesley

INDIFFERENCE

(See also: Apathy; Complacency)

Doctrinal indifference is no solution to the problem of doctrinal differences.

Men boast of their tolerance who should be ashamed of their indifference. *Will H. Houghton*

I believe that if there is one thing which pierces the Master's heart with unutterable grief it is not the world's iniquity but the church's indifference.
F. B. Meyer

The refusal to be committed and the attitude of indifference can in fact never be neutral.
J. B. Phillips

Indifference *in* religion is the first step to apostasy *from* religion.
William Secker

INDOLENCE

Inaction speaks louder than words.

It is often said that it is difficult to get the sinners in – but it is often just as difficult to get the saints out.

An idle brain is the devil's workshop. *Anon.*

God's biggest problem with labourers in his vineyard is absenteeism. *Anon.*

No farmer ever ploughed a field by turning it over in his mind. *Anon.*

Our idle days are Satan's busy days. *Anon.*

The only thing necessary for the triumph of evil is that good men do nothing. *Anon.*

If you are idle, you are on the road to ruin, and there are few stopping-places upon it. It is rather a precipice than a road. *Henry Ward Beecher*

Idleness is the enemy of the soul. *Benedict*

We must not seek rest or ease in a world where he whom we love had none. *Horatius Bonar*

Our laziness after God is our crying sin . . . No man gets God who does not follow hard after him. *E. M. Bounds*

A lazy spirit is always a losing spirit. *Thomas Brooks*

An idle life and a holy heart is a contradiction. *Thomas Brooks*

Lose an hour in the morning and you will be looking for it the rest of the day. *Philip Chesterfield*

It is better to wear out than to rust out. *Richard Cumberland*

An idle man does none good, and himself most harm. *William Gurnall*

Salvation is a helmet, not a nightcap. *Vance Havner*

Idleness *tempts* God instead of *trusting* him. *Matthew Henry*

Ease is never good for the people of God. *Alexander Peden*

He is not only idle who does nothing, but he is idle who might be better employed. *Socrates*

Some temptations come to the industrious, but all temptations attack the idle. *C. H. Spurgeon*

Some people seem to me to have three hands: a right hand, a left hand, and a little behind hand. *C. H. Spurgeon*

Idleness is the burial of a living man. *Jeremy Taylor*

An idle man is the devil's tennis ball. *John Trapp*

Jesus has never slept for an hour while one of his disciples watched and prayed in agony.
H. Clay Trumbull

God has given no man a dispensation to be idle.
Ralph Venning

Idleness tempts the devil to tempt. *Thomas Watson*

INFLUENCE

(See also: Example)

A good man does good merely by living. *Anon.*

There is little we touch but we leave the print of our fingers behind.
Richard Baxter

No man is an island, entire of itself; every man is a piece of the continent.
John Donne

The tiniest post office can bear a letter that may wreck or bless a nation. And the simplest life can relay blessings that may rock a continent toward God. *Vance Havner*

To be a Christian is to be a key personality in the world situation today.
Geoffrey King

When I think of those who have influenced my life the most, I think not of the great but of the good.
John Knox

There is no such person as a person without influence.
J. A. Motyer

The serene, silent beauty of a holy life is the most powerful influence in the world, next to the might of the Spirit of God.
C. H. Spurgeon

Influence is the exhalation of character.
W. M. Taylor

The most serious thing in all the world is this matter of personal influence.
George Truett

INTEGRITY

(See also: Honesty; Truth)

It is better to go straight than to move in the best of circles.

Integrity of heart is indispensable. *John Calvin*

Knowledge without integrity is dangerous and dreadful.
Samuel Johnson

Integrity

The plainer the diamond the more it sparkles; the plainer the heart is the more it sparkles in God's eyes. *Thomas Watson*

JEALOUSY

(See also: Envy)

Jealousy is the raw material of murder. *Anon.*

Many lovely things pass out of life when jealousy comes in. *Anon.*

Jealousy never thinks itself strong enough.
John Bunyan

JESUS CHRIST – Ascension

When Jesus came to earth he did not cease to be God; when he returned to heaven he did not cease to be man.

Triumphant, Christ ascends
 on high,
The glorious work complete;
Sin, death and hell low van-
 quished lie
Beneath his awful feet.
Anne Steele

Our Lord is risen from
 the dead!
Our Jesus is gone up on
 high!
The powers of hell are
 captive led,
Dragged to the portals of
 the sky.
Charles Wesley

JESUS CHRIST – Death

(See also: Atonement; Cross; Forgiveness by God)

In taking the sinner's place on the cross, Jesus became as totally accountable for sin as if he was totally responsible for it.

Jesus is not a substitute for the symptoms – he is the cure for the cause.

He died that we might be
 forgiven,
He died to make us good,
That we might go at last
 to heaven,
Saved by his precious blood.
Cecil Frances Alexander

Christ's blood is heaven's key. *Thomas Brooks*

There is no tribunal so magnificent, no throne so stately, no show of triumph so distinguished, no chariot so elevated, as is the gibbet on which Christ hath subdued death and the devil.
John Calvin

The doctrine of the death of Christ is the substance of the gospel.
Stephen Charnock

When Jesus bowed his head,
And dying took our place,
The veil was rent, a way was found
To that pure home of grace.
John Elias

Though God loved Christ as a Son he frowned upon him as a Surety.
Matthew Henry

The cross is the key. If I lose this key I fumble. The universe will not open to me. But with the key in my hand I know I hold its secret. *E. Stanley Jones*

The dying of the Lord Jesus rescues us from eternal death, whilst the doing of the Lord Jesus obtains for us eternal life.
J. M. Killen

The whole world in comparison with the cross of Christ is one grand impertinence. *Robert Leighton*

One drop of Christ's blood is worth more than heaven and earth. *Martin Luther*

The wounds of Christ were the greatest outlets of his glory that ever were. The divine glory shone more out of his wounds than out of all his life before.
Robert Murray M'Cheyne

If I would appreciate the blood of Christ I must accept God's valuation of it, for the blood is not primarily for me but for God. *Watchman Nee*

This precious Lamb of God gave up his precious fleece for us.
Christopher Nesse

He suffered not as God, but he who suffered was God. *John Owen*

The death of Christ was the most dreadful blow ever given to the empire of darkness.
William S. Plumer

Death stung himself to death when he stung Christ.
William Romaine

If we would live aright it must be by the contemplation of Christ's death.
C. H. Spurgeon

Christ assumed every consequence of sin which was not itself sinful.
S. P. Tregelles

He himself was forsaken that none of his children

might ever need to utter his cry of loneliness.
J. H. Vincent

Was it for crimes that I had
  done,
He groaned upon the tree?
Amazing pity! grace un-
  known!
And love beyond degree!
Isaac Watts

Who delivered up Jesus to die? Not Judas, for money; not Pilate, for fear; not the Jews, for envy; but the Father, for love!
Octavius Winslow

JESUS CHRIST – Deity and Humanity

When Jesus came to earth he did not cease to be God; when he returned to heaven he did not cease to be man.

Christ was a complete man.
Augustine

Jesus Christ is God in the form of man; as completely God as if he were not man; as completely man as if he were not God.
A. J. F. Behrends

Jesus Christ, the condescension of divinity, and the exaltation of humanity.
Phillips Brooks

Christ uncrowned himself to crown us, and put off his robes to put on our rags, and came down from heaven to keep us out of hell. He fasted forty days that he might feast us to all eternity; he came from heaven to earth that he might send us from earth to heaven. *W. Dyer*

Jesus became as like us as God can be.
Donald English

Jesus did not become identical to us; he did become identified with us.
Donald English

It pleases the Father that *all* fulness should be in Christ; therefore there is nothing but emptiness anywhere else. *W. Gadsby*

Christ's humanity is the great hem of the garment, through which we can touch his Godhead.
Richard Glover

If ever the Divine appeared on earth, it was in the person of Christ.
Johannes Von Goethe

Christ is our temple, in whom by faith all believers meet. *Matthew Henry*

In Christ Jesus heaven meets earth and earth ascends to heaven.
Henry Law

Surely royalty in rags, angels in cells, is not descent compared to Deity in flesh! *Henry Law*

A man who was merely a man and said the sort of things Jesus said wouldn't be a great moral teacher. He'd be either a lunatic – on a level with a man who says he's a poached egg – or else he'd be the devil of hell. You must make your choice. Either this man was and is the Son of God, or else a madman or something worse . . . But don't let us come up with any patronizing nonsense about his being a great human teacher. He hasn't left that open to us. He didn't intend to.
C. S. Lewis

Jesus was man in guise, not in *dis*guise.
Handley C. G. Moule

He suffered not as God, but he suffered who was God. *John Owen*

The impression of Jesus which the gospels give . . . is not so much one of deity reduced as of divine capacities restrained. *J. I. Packer*

If the life and death of Socrates are those of a philosopher, the life and death of Jesus Christ are those of a God.
Jean Jacques Rousseau

If you want to know what God has to say to you, see what Christ was and is.
C. H. Spurgeon

Remember, Christ was not a deified man, neither was he a humanized God. He was perfectly God and at the same time perfectly man. *C. H. Spurgeon*

Christ was not half a God and half a man; he was perfectly God and perfectly man. *James Stalker*

Because Christ was God, did he pass unscorched through the fires of Gethsemane and Calvary? Rather let us say, because Christ was God he underwent a suffering that was absolutely infinite.
Augustus H. Strong

A cloud over the sun makes no change in the body of the sun; so, though the divine nature be covered with the human, it makes no change in the divine nature. *Thomas Watson*

JESUS CHRIST – Glory

Christ is lovely, Christ is very lovely, Christ is most lovely, Christ is always lovely, Christ is altogether lovely. *Thomas Brooks*

Christ is the most sparkling diamond in the ring of glory. *Thomas Brooks*

Christ is the ocean, in which every drop is infinite compassion. He is the mountain towering above the mountains, in which every grain is God's own goodness.
Henry Law

The world cannot bury Christ. The earth is not deep enough for his tomb, the clouds are not wide enough for his winding-sheet. *Edward Thomson*

The more you think about Christ, the more you think of him. *H. C. Trumbull*

JESUS CHRIST – Immutability

I change, he changes not,
The Christ can never die;
His love, not mine, the resting-place,
His truth, not mine, the tie.
Horatius Bonar

Christ's purse is always full, though he be always giving. *Thomas Brooks*

Christ is the still point of the turning world.
T. S. Eliot

The sea ebbs and flows, but the rock remains unmoved.
Robert Murray M'Cheyne

JESUS CHRIST – Intercession

He who for men their surety stood,
And poured on earth his precious blood,
Pursues in heaven his mighty plan,
The Saviour and the Friend of man.
Michael Bruce

If I could hear Christ praying for me in the next room, I would not fear a million of enemies. Yet the distance makes no difference; he is praying for me!
Robert Murray M'Cheyne

Christ has taken our nature into heaven to represent us, and has left us on earth with his nature to represent him. *John Newton*

Prayer as it comes from the saint is weak and languid;

but when the arrow of a saint's prayer is put into the bow of Christ's intercession it pierces the throne of grace. *Thomas Watson*

JESUS CHRIST – Life and Influence

All the armies that ever marched, and all the navies that ever were built, and all the parliaments that ever sat, and all the kings that ever reigned, put together, have not affected the life of mankind on this earth as powerfully as has that one solitary life.
Anon.

The name of Jesus is not so much written as ploughed into the history of the world.
Ralph Waldo Emerson

After reading the doctrine of Plato, Socrates, or Aristotle, we feel that the specific difference between their words and Christ's is the difference between an inquiry and a revelation.
Joseph Parker

Our Lord's life was ordered by his objective.
Ken Robins

Jesus Christ himself was a do-gooder from the beginning of his public ministry to the end of it. There is a sense in which he did nothing else.
Foy Valentine

Christ lived what he preached and preached what he lived.
Fernando Vangioni

JESUS CHRIST – Lordship

As Christ is the root by which a saint grows, so is he the rule by which a saint walks. *Anon.*

He values not Christ at all who does not value Christ above all. *Augustine*

The Lord who vacated his tomb has not vacated his throne.
G. R. Beasley-Murray

Christ with anything would have satisfied me; nothing without Christ could do it.
Thomas Boston

Miss Christ and you miss all.
Thomas Brooks

The rattle without the breast will not satisfy the child; the house without the husband will not satisfy the wife; the cabinet without the jewel will not satisfy the virgin; the world

without Christ will not satisfy the soul.
Thomas Brooks

They do not love Christ who love anything more than Christ.
Thomas Brooks

Jesus cannot be our Saviour unless he is first our Lord.
Hugh C. Burr

The system of human mediation falls away in the advent to our souls of the living Christ. Who wants stars, or even the moon, after the sun is up?
A. B. Cave

Christ is either both Saviour and Lord, or he is neither Saviour nor Lord.
John R. De Witt

Every blessing God has for man is in and through Jesus Christ.
A. Lindsay Glegg

You cannot have the gifts of Christ apart from the government of Christ.
A. Lindsay Glegg

Christ is now creation's sceptre-bearer, as he was once creation's burden-bearer. *A. J. Gordon*

A Christ supplemented is a Christ supplanted.
William Hendriksen

Tomorrow's history has already been written . . . at the name of Jesus every knee must bow.
Paul E. Kauffman

There's not a thumb's breadth of this universe about which Jesus Christ does not say, 'It is mine.'
Abraham Kuyper

Seek Christ, and you will find him, and with him everything else thrown in.
C. S. Lewis

When Jesus Christ utters a word, he opens his mouth so wide that it embraces all heaven and earth, even though that word be but in a whisper.
Martin Luther

Jesus Christ is the centre of everything, and the object of everything, and he that does not know him knows nothing of nature, and nothing of himself.
Blaise Pascal

The early Christians would have been quite surprised to hear 'Jesus is Lord' as a second experience. For them it was a baptismal confession!
Kenneth F. W. Prior

All history is incomprehensible without Christ.
Ernest Renan

Whatever may be the surprises of the future, Jesus will never be surpassed.
Ernest Renan

I have a great need for Christ; I have a great Christ for my need.
C. H. Spurgeon

It is as unbiblical as it is unrealistic to divorce the lordship from the Saviourhood of Jesus Christ.
John R. W. Stott

For the true Christian the one supreme test for the present soundness and ultimate worth of everything religious must be the place our Lord occupies in it.
A. W. Tozer

To present Christ's lordship as an option leaves it squarely in the category of stereo equipment for a new car. *Dallas Willard*

JESUS CHRIST – Love

Christ's love to his people is not a lip-love, from the teeth outwardly, but a real love, from the heart inwardly. *W. Dyer*

I stand amazed in the presence
Of Jesus the Nazarene,
And wonder how he could love me,
A sinner, condemned, unclean.
Charles Homer Gabriel

We are never nearer Christ than when we find ourselves lost in a holy amazement at his unspeakable love. *John Owen*

Though our Saviour's passion is over, his compassion is not. *William Penn*

Every day we may see some new thing in Christ. His love has neither brim nor bottom.
Samuel Rutherford

In our fluctuations of feeling, it is well to remember that Jesus admits no change in his affections; your heart is not the compass Jesus saileth by.
Samuel Rutherford

JESUS CHRIST – Perfection

Jesus perfectly lived what he perfectly taught.
Herman H. Horne

The most destructive criticism has not been able to dethrone Christ as the incarnation of perfect holiness. *Herrick Johnson*

Jesus Christ – Perfection

It is a lovely sight to see man treading earth and no mire clinging to his feet; and breathing our polluted air without infection's taint.

Henry Law

Christ, if not good, is not God. *Augustus H. Strong*

Jesus Christ is both the most absolute grace and the most perfect law; so that to believe in him is to embrace at once both law and grace.

Alexandre Vinet

JESUS CHRIST – Power

Christ is the dynamic of all his demands.

Christ's performances outstrip his promises.

Nehemiah Rogers

The great maker of the will is alive to carry out his own intentions.

C. H. Spurgeon

JESUS CHRIST–Sympathy

Jesus takes to heart the sufferings of his friends.

William Hendriksen

Jesus Christ is not only the Son of God mighty to save, but the Son of man able to feel.

J. C. Ryle

O Saviour Christ, thou too
art man;
Thou hast been troubled,
tempted, tried;
Thy kind but searching
glance can scan
The very wounds that
shame would hide.

Henry Twells

Touched with a sympathy
within,
He knows our feeble frame;
He knows what sore tempta-
tions mean,
For he has felt the same.

Isaac Watts

JESUS CHRIST – Teaching

Christ's statements are either cosmic or comic.

How is it that nobody has dreamed up any moral advances since Christ's teaching? What was there in his heredity and his environment to account for this unique teacher, and the remarkable fact that no greater has ever looked like emerging?

Michael Green

Certainly, no revolution that has ever taken place in

society can be compared to that which has been produced by the words of Jesus Christ. *Mark Hopkins*

The discrepancy between the depth, sincerity and, may I say, shrewdness of Christ's moral teaching and the rampant megalomania which must lie behind his theological teaching unless he is indeed God, has never been got over.
C. S. Lewis

JESUS CHRIST – Uniqueness

Jesus was not the first Christian; he was and is the Christ. *Herman Bavinck*

Between Jesus and whomsoever else in the world there is no possible comparison.
Napoleon Bonaparte

There is more of power to sanctify, elevate, strengthen and cheer in the word *Jesus* (Jehovah - Saviour) than in all the utterances of man since the world began. *Charles Hodge*

In his life Christ is an example showing us how to live; in his death, he is a sacrifice satisfying for our sins; in his resurrection, a conqueror; in his ascension, a king; in his intercession, a high priest.
Martin Luther

Jesus Christ cannot be adequately understood in terms of any category applicable to man . . . He is a category by himself.
Donald MacLeod

Jesus was the greatest religious genius that ever lived. His beauty is eternal and his reign will never end. He is in every respect unique and nothing can be compared with him.
Ernest Renan

He is not the Great – he is the Only!
Carnegie Simpson

Christ is the most unique person in history. No man can write a history of the human race without giving first and foremost place to the penniless teacher of Nazareth. *H. G. Wells*

JOY

(See also: Happiness)

Joy is the natural outcome of the Christian's obedience to the revealed will of God.

True joy glows in the dark.

Joy is the flag that is flown from the citadel of the heart when the King is in residence. *Anon.*

The Christian should be an alleluia from head to foot. *Augustine*

There may be joy *in* God when there is little joy *from* God.
Stephen Charnock

Take a saint, and put him in any condition, and he knows how to rejoice in the Lord.
Walter Cradock

A joyless Christian is a libel on his Master.
Northcote Deck

Job was a happier man on the dunghill than Adam was in paradise. *John Flavel*

'Pleasure' and 'joy' not only are not synonymous, but may be as profoundly different as heaven and hell. *Sidney J. Harris*

Holy joy is the oil to the wheels of our obedience.
Matthew Henry

Joy is the serious business of heaven. *C. S. Lewis*

The Christian ought to be a living doxology.
Martin Luther

We can do nothing well without joy, and a good conscience which is the ground of joy.
Richard Sibbes

If you have no joy in your religion, there's a leak in your Christianity somewhere. *Billy Sunday*

There is as much difference between spiritual joys and earthly as between a banquet that is eaten and one that is painted on the wall. *Thomas Watson*

JUDGEMENT

(See also: Eternal Life; Eternity; Heaven; Hell; Punishment)

The fact that the Christian can face the day of judgement secure in the knowledge that he will not be rejected does not mean that he is to think of it in terms of a glorified prize-giving.

That which a man spits against heaven shall fall back on his own face.
Thomas Adams

The day of judgement is remote; *thy* day of judgement is at hand. *Anon.*

As death leaves us, so judgement will find us.
Thomas Brooks

Those whose hearts are not pierced by the sword of God's justice shall certainly be cut down and destroyed by the axe of his judgements.

Francis Burkitt

It is no inconsiderable security that we shall stand before no other tribunal than that of our Redeemer.

John Calvin

If we are believers in Jesus Christ we have already come through the storm of judgement. It happened at the cross.

Billy Graham

Heaven will be filled with such as have done good works, and hell with such as intended to do them.

Antonio Guevasa

God's fork follows the wicked's rake.

William Gurnall

Those that love darkness rather than light shall have their doom accordingly.

Matthew Henry

Those who will not deliver themselves into the hand of God's mercy cannot be delivered out of the hand of his justice.

Matthew Henry

Men must choose between an exceeding great and eternal weight of glory and an exceeding great and eternal weight of wrath.

Thomas V. Moore

The power of man can never reverse the sentence of God.

Thomas V. Moore

The punishment of the sinner is not an arbitrary vengeance, but the due process of moral providence. *J. A. Motyer*

Time shall be no more when judgement comes, and when time is no more change is impossible.

C. H. Spurgeon

The Lord has a golden sceptre and an iron rod. Those who will not bow to the one shall be broken by the other.

Thomas Watson

Just as the tree cut down,
  that falls to
North or southward, there
  it lies;
So man departs to heav'n
  or hell,
Fix'd in the state wherein
  he dies.

Isaac Watts

JUSTIFICATION

(See also: Faith – and Deeds; Holiness – and Justification)

In justification, the sinner is not only pardoned, he is promoted.

Christ's righteousness, pleaded in the court of justice, is our full and final discharge. *Anon.*

God hath two hands, a right hand of mercy and a left hand of justice.
John Boys

Justification takes place in the mind of God and not in the nervous system of the believer.
C. I. Schofield

Nobody has understood Christianity who does not understand . . . the word 'justified'.
John R. W. Stott

Justification is the very hinge and pillar of Christianity. *Thomas Watson*

KINDNESS

(See also: Compassion; Love for Others; Mercy to Others)

Kindness is a language that the deaf can hear and the blind can see.

He is too busy who is too busy to be kind.
James W. Alexander

Every moment is the right one to be kind. *Anon.*

The best exercise for strengthening the heart is reaching down and lifting people up. *Ernest Blevins*

Kind words are the music of the world.
Frederick W. Faber

Kindness in ourselves is the honey that blunts the sting of unkindness in another.
Walter Savage Landor

God has a secret method by which he recompenses his saints: he sees to it that they become the prime beneficiaries of their own benefactions!
I. D. E. Thomas

Be kind. Remember that everyone you meet is fighting a hard battle.
Harry Thompson

KINGDOM OF GOD

The only kingdom that will prevail in this world is the kingdom that is not of this world. *Anon.*

Ten million roots are pumping in the streets: do you hear them? Ten million buds are forming in the axles of the leaves: do you hear the sound of the saw or the hammer? All next summer is at work in the world: but it is unseen by us. And so 'the kingdom of God comes not with observation'.
Henry Ward Beecher

The entrance fee into the kingdom of God is nothing; the annual subscription is all we possess.
Henry Drummond

The Bible is the statute-book of God's kingdom.
Ezekiel Hopkins

The kingdom of God does not exist because of your effort or mine. It exists because God reigns. Our part is to enter this kingdom and bring our life under his sovereign will.
T. Z. Koo

The kingdom of God has come into the world and the powers of the age to come are operative even in the age that now is.
Peter Lewis

The key to the history of the world is the kingdom of God.
D. Martyn Lloyd-Jones

The kingdom of God is like a grain of mustard seed, not like a can of nitro-glycerine.
J. B. Thomas

KNOWLEDGE

(See also: Education; Mind; Reason)

Knowledge directs conscience; conscience perfects knowledge.
Thomas Adams

Practice is the soul of knowledge.
Thomas Adams

To be aware that you are ignorant is a great step to knowledge. *Anon.*

Ignorance is your disease; knowledge must be your cure. *Richard Baxter*

That knowledge which puffs up will at last puff down. *Joseph Caryl*

Knowledge in the head is as money in the purse; knowledge in the heart is as money for our use.
Stephen Charnock

You cannot find knowledge by rearranging your ignorance. *Ronald Eyre*

Action is the proper fruit of knowledge.
Thomas Fuller

Knowledge is but folly unless it is guided by grace.
George Herbert

Knowledge without integrity is dangerous and dreadful. *Samuel Johnson*

Sins of omission are aggravated by knowledge.
Thomas Manton

What use is deeper knowledge if we have shallower hearts? *Leonard Ravenhill*

True faith and saving knowledge go together.
George Swinnock

To be proud of learning is the greatest ignorance.
Jeremy Taylor

Knowledge is the eye that must direct the foot of obedience.
Thomas Watson

Many a man's knowledge is a torch to light him to hell. *Thomas Watson*

Not ignorance, but the ignorance of ignorance, is the death of knowledge.
Alfred North Whitehead

KNOWLEDGE OF GOD

(See also: Revelation)

To many people, God is no more than an upright blur.

The evidence of knowing God is obeying God.
Eric Alexander

There is but one thing in the world really worth pursuing – the knowledge of God.
Robert H. Benson

Knowledge of God can no more connect a man with God than the sight of the sun can carry him to heaven. *John Calvin*

Little knowledge of God is worth a lot more than a great deal of knowledge about him. *J. I. Packer*

Once you become aware that the main business that you are here for is to know God, most of life's problems fall into place of their own accord.
J. I. Packer

One can know a great deal about godliness without much knowledge of God. *J. I. Packer*

Divine knowledge leaves no man stationary.
W. Graham Scroggie

Divine knowledge is not as the light of the moon to sleep by, but as the light of the sun to work by.
William Secker

LAW OF GOD

Christ abolished the law as a means of justification not by destroying it but by fulfilling it.

God's law was given to reveal sin, not to remove it.

The law gives menaces; the gospel gives promises.
Thomas Adams

The law can pursue a man to Calvary, but no farther.
Anon.

The law sends us to the gospel, that we may be justified, and the gospel sends us to the law again to enquire what is our duty, being justified.
Samuel Bolton

The Bible's God, and none other, can satisfy human needs. His moral code for centuries has passed through the flames of controversy, but it does not even have the smell of fire upon it. *D. J. Burrell*

The law is a hammer to break us, the gospel God's oil to cure us.
Stephen Charnock

When the law of God is written in our hearts, our duty will be our delight.
Matthew Henry

The divine law, as seen by the Christian, exhibits liberty, gives liberty, is liberty.
Robert Johnstone

Law says 'Do', grace says 'Done'. *John Henry Jowett*

God is love, and law is the way he loves us. But it is also true that God is law, and love is the way he rules us. *G. S. Lee*

People make excuses for not keeping the law of God, which is proof how deeply they believe in the law. *C. S. Lewis*

The law discovers the disease. The gospel gives the remedy.
Martin Luther

The law is what we must do; the gospel is what God will give.
Martin Luther

The giving of the law is part of the dispensation of the covenant of grace.
Donald MacLeod

The law demands what it cannot give; grace gives all it demands.
Blaise Pascal

Christ has redeemed his people from the curse of the law and not from the command of it; he has saved them from the wrath of God, but not from his government. *A. W. Pink*

There was grace under law and there is law under grace.
Charles Caldwell Ryrie

He who really, and in good faith, preaches the cross, never opposes the preaching of the law.
W. G. T. Shedd

The needle of the law must precede the thread of the gospel.
C. H. Spurgeon

The law is a court of justice, but the gospel is a throne of grace.
George Swinnock

LEGALISM

The believer mortifies because God is pacified towards him; the legalist mortifies that he may pacify God by his mortification . . . that he may have whereof to glory.
Ralph Erskine

Legalism is an abuse of the law; it is a reliance on law-keeping for acceptance with God, and the proud observance of laws is no part of the grace of God.
Ernest F. Kevan

Legalism is bound to produce pride of heart.
Watchman Nee

LEISURE

It is what you do when you have nothing to do that reveals what you are.
Anon.

Leisure is a beautiful garment, but it will not do for constant wear. *Anon.*

Tell me how a young person spends his leisure time and I will tell you the kind of person he is.
Billy Graham

Temptation rarely comes in working hours. It is in their leisure time that men are made or marred.
W. T. Taylor

LIBERALISM

Liberalism is a miscarriage of truth.

Those who preach liberal theology are robbers; they rob God of his sovereignty,

Jesus of his divinity, the Holy Spirit of his ministry, the miracles of their credibility, Mary of her virginity, the apostles of their authority, the church of its history and the new birth of its necessity.

A liberal is one who transforms biblical terms into theological bubble gum.
Anon.

Liberalism is not the answer to a heart longing for a vital faith. We must look in some other direction.
Vance Havner

An examination of the teachings of liberalism in comparison with those of Christianity will show that at every point the two movements are in direct opposition.
J. Gresham Machen

Historic Christianity and either the old or the new liberal theology are two separate religions with nothing in common except certain terms which they use with totally different meanings.
Francis Schaeffer

LIBERTY

Liberty is not the same as licence; to be free is not to be free and easy; the Christian is not free to please himself but to please God.

Freedom is not the right to do as you please; it is the liberty to do as you ought. *Anon.*

Man is most free when controlled by God alone.
Augustine

Liberty means ability not to violate the law of God. Licence means personal insistence on doing what I like. *Oswald Chambers*

Liberty is turned to licence by self. *Walter Chantry*

Perfect conformity to the will of God is the sole sovereign and complete liberty.
J. H. Merle D'Aubigné

True freedom is only to be found when one escapes from oneself and enters into the liberty of the children of God.
François Fenelon

Gospel liberty is a liberty *from* sin, not *to* sin.
Thomas Hall

The truth makes us free *from* our spiritual enemies, free *in* the service of God, free *to* the privileges of sons. *Matthew Henry*

My liberty is controlled by my love for my brothers and sisters. *Jan Kaleta*

Liberty has brought us the freedom to be the slaves of righteousness.
Charles Caldwell Ryrie

To obey God is perfect liberty. *Seneca*

A Christian is the greatest freeman in the world . . . yet in regard of love he is the greatest servant.
Richard Sibbes

True freedom consists with the observance of law.
W. L. Thornton

LIFE

If life is an accident, it cannot conceivably have any purpose, for accident and purpose are mutually exclusive.

Life at its best means putting God first.

How frail is human life! A thin texture of living flesh is the only screen between never-dying souls and their eternal condition.
Anon.

Life asks no questions that faith cannot answer.
Anon.

The world is only a passage-room to eternity; the world is to us as the wilderness was to Israel, not to rest in but to travel through.
Anon.

This life is all the heaven the worldling has, and all the hell the saint ever sees.
Anon.

As soon as man is born he begins to sicken; he only terminates his sickness by his death. *Augustine*

Life is a long lesson in humility.
James M. Barrie

Age and youth look upon life from the opposite ends of the telescope; to the one it is exceedingly long, to the other exceedingly short.
Henry Ward Beecher

Be such a man, and live such a life, that if every man were such as you, and every life a life like yours, this earth would be God's paradise.
Phillips Brooks

If it were not that ingratitude had blinded our eyes,

every birth would fill us with amazement.
John Calvin

The quality of life is more important than life itself.
Alexis Carrel

The man who regards his own life and that of his fellow creatures as meaningless is not merely unfortunate but almost disqualified for life. *Albert Einstein*

What makes life dreary is absence of motive. What makes life complicated is multiplicity of motive. What makes life victorious is singleness of motive.
George Eliot

Life is a path trodden by all men, *and but once.*
John Gill

A useless life is only an early death.
Johannes Von Goethe

Nothing is trivial here if heaven looks on.
Vance Havner

The business of our lives is not to please ourselves but to please God.
Matthew Henry

Of what does life essentially consist? . . . the Bible answers that life is composed of relationships.
Robert Horn

It is not possible to set out in the Christian profession with a more instructive or impressive idea than this – *life is the seed-time for eternity.*
John Angell James

Sow an action and you reap a habit; sow a habit and you reap a character; sow a character and you reap a destiny.
William James

Whatever we do in this life is seed.
Thomas Manton

Make sure the thing you are living for is worth dying for.
Charles Mayes

How short is human life!
The very breath
Which frames my words
accelerates my death.
Hannah More

The whole of life is a test, a trial of what is in us, so arranged by God himself.
William S. Plumer

We must not live only to live. *Richard Sibbes*

Let us live as people who are prepared to die, and die as people who are prepared to live.
James S. Stewart

Take care of your life and the Lord will take care of your death.
George Whitefield

We are immortal till our work is done.
George Whitefield

Ask the Lord to make your life a glory to him, a menace to the devil, a strength to your church and a witness to the world.
Frederick P. Wood

LITERATURE

The printed page is a visitor who gets inside the home and stays there; it always catches a man in the right mood, for it speaks to him only when he is reading it. *Anon.*

If I might control the literature of the household, I would guarantee the well-being of the church and state. *Francis Bacon*

Books may preach when the author cannot, when the author may not, when the author dares not, yea, and which is more, when the author is not.
Thomas Brooks

The devil hates goose quills.
Martin Luther

We must throw the printer's inkpot at the devil.
Martin Luther

The smallest tract may be the stone in David's sling. In the hands of Christ it may bring down a giant soul.
Robert Murray M'Cheyne

We become what we read.
Matilda Nordtvedt

Literature is the immortality of speech.
August Schlegel

Be careful what books you read; for as water tastes of the soil it runs through, so does the soul of the authors that a man reads.
John Trapp

No other agency can penetrate so deeply, witness so daringly, abide so persistently and influence so irresistibly as the printed page. *Samuel Zwemmer*

LONELINESS

When Christ saves a man, he not only saves him

from his sin, he also saves him from his solitude.
Frank Colquhoun

Walking with our divine Lord we should never feel lonely and never feel lost.
Frank Farley

Loneliness is the first thing which God's eye named not good. *John Milton*

Christ understands loneliness; he's been through it.
Paul S. Rees

The soul hardly ever realizes it, but whether he is a believer or not, his loneliness is really a homesickness for God.
Hubert Van Zeller

The world is filled with rootless people. So many cannot say the lovely, necessary little phrase 'I belong'. *Alan Walker*

LORD'S DAY

See that the Lord's day be spent in holy preparation for eternity.
Richard Baxter

Profaning of the Lord's sabbath is as great an argument of a profane heart as any that can be found in the whole book of God.
Thomas Brooks

Make the Lord's day the market for thy soul.
John Bunyan

Sunday is a divine and priceless institution.
Winston Churchill

Where sabbaths are neglected all religion sensibly goes to decay.
Matthew Henry

The essence of the sabbath could not be changed without changing the nature of man. *A. A. Hodge*

The sabbath is the golden clasp that binds together the volume of the week.
J. C. MacAuley

The murderer who is dragged to the gibbet and the polished sabbath-breaker are one in the sight of God.
Robert Murray M'Cheyne

You show me a nation that has given up the sabbath and I will show you a nation that has got the seed of decay.
D. L. Moody

Man was made to worship every day, but work is eliminated on the sabbath to show its proper perspective in God's divine plan.
Clyde Narramore

A weekly sabbath walls in our wild nature.
Christopher Nesse

Common sense, reason, conscience, will combine, I think, to say that if we cannot spare God one day in a week we cannot be living as those ought to live who must die one day.
J. C. Ryle

The day of the Lord is likely to be a dreadful day to them that despise the Lord's day.
George Swinnock

If you want to kill Christianity you must abolish Sunday.
François Voltaire

He that would prepare for heaven must honour the sabbath upon earth.
Daniel Wilson

LOVE FOR CHRIST

(See also: Communion with Christ; Meditation; Prayer)

The question is still the same: Do you love Jesus? Affection is the answer to apathy. *Vance Havner*

The surest evidence of our love to Christ is obedience to the laws of Christ . . . Love is the root, obedience is the fruit.
Matthew Henry

Of all the things that will surprise us in the resurrection morning, this, I believe, will surprise us most: that we did not love Christ more before we died.
J. C. Ryle

LOVE FOR GOD

(See also: Communion with God; Meditation; Prayer)

The greatest and best thing that can be said of a man is that he loved the Lord.
Anon.

I would hate my own soul if I did not find it loving God. *Augustine*

Love to God and obedience to God are so completely involved in each other that any one of them implies the other too.
F. F. Bruce

Obedience to God is the most infallible evidence of sincere and supreme love to him.
Nathaniel Emmons

Our love to the Lord is not worth speaking of but his to us can never be enough spoken of.
Matthew Henry

Even the heart of God thirsts after love.
Abraham Kuyper

Don't throw God a bone of your love unless there's the meat of obedience on it. *John MacArthur*

Love of the creature toward the Creator must include obedience or it is meaningless.
Francis Schaeffer

Love is the only thing in which we can retaliate with God . . . We must not give him word for word, but we must give him love for love.
Thomas Watson

LOVE FOR OTHERS – Definition

Jealousy, properly considered, is an essential element of true love: it is . . . an unceasing longing for the loved one's welfare.
J. A. Motyer

Love = to live for.
Mary Slessor

Love is service rather than sentiment.
John R. W. Stott

Love is the outgoing of the entire nature in self-sacrificing service.
W. H. Griffith Thomas

LOVE FOR OTHERS – Effects

Love is the master key to a happy home. *Anon.*

One loving heart sets another on fire.
Augustine

Duty makes us do things well, but love makes us do them beautifully.
Phillips Brooks

If you work at love, you will find love at work.
Peter Jackson

Suspicions subtract, faith adds, but love multiplies. It blesses twice – him who gives it and him who gets it.
C. T. Studd

LOVE FOR OTHERS – Importance

Christian love is the distinguishing mark of Christian life.

It is possible to give without loving, but it is

impossible to love without giving.
Richard Braunstein

We are shaped and fashioned by what we love.
Johannes Von Goethe

Brotherly love is the badge of Christ's disciples.
Matthew Henry

Love is the leading affection of the soul.
Matthew Henry

Whatever of outward service or obedience we render to God or man, if love is withheld, the law is not fulfilled.
F. B. Meyer

Love is the binding power which holds the body of the Christian church together. *Stephen Olford*

Love is the oxygen of the kingdom.
Juan Carlos Ortiz

Love is the hardest lesson in Christianity; but for that reason it should be our most care to learn it.
William Penn

Love is the queen of all the Christian graces.
A. W. Pink

Love should be the silver thread that runs through all your conduct. *J. C. Ryle*

We are as we love, not as we know. *Richard Sibbes*

You never so touch the ocean of God's love as when you forgive and love your enemies. *Corrie Ten Boom*

If a man says he is a Christian but has no love he is simply deluding himself.
Geoffrey Thomas

LOVE FOR OTHERS – Contrasted with Lust

(See also: Lust)

The world is littered with the debris of what *eros* has promised but been unable to provide.
Jill Briscoe

Love can wait to give; it is lust that can't wait to get. *Josh McDowell*

Love is not blind. Lust is blind. If love is blind, God is blind.
Gordon Palmer

It is the difference betwixt lust and love, that this is fixed, that volatile. Love grows, lust wastes, by enjoyment; and the reason is that one springs from a union of souls, and the other springs from a union of sense. *William Penn*

The expression 'free love' is a contradiction in terms. If it's free, it's not love; if it's love, it's not free.
David Watson

LOVE FOR OTHERS – Measure

The proof of love is its capacity to suffer for the object of its affection.
Anon.

Of love there be two principal offices, one to give, another to forgive.
John Boys

Love's mantle is very large.
Thomas Brooks

Love must love even when it gets nothing out of it.
Roger Forster

The chains of love are stronger than the chains of fear. *William Gurnall*

Love seeks one thing only: the good of the one loved. It leaves all the other secondary effects to take care of themselves.
Thomas Merton

The measure of our love for others can largely be determined by the frequency and earnestness of our prayers for them.
A. W. Pink

Love goes beyond safety.
Frederick Sampson

No man can love a saint, as a saint, but a saint.
Richard Sibbes

Love is the livery of Christ.
C. H. Spurgeon

Perfect love knows no *because*. *A. W. Tozer*

LOVE FOR OTHERS – Practical

Many love at their tongue's end, but the godly love at their fingers' end. *Anon.*

Love does not say, 'Give me', but 'Let me give you'.
Jill Briscoe

Love is practical or it is not love at all.
P. W. Heward

Nobody will know what you mean by saying that 'God is Love' unless you act it as well.
Lawrence Pearsall Jacks

Whereas obedience is righteousness in relation to God, love is righteousness in relation to others.
A. Plummer

Whatever else love is, it is not passive.
Frederick Sampson

Christian love is not the victim of our emotions but the servant of our will. *John R. W. Stott*

Love without obedience is a satanic substitute for God's plan.
John C. Whitcomb

LUST

(See also: Desires; Sex)

The world is littered with the debris of what *eros* has promised but been unable to provide.
Jill Briscoe

A little will satisfy nature; less will satisfy grace; nothing will satisfy men's lusts. *Thomas Brooks*

Our eyes, when gazing on sinful objects, are out of their calling and God's keeping. *Thomas Fuller*

What lust is so sweet or profitable that is worth burning in hell for?
William Gurnall

Love can wait to give; it is lust that can't wait to get. *Josh McDowell*

Lust is appetite run wild.
F. B. Meyer

Love is not blind. Lust is blind. If love is blind, God is blind.
Gordon Palmer

The expression 'free love' is a contradiction in terms. If it's free, it's not love; if it's love, it's not free.
David Watson

LUXURY

(See also: Materialism; Money; Possessions; Prosperity; Riches; Wealth)

Christ did not die to purchase this world for us.
Thomas Adams

Comfort comes as a guest, lingers to become a host, and stays to enslave us.
Anon.

Luxury is a sin that never goes alone.
Thomas Brooks

God rarely seems to use a man who pampers himself with luxury.
Kenneth F. W. Prior

LYING

(See also: Dishonesty)

It is easy to tell one lie, but not easy to tell just one lie.

Nothing is rarer than a solitary lie; for lies breed like toads; you cannot tell one but out it comes with a hundred young ones on its back.
Washington Allston

A good memory is needed once you have lied.
Anon.

The ability to lie is always a liability. *Anon.*

All that one gains by falsehood is not to be believed when he speaks the truth.
Aristotle

Better to die than to lie.
Thomas Brooks

Liars pervert the end for which God created speech.
Thomas Brooks

Sin has many tools, but a lie is the handle that fits them all.
Oliver Wendell Holmes

None but cowards lie.
Arthur Murphy

One lie must be thatched with another or it will soon rain through.
John Jason Owen

MAN – A Failure

Man, in his fallen nature, is a dissatisfied and frustrated rainbow-chaser.
Anon.

Surely the best of men are but men at the best.
Thomas Brooks

What shadows we are, and what shadows we pursue!
Edmund Burke

Whatever else is or is not true, this one thing is certain – man is not what he was meant to be.
G. K. Chesterton

Man is a jewel robbed of its precious stone, with only the costly setting left, and even of that we must exclaim, 'How is the gold become dim and the most fine gold changed!'
Henry Gill

Every natural man is a fool.
Thomas Granger

It is becoming more and more obvious that it is not starvation, not microbes, not cancer, but man himself who is mankind's greatest danger. *Carl Gustav Jung*

For the first time I examined myself with a serious practical purpose. And there I found what appalled me: a zoo of lusts, a bedlam of ambitions, a nursery of fear, a harem of fondled hatreds. My name was Legion. *C. S. Lewis*

Man was created for an empire but is living in a pit. *H. G. Wells*

MAN – God's Creation and Concern

His creation by God is man's only claim to dignity, importance or value.

God made man to be somebody – not just to have things. *Anon.*

The yearning of man's heart is homesickness for God. *Anon.*

The most profound essence of my nature is that I am capable of receiving God. *Augustine*

Man without God ceases to be a man. *Nicolas Berdyaev*

It is only an infinite God, and an infinite good, that can fill and satisfy the precious and immortal soul of man. *Thomas Brooks*

A circle cannot fill a triangle; no more can the whole world fill the heart of man. *Thomas Brooks*

Jesus Christ never met an unimportant person. That is why God sent his Son to die for us. If someone dies for you, you must be important. *M. C. Cleveland*

In God's sight there are two men – Adam and Jesus Christ – and these two men have all other men hanging at their girdle strings. *Thomas Goodwin*

Because he is made in the image of God, man is inviolable. *Os Guinness*

If God is God and man is made in his image, then *each* man is significant. *Os Guinness*

Historic Christianity sees man as distinct, but not divorced, from nature. *Os Guinness*

Man still stands in the image of God – twisted,

broken, abnormal, but still the image-bearer of God.
Francis Schaeffer

Because we are the handiwork of God it follows that all our problems and their solutions are theological. *A. W. Tozer*

The man who denies that fallen man bears upon him something of the ruined relic of what he once was is no true friend of the Bible. *A. W. Tozer*

MAN – a Paradox

Man is harder than rock, and more fragile than an egg. *Anon.*

I have become a puzzle to myself. *Augustine*

Although modern man zestfully explores outer space, he seems quite content to live in a spiritual kindergarten and to play in a moral wilderness.
Carl F. H. Henry

Man is an enigma to himself. *Carl Gustav Jung*

Man's conquest of nature has been astonishing. His failure to conquer human nature has been tragic.
Julius Mark

All the evidence of history suggests that man is indeed a rational animal, but with a nearly infinite capacity for folly . . . He draws blueprints for Utopia but never quite gets it built.
Robert McNamara

What a chimera, then, is man! What a novelty! What a chaos, what a contradiction, what a prodigy! Judge of all things, imbecile worm of the earth; depository of truth; a sink of uncertainty and error; the pride and refuse of the universe. *Blaise Pascal*

Man is a peculiar, puzzling paradox, groping for God and hoping to hide from him at the selfsame time.
William A. Ward

MAN – a Religious Being

(See also: Religion)

Man must and will have some religion. If he has not the religion of Jesus he will have the religion of Satan. *William Blake*

Man is by his constitution a religious animal.
Edmund Burke

Men are religious beings. Religion can't be got rid of by seeking to ignore it.
A. A. Hodge

Man – a Religious Being

Man must have a God or an idol. *Martin Luther*

Man is incurably religious.
Paul Sabatier

MAN – a Sinner

(See also: Depravity; Sin; Sinful Nature)

Man was made to dwell in a garden, but his sin has turned it into a wilderness.

The Bible does not picture man as a risen creature but as a fallen one.

Civilized man is psychologically sick, and the more cultured and civilized he becomes, the more sick he will be, for modern man is seeking to feel at home in the world without any reference to God.
Akbar Abdul-Haqq

Modern man wants to be treated as an invalid rather than a sinner.
Eric Alexander

Man is a good thing spoiled.
Augustine

The natural man's affections are wretchedly misplaced; he is a spiritual monster. His heart is where his feet should be, fixed on earth; his heels are lifted up against heaven, where his heart should be set. *Thomas Boston*

The dilemma for man is not who he is but what he has done. His predicament is not that he is small but that he is sinful.
Os Guinness

Everything man touches he perverts. *Philip E. Hughes*

The history of man is his attempt to escape his own corruption.
Daniel Mullis

Sin has so degraded man that from what he is now we can form no conception of what he was meant to be. *Andrew Murray*

Men may be changed by divine grace, but *man* is unchanged.
William S. Plumer

Any natural man, he is iron to God and wax to the devil. *Richard Sibbes*

Man is a skin-encapsulated ego. *Alan Watts*

MARRIAGE

(See also: Family Life)

As God by creation made two of one, so again by

marriage he made one of two. *Thomas Adams*

Don't look around for a life partner, look *up*. Any other choice than God's will mean disaster.
Anon.

Marriage is more than finding the right person; it is being the right person.
Anon.

Never be yoked to one who refuses the yoke of Christ. *Anon.*

A pledge to take a woman for his wife commits a man to sharing life in its entirety.
Walter J. Chantry

How soon marriage counselling sessions would end if husbands and wives were competing in thoughtful self-denial!
Walter J. Chantry

God made the human pair in such a manner that it is natural for the husband to lead, for the wife to follow.
William Hendriksen

A man's children are pieces of himself, but his wife *is* himself.
Matthew Henry

The woman was made of a rib out of the side of Adam; not made out of his head to rule over him, nor out of his feet to be trampled on by him; but out of his side to be equal to him, under his arm to be protected, and near his heart to be loved.
Matthew Henry

One plus one equals one may not be an accurate mathematical concept, but it is an accurate description of God's intention for the marriage relationship.
Wayne Mack

God is the witness to every marriage ceremony, and will be the witness to every violation of its vows. *Thomas V. Moore*

Successful marriage is always a triangle: a man, a woman and God.
Cecil Myers

God did not create woman to be a competitor but to be a companion.
Frederick Sampson

Before man had any other calling he was called to be a husband. *Henry Smith*

There is always a danger of marriage taking the razor edge off the passion for Jesus and souls.
C. T. Studd

Try praising your wife, even if it does frighten her at first. *Billy Sunday*

Marriage is both honourable and onerable. *George Swinnock*

God's love ties the marriage-knot so fast that neither death nor hell can break it. *Thomas Watson*

MARTYRDOM

(See also: Persecution)

The martyrs were bound, imprisoned, scourged, racked, burnt, rent, butchered – and they multiplied. *Augustine*

Divine presence made the martyrs as willing to die as to dine. *Thomas Brooks*

It is not the blood but the cause that makes a martyr. *Thomas Brooks*

The Lord knows I go up this ladder [to be hung as a martyr] with less fear, confusion or perturbation of mind than ever I entered a pulpit to preach. *Donald Cargill*

Christianity has made martyrdom sublime and sorrow triumphant. *E. H. Chapin*

God sometimes raises up many faithful ministers out of the ashes of one. *Matthew Henry*

Martyrdom came into the world early; the first man that died died for religion. *William Jenkyn*

Most joyfully will I confirm with my blood that truth which I have written and preached. *Jan Hus*

It is better for me to be a martyr than a monarch. *Ignatius*

The blood of the martyrs is the seed of the church. *Jerome*

You may kill us, but you can never hurt us. *Justyn Martyr*

The martyrs shook the powers of darkness with the irresistible power of weakness. *John Milton*

It is a small matter to die once for Christ; if it might be, I could wish I might die a thousand deaths for him. *Lewis Paschalis*

Weak grace may *do* for God, but it must be strong grace that will *die* for God. *William Secker*

MATERIALISM

(See also: Luxury; Possessions; Prosperity; Riches; Wealth)

A man caught up with this world is not ready for the next one. Materialism is no preparation for judgement or for heaven.

In the world in which we live today it takes a miracle for a man not to be a materialist.

Materialism is every bit as dangerous as modernism.

It is a very high point of Christian wisdom and prudence always to look upon the good things and the great things of this world as a man will certainly look upon them when he comes to die.
Thomas Brooks

Death is the final mockery of materialism. We brought nothing into this world and it is certain we can carry nothing out. If a man has lived to accumulate good, how indescribably tragic his dying!
Herbert M. Carson

May God pity a nation whose factory chimneys rise higher than her church steeples. *John Kelman*

There is not a vice which more effectually contracts and deadens the feelings, which more completely makes a man's affections centre in himself and excludes all others from partaking in them, than the desire of accumulating possessions.
Thomas Manton

Build your nest in no tree here . . . for the Lord of the forest has condemned the whole woods to be demolished.
Samuel Rutherford

No oriental monarch ever ruled his cowering subjects with any more cruel tyranny than things, visible things, audible things, tangible things, rule mankind.
A. W. Tozer

MEDITATION

(See also: Communion with God; Love for God; Prayer)

Meditation has a digesting power and turns special truth into nourishment.
Anon.

The hearer of God's Word ought to be like those animals that chew the cud; he ought not only to feed upon it, but to ruminate upon it. *Augustine*

The vessels are fullest of grace which are nearest its spring. The more Christ's glory is beheld, the more men are changed.
William Bagshawe

A man may think on God every day and meditate on God no day.
William Bridge

There is no place like the feet of Jesus for resolving the problems that perplex our hearts.
G. B. Duncan

If we hope to move beyond the superficialities of our culture . . . we must be willing to go down into the recreating silences.
Richard Foster

Meditation is the best help to memory.
Matthew Henry

It is easier to go six miles to hear a sermon, than to spend one quarter of an hour in meditating on it when I come home.
Philip Henry

Meditation is a scriptural duty . . . as binding as Bible reading and prayer.
John J. Murray

Meditate on the Word in the Word. *John Owen*

Meditation is the activity of calling to mind, and thinking over, and dwelling on, and applying to oneself, the various things that one knows about the works and ways and purposes and promises of God.
J. I. Packer

Our design in meditation must be rather to cleanse our hearts than to clear our minds.
George Swinnock

Meditation is the bellows of the affections.
Thomas Watson

Reading and conversation may furnish us with many ideas of men and things, yet it is our own meditation that must form our judgement. *Isaac Watts*

MEEKNESS

(See also: Humility; Self-Crucifixion)

A meek and quiet spirit is an incorruptible ornament, much more valuable than gold. *Thomas Brooks*

You must have meekness stamped upon you. You assent to it today, but meekness is often forgotten when most needed.
Alfred Buxton

Learn the blessedness of the unoffended in the face of the unexplainable.
Amy Carmichael

A lion in God's cause must be a lamb in his own.
Matthew Henry

Poverty of spirit is the bag into which Christ puts the riches of his grace.
Rowland Hill

Keep thy heart in a soft and tractable state lest thou lose the imprints of God's hands. *Irenaeus*

The most difficult thing in the world is to become poor in spirit.
D. Martyn Lloyd-Jones

The meek person has a preference for the will of God. *J. Oswald Sanders*

A meek man is a good neighbour.
George Swinnock

Meekness is the mark of a man who has been mastered by God.
Geoffrey B. Wilson

MERCY FROM GOD

(See also: Forgiveness by God)

A Christian should always remember that his mercies are greater than his miseries.

God gives his anger by weight but his mercy without measure. *Anon.*

Grace is especially associated with men in their sins: mercy is usually associated with men in their misery. *Anon.*

God hath two hands, a right hand of mercy and a left hand of justice.
John Boys

Mercy and punishment, they flow from God, as the honey and the sting from the bee.
Thomas Brooks

Shall light troubles make you forget weighty mercies? *John Flavel*

Mercy in the promise is as the apple in the seed.
William Gurnall

As God's mercies are new every morning toward his people, so his anger is new every morning against the wicked. *Matthew Henry*

If the end of one mercy were not the beginning of another, we were undone.
Philip Henry

Mercies are such gifts as advance our debts.
William Secker

Mercy is God's Benjamin; the last born and best beloved of his attributes.
C. H. Spurgeon

A debtor to mercy alone,
Of covenant mercy I sing;
Nor fear, with thy righteousness on,
My person and offering to bring;
The terrors of law and of God
With me can have nothing to do;
My Saviour's obedience and blood
Hide all my transgressions from view.
Augustus M. Toplady

Mercies are never so savoury as when they savour of a Saviour. *Ralph Venning*

Those are the best prepared for the greatest mercies that see themselves unworthy of the least. *Thomas Watson*

MERCY TO OTHERS

(See also: Forgiveness of Others)

He that demands mercy and shows none ruins the bridge over which he himself is to pass.
Thomas Adams

The more godly any man is, the more merciful that man will be.
Thomas Brooks

The merciful fall into the arms of mercy.
J. P. Lange

Mercy turns her back on the unmerciful.
Francis Quarles

Mercy is one end of patience. *Henry Smith*

Show your piety by your pity. *Thomas Watson*

MIND

(See also: Education; Imagination; Knowledge; Reason; Thoughts)

It is good to have an open mind, provided it isn't open at both ends.
Doug Barnett

Our greatest sins are those of the mind.
Thomas Goodwin

Let us never forget that the message of the Bible is addressed primarily to the mind, to the understanding.
D. Martyn Lloyd-Jones

It doesn't take a great mind to be a Christian, but it takes all the mind a man has. *Richard C. Raines*

Speech is the index of the mind. *Seneca*

The secret of holy living is in the mind.
John R. W. Stott

The purpose of an open mind is to close it on something.
William Temple

The mind is good – God put it there. He gave us our heads and it was not his intention that our heads would function just as a place to hang a hat.
A. W. Tozer

MIRACLES

The miraculous is absolutely basic to Christianity.
E. H. Andrews

Miracles are not breaches of natural but revelations of spiritual law. *Anon.*

The church that does not work miracles is dead and ought to be buried.
Samuel Chadwick

Miracles are the great bell of the universe, which draws men to God's sermon. *John Foster*

Miracles are the swaddling-clothes of the infant church.
Thomas Fuller

The miracles were to the gospel as seals are to a writing. *William Gurnall*

Grace will bring a man to heaven without working miracles, but working miracles will never bring a man to heaven without grace. *Matthew Henry*

Miracles are not to be expected when ordinary means are to be used.
Matthew Henry

We rob Christianity of all excitement when we evacuate the miraculous.
Stephen Olford

A religion without wonders is false. A theology without wonders is heretical.
William S. Plumer

MONEY

(See also: Luxury; Materialism; Possessions; Prosperity; Riches; Wealth)

Few things test a person's spirituality more accurately than the way he uses money.

Money is like sea-water; the more a man drinks, the more thirsty he becomes.
Anon.

There are no pockets in a shroud. *Anon.*

You can blot out the sun if you hold a penny close enough to your eye.
Anon.

Money is like muck, no good unless it is spread.
Francis Bacon

The love of money is a greater curse to the church than the aggregate of all the other evils in the world. *Samuel Chadwick*

Time and money are the heaviest burdens of life, and the unhappiest of all mortals are those who have more of either than they know how to use.
Samuel Johnson

The real measure of our wealth is how much we'd be worth if we lost all our money.
John Henry Jowett

He that serves God for money will serve the devil for better wages.
Roger L'Estrange

If a man's religion does not affect his use of money, that man's religion is vain.
Hugh Martin

The key to our whole relationship to money lies in the attitude of our minds towards it.
Kenneth F. W. Prior

The poorest man I know is the man who has nothing but money.
John D. Rockefeller

Two-thirds of all the strifes, quarrels and lawsuits in the world arise from one simple cause – money!
J. C. Ryle

Mammon is the largest slave-holder in the world.
Frederick Saunders

Money has never yet made anyone rich. *Seneca*

Money – the greatest god below the sky.
Herbert Spencer

I fear money. Mother Hubbard's cupboard is safe; a full cupboard is very risky. *C. T. Studd*

Nothing that is God's is obtainable by money.
Tertullian

When I have any money I get rid of it as quickly as possible, lest it find a way into my heart.
John Wesley

MORALITY

(See also: Ethics; Goodness)

The Christian life is a moral marathon.

We were not redeemed merely to be legally safe, but also to be morally sound.

Men are more accountable for their motives than for anything else; and primarily, morality consists in the motives, that is in the affections.
Archibald Alexander

No man can be a true member of the church of God who is a stranger to moral righteousness.
Anon.

The Bible's God, and none other, can satisfy human needs. His moral code for centuries has passed through the flames of controversy, but it does not even have the smell of fire upon it.
D. J. Burrell

Morality, taken as apart from religion, is but another name for decency in sin.
Horace Bushnell

It is not guided missiles but guided morals that is our great need today.
George L. Ford

The immutability of God's holy character is itself the absolute and the final court of morality.
Os Guinness

Nothing is ever settled until it is settled right; and nothing is ever settled right until it is settled with God.
Vance Havner

Atheistic morality is not impossible, but it will never answer our purpose.
Roswell D. Hitchcock

All moral obligation resolves itself into the obligation of conformity to the will of God. *Charles Hodge*

Morality is not merely the purity patter of preachers – it is the law of God.
W. E. Sangster

No man's religion ever survives his morals.

Robert South

As the sailor locates his position on the sea by 'shooting' the sun, so we may get our moral bearings by looking at God.

A. W. Tozer

MURMURING

The frog and the murmurer, both of them are bred of the mud. *Thomas Adams*

It is better to be mute than to murmur.

Thomas Brooks

Murmuring uncrowns a man. *Thomas Brooks*

Those who complain most are most to be complained of. *Matthew Henry*

Our murmuring is the devil's music.

Thomas Watson

MUSIC

Among other things adapted for man's pleasure and for giving them pleasure, music is either the foremost, or one of the principal; and we must esteem it a gift from God designed for that purpose.

John Calvin

He who does not find [the great and perfect wisdom of God] in his wonderful work of music is truly a clod and is not worthy to be considered a man!

Martin Luther

MYSTERY

(See also: God – Inscrutability)

A religion without mystery must be a religion without God. *Anon.*

A science without mystery is unknown; a religion without mystery is absurd.

Henry Drummond

Mystery is but another name for our ignorance; if we were omniscient all would be perfectly plain.

Tryon Edwards

Mystery is beyond human reason but it is not against reason. *Os Guinness*

NATURE

(See also: Creation; Evolution)

The world is the first Bible that God made for the instruction of man.

Clemens Alexandrinus

Open your eyes, and the whole world is full of God.
Jacob Boehme

What are the heavens, the earth, the sea, but a sheet of royal paper, written all over with the wisdom and power of God?
Thomas Brooks

Nature is the art of God.
Thomas Browne

If we would avoid a senseless natural philosophy we must always start with this principle, that everything in nature depends upon the will of God, and that the whole course of nature is only the prompt carrying into effect of his orders. *John Calvin*

Nature is but a name for an effect whose cause is God. *William Cowper*

The laws of nature are but the thoughts and agencies of God, the modes in which he works and carries out the designs of his providence and will.
Tryon Edwards

Nature is a first volume, in itself incomplete, and demanding a second volume, which is Christ.
Charles Gore

God's will is the law of universal nature.
William S. Plumer

Causes in nature do not obviate the necessity of a Cause in nature.
George John Romanes

OBEDIENCE – Blessing

Joy is the natural outcome of the Christian's obedience to the revealed will of God.

Obedience changes things.

All heaven is waiting to help those who will discover the will of God and do it. *J. Robert Ashcroft*

Obedience won't stop the decomposition of our physical lives but it will halt the decay of our spiritual lives. *Ian Barclay*

By obeying Christ's commands you will gain more than you can give.
Thomas Brooks

Though no man merits assurance by his obedience, yet God usually crowns obedience with assurance.
Thomas Brooks

Peace and comfort can be found nowhere except in simple obedience.
François Fenelon

Holy joy is the oil to the wheels of our obedience.
Matthew Henry

To obey God is perfect liberty. *Seneca*

The reward of sin is more sin and the reward of obedience is the power to obey again.
David Shepherd

The fundamental deception of Satan is the lie that obedience can never bring happiness. *R. C. Sproul*

Before faith and obedience become acts of man they are gifts of God.
R. B. Kuyper

Knowledge is the eye that must direct the foot of obedience.
Thomas Watson

The true obedience of faith is a cheerful obedience.
Thomas Watson

OBEDIENCE – Characteristics

Christian obedience is not slavery to dominating legalism but it is submission to divine law.

It is only by the grace of God that a man can obey the law of God.

The difference between disobedience and obedience is marked by the individual's attitude toward sin.
Donald Grey Barnhouse

OBEDIENCE – Importance

Obedience is not the essence of a right relationship with God, but it is the evidence of it.

Obedience is the positive side of repentance.

The evidence of saving faith is not how much you believe but how well you behave.

The evidence of knowing God is obeying God.
Eric Alexander

Christ's sheep are marked in the ear and the foot; they hear his voice and they follow him. *Anon.*

Christianity is obedience.
Anon.

One act of obedience is better than a hundred sermons.
Dietrich Bonhoeffer

Every man obeys Christ as he prizes Christ, and no otherwise.
Thomas Brooks

He who obeys sincerely endeavours to obey thoroughly.
Thomas Brooks

The obedience that springs from faith is the obedience of a son, not of a slave.
Thomas Brooks

Love to God and obedience to God are so completely involved in each other that any one of them implies the other too.
F. F. Bruce

We cannot rely on God's promises without obeying his commandments.
John Calvin

Faith is the starting-post of obedience.
Thomas Chalmers

The best measure of a spiritual life is not its ecstasies but its obedience.
Oswald Chambers

The golden rule for understanding in spiritual matters is not intellect, but obedience. *Oswald Chambers*

My gracious Lord, I own thy right
To every service I can pay;
And call it my supreme delight
To hear thy dictates and obey.
Philip Doddridge

Obedience to God is the most infallible evidence of sincere and supreme love to him.
Nathanael Emmons

Faith that saves has one distinguishing quality: saving faith is a faith that produces obedience; it is a faith that brings about a way of life. *Billy Graham*

Understanding can wait. Obedience cannot.
Geoffrey Grogan

Sacrifice without obedience is sacrilege.
William Gurnall

What our Lord said about cross-bearing and obedience is not in fine type. It is in bold print on the face of the contract.
Vance Havner

The surest evidence of our love to Christ is obedience to the laws of Christ . . .

Love is the root, obedience is the fruit.
Matthew Henry

God calls people to worship him with their obedience, and instead they try to fob him off with their religion.
John Hercus

God is not otherwise to be enjoyed than as he is obeyed. *John Howe*

I had rather obey than work miracles.
Martin Luther

Don't throw God a bone of your love unless there's the meat of obedience on it. *John MacArthur*

There is no experience of sanctification which absolves us from the responsibility of day-to-day obedience. *David McKee*

Obedience is the best commentary on the Bible.
Theodore Monod

The believer is not redeemed by obedience to the law but he is redeemed unto it. *John Murray*

Love of the creature toward the Creator must include obedience or it is meaningless. *Francis Schaeffer*

Believing and obeying always run side by side.
C. H. Spurgeon

Faith and obedience are bound up in the same bundle. He that obeys God, trusts God; and he that trusts God, obeys God.
C. H. Spurgeon

Where the right is absolute, the obedience must not be conditional.
George Swinnock

To escape the error of salvation by works we have fallen into the opposite error of salvation without obedience. *A. W. Tozer*

Doers of the Word are the best hearers.
Thomas Watson

Love without obedience is a satanic substitute for God's plan.
John C. Whitcomb

OLD AGE

Don't resent growing old; many do not have the opportunity of doing so.
Anon.

Life's evening will take its character from the day that has preceded it.
Anon.

An aged Christian with the snow of time on his head may remind us that those points of earth are whitest that are nearest heaven. *E. H. Chapin*

Forty is the old age of youth; fifty is the youth of old age. *Victor Hugo*

The evening of a well-spent life brings its lamps with it. *Joseph Joubert*

The last ten years of life are the best, because we are freest from illusions and fullest of experience.
Benjamin Jowett

No wise man ever wished to be younger.
Jonathan Swift

ORTHODOXY

There is nothing more ugly than orthodoxy without understanding or compassion. *Anon.*

Biblical orthodoxy without compassion is surely the ugliest thing in the world.
Francis Schaeffer

Orthodoxy is my doxy; heterodoxy is another man's doxy.
William Warburton

You may be as orthodox as the devil, and just as wicked. *John Wesley*

PAIN

(See also: Sickness; Suffering; Trials)

If anybody is not disturbed by the problem of pain, it is for one of two reasons: either because of hardening of the heart or else because of softening of the brain.
G. A. Studdert Kennedy

God whispers to us in our pleasures, speaks in our consciences, but shouts in our pains; it is his megaphone to rouse a deaf world. *C. S. Lewis*

PATIENCE

Biblical patience is not rooted in fatalism that says everything is out of control. It is rooted in faith that says everything is in God's control.

Waiting for an answer to prayer is often part of the answer.

Patience must not be an inch shorter than affliction.
Thomas Adams

Life is a symphony, and we lose a third of it by

cutting out the slow movement. *Anon.*

Long-suffering is a grace of silence.
William Bagshawe

There is no place for faith if we expect God to fulfil immediately what he promises. *John Calvin*

Patient waiting is often the highest way of doing God's will.
Jeremy Collier

Though God take the sun out of heaven, yet we must have patience.
George Herbert

Hope is the mother of patience. *William Jenkyn*

Our impatience only learns patience through the thorn of delay and darkness.
J. Charles Stern

To lengthen my patience is the best way to shorten my troubles.
George Swinnock

Patience in prayer is nothing but faith spun out.
Thomas Watson

PEACE

(See also: Peace-Making)

The peace of God means being grateful for his past mercies, conscious of his present mercies, and certain of his future mercies.

Peace is the establishment of harmonious relationships with that for which we are constituted.
Douglas Adam

Peace is the conscious possession of adequate resources. *Anon.*

Peace is the deliberate adjustment of my life to the will of God. *Anon.*

If we have not quiet in our minds, outward comfort will do no more for us than a golden slipper on a gouty foot.
John Bunyan

Peace and comfort can be found nowhere except in simple obedience.
François Fenelon

The peace of the soul consists in an absolute resignation to the will of God. *François Fenelon*

Peace is never to be obtained but by the rooting out of sin. *Francis Hall*

Stayed upon Jehovah
Hearts are fully blest,
Finding, as he promised,
Perfect peace and rest.
Frances Ridley Havergal

Peace is not real peace until it has been tested in the storm. *Eric Hayman*

Peace is the smile of God reflected in the soul of the believer.
William Hendriksen

Peace is such a precious jewel that I would give anything for it but truth.
Matthew Henry

What peace can they have who are not at peace with God? *Matthew Henry*

You will never find peace and happiness until you are ready to commit yourself to something worth dying for.
Jean Paul Sartre

Peace is the fruit of believing prayer. *M. R. Vincent*

Peace flows from purity.
Thomas Watson

The seeming peace a sinner has is not from the knowledge of his happiness but the ignorance of his danger.
Thomas Watson

PEACE-MAKING

(See also: Peace)

He that is not a son of peace is not a son of God.
Richard Baxter

Labour mightily for a healing spirit.
Thomas Brooks

The oilcan is mightier than the sword.
Everett Dirksen

Few things more adorn and beautify a Christian profession than exercising and manifesting the spirit of peace. *A. W. Pink*

PENITENCE

(See also: Confession; Contrition; Conviction of Sin; Repentance)

A penitent's prayer is an undeniable ambassador.
Anon.

When the soul has laid down its faults at the feet of God, it feels as though it had wings.
Eugene de Guerin

Godly mourning is better than carnal rejoicing.
William S. Plumer

PERFECTION

This life was not intended to be the place of our

perfection but the preparation for it.
Richard Baxter

I would rather aim at perfection and fall short of it than aim at imperfection and fully attain it.
A. J. Gordon

We shall never come to the perfect man till we come to the perfect world.
Matthew Henry

A great deal of perfectionism is rotten to the core.
A. A. Hodge

The perfect Christian is the one who, having a sense of his own failure, is minded to press towards the mark.
Ernest F. Kevan

The nearer men are to being sinless, the less they talk about it.
D. L. Moody

As soon as I learn that a brother states that he has lived for months without sin . . . I feel sure that somewhere or other there is a leak in the ship.
C. H. Spurgeon

I met only one perfect man and he was a perfect nuisance! *C. H. Spurgeon*

What is Christian perfection? Loving God with all our heart, mind, soul and strength. *John Wesley*

PERMISSIVENESS

Permissiveness is man thinking he can take God's law into his own hands.

Permissiveness is nothing less than moral mutiny.

If God did not exist, all would be permitted.
Feodor Dostoevsky

A permissive home is a home where you don't love enough to exercise the authority that Christ gave you. *Ben Haden*

Permissiveness is not a policy; it is the abandonment of policy and its apparent advantages are illusory. *B. F. Skinner*

PERSECUTION

(See also: Martyrdom)

Persecution is one of the surest signs of the genuineness of our Christianity.
Benjamin E. Fernando

Crushing the church is like smashing the atom: divine

energy of high quality is released in enormous quantity and with miraculous effects.
Benjamin E. Fernando

Who more innocent than Christ? And who more persecuted? The world is the world still.
John Flavel

Christ's followers cannot expect better treatment in the world than their Master had. *Matthew Henry*

Persecution is no novelty . . . the offence of the cross will never cease till all flesh shall see the salvation of God.
William S. Plumer

The fire of God can't be damped out by the waters of man's persecution.
A. W. Tozer

PERSEVERANCE

(See also: Determination)

If you fall, don't give up, *get up!* *Anon.*

The difference between perseverance and obstinacy is that one often comes from a strong will and the other from a strong won't.
Henry Ward Beecher

The root of all steadfastness is in consecration to God.
Alexander MacLaren

PHILOSOPHY

Philosophy is the search for truth. In Jesus, the search ends.

Any philosophy which deals only with the here and now is not adequate for man.
Billy Graham

I have looked into most philosophical systems, and I have seen that none will work without a God.
Clerk Maxwell

What philosophy is striving to find, theology asserts has been found.
Augustus H. Strong

Philosophy is saying what everybody knows in language that no one can understand. *J. F. Taviner*

PIETY

Piety means letting God bend your will, not just your knees. *Anon.*

The path of piety avoids ritualism and rationalism.
Richard Glover

Piety is God sensible to the heart. *Blaise Pascal*

Practice is the very life of piety.
William S. Plumer

True piety is never separate from the fear of God.
William S. Plumer

Piety is the best parentage.
William Secker

Show your piety by your pity. *Thomas Watson*

PLEASURES

Consider pleasures as they depart, not as they come.
Aristotle

'Pleasure' and 'joy' not only are not synonymous, but may be as profoundly different as heaven and hell. *Sidney J. Harris*

The Christian tastes God in all his pleasures.
J. I. Packer

That this world is a playground instead of a battlefield has now been accepted in practice by the vast majority of fundamentalist Christians. *A. W. Tozer*

Soft pleasures harden the heart. *Thomas Watson*

POSSESSIONS

(See also: Luxury; Materialism; Money; Prosperity; Riches; Wealth)

Worldly possessions have ruined many people but redeemed none.

If we have God in all things while they are ours, we shall have all things in God when they are taken away. *Anon.*

You actually possess everything you can see when you close your eyes.
Anon.

It is easier to renounce worldly possessions than it is to renounce the love of them. *Walter Hilton*

All the possessions of mortals are mortal.
Metrodorus

Nothing influences a man so much as that which he calls his own.
C. H. Spurgeon

POVERTY

It is good to run short, that we may be driven to Christ with our necessity.
Anon.

He who is not contented with a little will never be satisfied with much.
Thomas Brooks

Worry over poverty is as fatal to spiritual fruitfulness as is gloating over wealth.
A. W. Pink

Poverty and affliction take away the fuel that feeds pride. *Richard Sibbes*

Poverty is a friend to prayer.
George Swinnock

I am mended by my sickness, enriched by my poverty, and strengthened by my weakness.
Abraham Wright

POWER

Almighty must be that power whose sufficient strength is weakness.
Anon.

The Christian needs won't power as well as will power.
Anon.

Nothing will so avail to divide the church as love of power. *Chrysostom*

Remember Jesus *for us* is all our righteousness before a holy God, and Jesus *in us* is all our strength in an ungodly world.
Robert Murray M'Cheyne

We have no power from God unless we live in the persuasion that we have none of our own.
John Owen

We only lose our weaknesses through discovery of them. *J. Charles Stern*

PRAISE

(See also: Worship)

The best atmosphere for prayer is praise.
Peter Anderson

Praise . . . decentralizes self. *Paul E. Billheimer*

Had I a thousand tongues, I would praise God with them all. *Peter Boehler*

We should be always wearing the garment of praise, not just waving a palm-branch now and then.
Andrew Bonar

Men in general praise God in such a manner that he scarcely obtains the tenth part of his due.
John Calvin

Be not afraid of saying too much in the praises of God; all the danger is of saying too little.
Matthew Henry

What we win by prayer we must wear with praise.
Matthew Henry

If Christians praised God more, the world would doubt him less.
Charles E. Jefferson

Give unlimited credit to our God.
Robert Murray M'Cheyne

Come, thou fount of every blessing,
Tune my heart to sing thy grace;
Streams of mercy, never ceasing,
Call for songs of loudest praise.
Teach me some melodious measure,
Sung by flaming tongues above;
Oh, the vast, the boundless treasure
Of my Lord's unchanging love!
Robert Robinson

A drop of praise is an unsuitable acknowledgement for an ocean of mercy. *William Secker*

The concealment of praise is tantamount to depriving the Lord of half his glory.
Friedrich Tholuck

In prayer we act like men; in praise we act like angels.
Thomas Watson

PRAYER – Answers
(See also: Prayer – Unanswered)

Waiting for an answer to prayer is often part of the answer.

We dare not limit God in our asking, nor in his answering.

To spend an hour worrying on our knees is not prayer. Indeed, there are times when it is our duty, having committed a problem to God in prayer, to stop praying and to trust and to do the necessary work to arrive at a solution.
Oliver Barclay

God can no more divest himself of his attribute of hearing prayer than of being. *John Calvin*

Pure prayers have pure blessings.
Thomas Goodwin

Those blessings are sweetest that are won with

prayers and worn with thanks. *Thomas Goodwin*

Good prayers never come weeping home. I am sure I shall receive either what I ask or what I should ask. *Joseph Hall*

Our prayer and God's mercy are like two buckets in a well; while the one ascends, the other descends.
Mark Hopkins

We should be glad that God makes us wait for mercy. A great part of our sanctification is waiting for answer to our prayers.
Humphrey Mildred

If it were the case that whatever we ask God was pledged to give, then I for one would never pray again, because I would not have sufficient confidence in my own wisdom to ask God for anything. *J. A. Motyer*

I live in the spirit of prayer. I pray as I walk about, when I lie down and when I rise up. And the answers are always coming.
George Muller

All my discoveries have been made in answer to prayer. *Isaac Newton*

God's condescension is nowhere more conspicuous than in his hearing of prayer. *Austin Phelps*

Genuine prayer will be looking out for answers.
William S. Plumer

Heaven finds an ear when sinners find a tongue.
Francis Quarles

We should believe that nothing is too small to be named before God. What should we think of the patient who told his doctor he was ill, but never went into particulars?
J. C. Ryle

When we shoot an arrow, we look to the fall of it; when we send a ship to sea, we look for the return of it; and when we sow seed, we look for a harvest; and so when we sow our prayers into God's bosom, shall we not look for an answer?
Richard Sibbes

PRAYER – and Christ's Intercession

Let not our prayers die while our Intercessor lives.
Anon.

Prayer – and Christ's Intercession

The impulse to prayer, within our hearts, is evidence that Christ is urging our claims in heaven.
Augustus H. Strong

Prayer as it comes from the saint is weak and languid; but when the arrow of a saint's prayer is put into the bow of Christ's intercession it pierces the throne of grace.
Thomas Watson

PRAYER – Earnestness

Praying is much more difficult than saying words to God.

We need to agonize as well as organize.

Our prayers must mean something to us if they are to mean anything to God. *Maltbie D. Babcock*

To pray aright is right earnest work.
Jacob Boehm

God hears no more than the heart speaks, and if the heart be dumb God will certainly be deaf.
Thomas Brooks

When thou prayest, rather be thy heart without words than thy words without heart. *John Bunyan*

In God's name I beseech you, let prayer nourish your soul as your meals nourish your body.
François Fenelon

Those prayers that awaken God must awaken us.
Thomas Goodwin

We must pray with our hand at the pump, or the ship will sink in sight of our prayers.
William Gurnall

I like ejaculatory prayer; it reaches heaven before the devil can get a shot at it. *Rowland Hill*

Prayer is the sweat of the soul. *Martin Luther*

Much of our praying is just asking God to bless some folks that are ill, and to keep us plugging along. But prayer is not merely prattle, it is warfare. *Alan Redpath*

Let your fleece lie on the threshing floor of supplication till it is wet with the dew of heaven.
C. H. Spurgeon

Prayer is the gun we shoot with, fervency is the fire that discharges it, and faith the bullet that pierces the throne of grace.
John Trapp

PRAYER – Essence

Effective prayer is a quartet – the Father, the Son, the Spirit and the Christian.

Prayer is not so much submitting our needs to God but submitting ourselves to him.

The real secret of prayer is secret prayer.

Prayer is the wing wherewith the soul flies to heaven and meditation the eye wherewith we see God. *Ambrose*

Prayer is something more than asking God to run errands for us. *Anon.*

When you pray, there is a clash of arms in the heavenly sphere. *Anon.*

Between the humble and contrite heart and the majesty of heaven there are no barriers. The only password is prayer.
H. Ballou

Talking to men for God is a great thing, but talking to God for men is greater still.
E. M. Bounds

A prayer in its simplest definition is merely a wish turned Godward.
Phillips Brooks

He who wants anything from God must approach him with empty hands.
Robert Cunningham

God is still on the throne, we're still on his footstool, and there's only a knee's distance between.
Jim Elliot

The Bible is a letter God has sent to us; prayer is a letter we send to him.
Matthew Henry

The greatest of men must turn beggars when they have to do with Christ.
Matthew Henry

Prayer is a summit meeting in the throne room of the universe.
Ralph A. Herring

Prayer is a time exposure of the soul to God.
E. Stanley Jones

Prayer is the nearest approach to God and the

highest enjoyment of him that we are capable of in this world. *William Law*

For what is prayer in the last analysis? It is a conscious spreading out of my helplessness before God.
Al Martin

Prayer is the simplest form
of speech
That infant lips can try;
Prayer the sublimest strains
that reach
The Majesty on high.
James Montgomery

We talk about heaven being so far away. It is within speaking distance to those who belong there.
D. L. Moody

Prayer is not eloquence, but earnestness; not the definition of helplessness, but the feeling of it.
Hannah More

The great secret of a right waiting upon God is to be brought down to utter impotence.
Andrew Murray

Prayer is not designed for the furnishing of God with the knowledge of what we need, but it is designed as a confession to him of our sense of need.
A. W. Pink

Prayer is a swift messenger, which in the twinkling of an eye can go and return with an answer from heaven.
William S. Plumer

Prayer prompted by the Holy Spirit is the footfall of the divine decree.
C. H. Spurgeon

The goal of prayer is the ear of God.
C. H. Spurgeon

Could we be content to meet a loved one only in public?
J. Hudson Taylor

The chief purpose of prayer is that God may be glorified in the answer.
R. A. Torrey

The pulse of prayer is praise. The heart of prayer is gratitude. The voice of prayer is obedience. The arm of prayer is service.
William A. Ward

Prayer is the key of heaven; faith is the hand that turns it. *Thomas Watson*

Prayer is not something that I *do*; prayer is something that I am.
Warren Wiersbe

PRAYER – and Faith

(See also: Faith – and Prayer)

There are no depths from which the prayer of faith cannot reach heaven.

We are encouraged to come freely to God but not flippantly.

We dare not limit God in our asking, nor in his answering.

Prayer is possession by anticipation. *Anon.*

Praying without faith is like shooting without a bullet; it makes a noise but does no execution.
Francis Burkitt

Prayer, it is the very natural breath of faith.
William Gurnall

If we cannot go to the house of the Lord we can go by faith to the Lord of the house.
Matthew Henry

All the storehouses of God are open to the voice of faith in prayer.
D. M. McIntyre

When the Lord is to lead a soul to great faith he leaves its prayers unheard.
Andrew Murray

Believing supplications are forecasts of the future.
C. H. Spurgeon

Large asking and large expectation on our part honour God. *A. L. Stone*

PRAYER – A Gift

The nature of the divine goodness is not only to open to those who knock, but also to *cause them* to knock and ask.
Augustine

To pray rightly is a rare gift. *John Calvin*

If you love God, you cannot be at a loss for something to say to him, something for your hearts to pour out before him, which his grace has already put there.
Matthew Henry

When God intends great mercy for his people, the first thing he does is set them a-praying.
Matthew Henry

Prayer comes from God and . . . all the time God is training us to pray.
Iain H. Murray

Prayer – a Gift

True prayers are like those carrier pigeons which find their way so well; they cannot fail to go to heaven, for it is from heaven that they came; they are only going home.
C. H. Spurgeon

The greatest and best talent that God gives to any man or woman in the world is the talent of prayer.
Alexander Whyte

The little estimate we put on prayer is evident from the little time we give to it. *E. M. Bounds*

Most of modern man's troubles stem from too much time on his hands and not enough on his knees. *Ivern Boyett*

Cold prayers do always freeze before they reach to heaven.
Thomas Brooks

PRAYER – Hindrances

No man can pray scripturally who prays selfishly.

Never tell me of a humble heart where I see a stubborn knee. *Thomas Adams*

Prayer that costs nothing is worth nothing; it is simply a by-product of a cheap Christianity.
Anon.

Some people treat God as they do a lawyer; they go to him only when they are in trouble.
Anon.

Nothing whatever can atone for the neglect of praying.
E. M. Bounds

He who runs from God in the morning will scarcely find him the rest of the day.
John Bunyan

Hurry is the death of prayer. *Samuel Chadwick*

What various hindrances we meet
In coming to the mercy-seat;
Yet who, that knows the worth of prayer,
But wishes to be often there?
William Cowper

Cold prayers, like cold suitors, are seldom effective in their aims. *Jim Elliot*

Leave not off praying to God; for either praying will make thee leave off sinning, or continuing in sin will make thee desist from praying. *Thomas Fuller*

Prayer is never an excuse for laziness.
Gerald B. Griffiths

Satan rocks the cradle when we sleep at our devotions.
Joseph Hall

It is not much *praying* that is condemned . . . but much *speaking*; the danger of this error is when we only *say* our prayers, not when we *pray* them. *Matthew Henry*

If I fail to spend two hours in prayer each morning, the devil gets the victory through the day.
Martin Luther

Means without prayer is presumption. Prayer without means is tempting God.
Al Martin

Beware in your prayer above everything of limiting God, not only by unbelief but by fancying that you know what he can do.
Andrew Murray

The self-sufficient do not pray, the self-satisfied will not pray, the self-righteous cannot pray.
Leonard Ravenhill

Many people pray for things that can only come by work and work for things that can only come by prayer. *W. E. Sangster*

Prayer without love has no suction. It does not draw the blessing down.
W. E. Sangster

Yank some of the groans out of your prayers, and shove in some shouts.
Billy Sunday

Prayer is often conceived to be little more than a technique for self-advancement, a heavenly method for achieving earthly success.
A. W. Tozer

When we become too glib in prayer we are almost certainly talking to ourselves. *A. W. Tozer*

It is foolish to pray against sin and then sin against prayer. *John Trapp*

Lifeless prayer is no more prayer than the picture of a man is a man.
Thomas Watson

PRAYER – and Holy Living

We cannot expect to live defectively and pray effectively.

A holy mouth is made by praying. *E. M. Bounds*

Prayer and a holy life are one. They mutually act and react. Neither can survive alone. The absence of the one is the absence of the other. *E. M. Bounds*

If you would have God hear you when you pray, you must hear him when he speaks.
Thomas Brooks

Prayer will make a man cease from sin, or sin will entice a man to cease from prayer. *John Bunyan*

Pray, and then start answering your prayer.
Deane Edwards

There is nothing that makes us love a man so much as praying for him.
William Law

There is nothing that tells the truth about us as Christians so much as our prayer life.
D. Martyn Lloyd-Jones

What a man is on his knees before God, that he is – and nothing more.
Robert Murray M'Cheyne

How our prayer avails depends upon what we are and what our life is.
Andrew Murray

The decisive preparation for prayer lies not in the prayer itself, but in the life prior to the prayer.
Handley C. G. Moule

He who prays as he ought will endeavour to live as he prays. *John Owen*

Prayer is conditioned by one thing alone and that is spirituality.
Leonard Ravenhill

Every prayer should begin with the confession that our lips are unclean.
Friedrich Tholuck

Abandon the secret chamber and the spiritual life will decay. *Isaac Watts*

PRAYER – Importance

Prayer is not the least we can do; it is the most.

To attempt any work for God without prayer is as futile as trying to launch a space probe with a peashooter.

We need more Christians for whom prayer is the first resort, not the last.

When problems get Christians praying they do more good than harm.

If your troubles are deep-seated or long-standing, try kneeling. *Anon.*

Mountains can only be climbed with the knees bent. *Anon.*

To give prayer the secondary place is to make God secondary in life's affairs.
E. M. Bounds

The best Christian is he that is the greatest monopolizer of time for private prayer. *Thomas Brooks*

Prayer is a shield to the soul, a sacrifice to God and a scourge for Satan.
John Bunyan

Prayer does not enable us to do a greater work for God. Prayer *is* a greater work for God.
Thomas Chalmers

To speak for God to men is a sacred and responsible task. To speak for men to God is not less responsible and is more solemn.
Robert Dabney

Prayer is the highest use to which speech can be put.
P. T. Forsyth

The greatest thing anyone can do for God and for man is to pray.
S. D. Gordon

To pray without labouring is to mock God: to labour without prayer is to rob God of his glory.
Robert Haldane

As long as we continue living we must continue praying. *Matthew Henry*

We need less travelling by jet planes from congress to congress . . . but more kneeling and praying and pleading to God to have mercy upon us, more crying to God to arise and scatter his enemies and make himself known.
D. Martyn Lloyd-Jones

As it is the business of tailors to make clothes and of cobblers to mend shoes, so it is the business of Christians to pray.
Martin Luther

There is nothing a natural man hates more than prayer.
Robert Murray M'Cheyne

To know how to speak to God is more important than knowing how to speak to men. *Andrew Murray*

Prayer is to religion what thinking is to philosophy.
Novalis

I am only as tall as I am on my knees.
Stephen Olford

The measure of our love for others can largely be determined by the frequency and earnestness of our prayers for them.
A. W. Pink

If we can bring our woes before God in prayer we have done the best possible thing. *William S. Plumer*

Satan is far more anxious to keep us off our knees than he is to keep us off our feet. *Ivor Powell*

No man is greater than his prayer life.
Leonard Ravenhill

Prayer is the very life-breath of true Christianity.
J. C. Ryle

If you are too busy to pray then you are too busy. *W. E. Sangster*

Prayer meetings are the throbbing machinery of the church.
C. H. Spurgeon

We shall never see much change for the better in our churches in general till the prayer meeting occupies a higher place in the esteem of Christians.
C. H. Spurgeon

If we ever forget our basic charter – 'My house is a house of prayer' – we might as well shut the church doors.
James S. Stewart

A prayerless Christian should be a non-existent species. *Geoff Treasure*

It is significant that there is no record of the Lord teaching his disciples how to preach; but he took time to teach them how to pray and how not to pray.
L. A. T. Van Dooren

Do with your hearts as you do with your watches, wind them up every morning by prayer, and at night examine whether your hearts have gone true all that day. *Thomas Watson*

God does nothing but in answer to prayer.
John Wesley

Prayer should be fundamental, not supplemental.
William J. C. White

Surely the experience of all good men confirms the proposition that without a due measure of private devotions the soul will grow lean.
William Wilberforce

Prayer is the pulse of the renewed soul; and the constancy of its beat is the test and measure of the spiritual life.
Octavius Winslow

PRAYER – Length

God looks not at the pomp of words and variety of expression, but at the sincerity and devotion of the heart. The key opens the door, not because it is gilt but because it fits the lock. *Anon.*

Lay no weight on the quantity of your prayers; that is to say, how long or how many they are. These things avail nothing with God, by whom prayers are not measured, but weighed. *Thomas Boston*

The worth of a prayer is not gauged by its dimensions.
Robert Murray M'Cheyne

It *is* necessary to draw near unto God, but it is not required of you to prolong your speech till everyone is longing to hear the word 'Amen'.
C. H. Spurgeon

PRAYER – Power

The Holy Spirit turns prayer from activity into energy.

Prayer can do anything that God can do.
E. M. Bounds

The church upon its knees would bring heaven upon the earth. *E. M. Bounds*

Units of prayer combined, like drops of water, make an ocean which defies resistance. *E. M. Bounds*

The one concern of the devil is to keep the saints from praying. He fears nothing from prayerless studies, prayerless work, prayerless religion. He laughs at our toil, he mocks at our wisdom, but he trembles when we pray.
Samuel Chadwick

Restraining prayer we cease
to fight;
Prayer makes the Christian's
armour bright;

And Satan trembles when
he sees
The weakest saint upon his
knees.

William Cowper

Prayer is the rope up in the belfry; we pull it, and it rings the bell up in heaven.

Christmas Evans

The man who kneels to God can stand up to anything. *Louis H. Evans*

Prayer is striking the winning blow . . . service is gathering up the results.

S. D. Gordon

Prayer is the slender sinew that moves the muscle of omnipotence.

J. Edwin Hartill

I judge that my prayer is more than the devil himself; if it were otherwise, Luther would have fared differently long before this.

Martin Luther

Prayer is that mightiest of all weapons that created natures can wield.

Martin Luther

There is no burden of the spirit but is lighter by kneeling under it.

F. B. Meyer

Most churches don't know that God rules the world by the prayers of his saints.

Andrew Murray

I can take my telescope and look millions of miles into space; but I can go away to my room and in prayer get nearer to God and heaven than I can when assisted by all the telescopes of earth.

Isaac Newton

Time spent on the knees in prayer will do more to remedy heart strain and nerve worry than anything else. *George D. Stewart*

When I pray coincidences happen, and when I do not, they don't.

William Temple

The power of prayer consists in the knowledge that God is *our* God.

Friedrich Tholuck

The Christian on his knees sees more than the philosopher on tiptoe.

Augustus M. Toplady

The strongest knees are those which bend most easily. *Mary S. Wood*

PRAYER – and the Promises of God

(See also: Promises of God)

Prayer is not wrestling with God's reluctance to bless us; it is laying hold on his willingness to do so.

Turn the Bible into prayer.
Robert Murray M'Cheyne

The Scriptures make prayer a reality and not a reverie.
Austin Phelps

Believing prayer never asks more than is promised.
William S. Plumer

God does not keep office hours. *A. W. Tozer*

PRAYER – Unanswered

(See also: Prayer – Answers)

The reason why we obtain no more in prayer is because we expect no more. God usually answers us according to our own hearts. *Richard Alleine*

If you do not get all you ask, it is because the Saviour intends to give you something better. *Anon.*

We ask for silver and God sometimes sends his denials wrapped in gold. *Anon.*

Prayer's perplexities are most often camouflaged discoveries, there for the making.
Donald Cranefield

I have lived to thank God that all my prayers have not been answered.
Jean Ingelow

The great tragedy of life is not unanswered prayer but unoffered prayer.
F. B. Meyer

When the Lord is to lead a soul to great faith he leaves its prayers unheard.
Andrew Murray

Patience in prayer is nothing but faith spun out.
Thomas Watson

PRAYER – and the Will of God

Nothing lies outside the reach of prayer except that which lies outside the will of God.

God shapes the world by prayer. *E. M. Bounds*

We are not at liberty in calling upon God to follow the suggestions of our own mind and will, but must seek God only in so far as he has invited us to approach him.

John Calvin

God answers only the requests which he inspires.

Ralph A. Herring

Prayer is a mighty instrument, not for getting man's will done in heaven, but for getting God's will done in earth. *Robert Law*

Did not God sometimes withhold in mercy what we ask, we should be ruined at our own request.

Hannah More

Prayer is not monologue, but dialogue; God's voice in response to mine is its most essential part. Listening to God's voice is the secret of the assurance that he will listen to mine.

Andrew Murray

In prayer, while we seek in appearance to bend God's will to ours, we are in reality bringing our will to his. *J. M. Neale*

To ask in the name of Christ is . . . to set aside our own will and bow to the perfect will of God.

A. W. Pink

To pray effectively we must want what God wants – that and that only is to pray in the will of God.

A. W. Tozer

PREACHING AND PREACHERS – Aim

Jesus told Peter to feed his sheep, not to flog them.

The skill of the evangelist, or the pastor who would do the work of an evangelist, is seen in the ability to present the limited body of redemptive truth repeatedly, yet with freshness and vitality.

Lewis Sperry Chafer

Put the hay down where the sheep can reach it.

Clovis Chappell

Preachers should never forget that preaching is destined for *immediate* effect. We always miss the mark when we preach with the idea of doing good at some other time.

Samuel Cook

If you shoot over the heads of your congregation, you don't prove anything except that you don't know how to shoot.

James Denney

Jesus said, 'Feed my sheep', not 'Feed my giraffes'.

William Evans

All ministers should be revival ministers, and all preaching should be revival preaching.
Charles G. Finney

Preach nothing down but the devil, and nothing up but Jesus Christ.
Rowland Hill

Aim at pricking the heart, not stroking the skin.
Jerome

The charge to Peter was 'Feed my sheep'; not 'Try experiments on my rats', or even 'Teach my performing dogs new tricks'.
C. S. Lewis

The Christian ministry exists for the promotion of holiness.
Donald MacLeod

My grand point in preaching is to break the hard heart, and to heal the broken one. *John Newton*

To preach means not to make capital out of people's felt frailties (the brainwasher's trick) but to measure their lives by the holy law of God.
J. I. Packer

Flowers are well enough, but hungry souls prefer bread. To allegorize with Origen may make men stare at you, but your work is to fill men's mouths with truth, not to open them with wonder.
C. H. Spurgeon

Exposition is the work of bringing to bear the authority of the Word of God on the totality of a man's being.
Andrew Swanson

Whenever you preach, be sure that you lift the Saviour high and lay the sinner low. *John Wilmot*

PREACHING AND PREACHERS – Christ the Message

If we can but teach *Christ* to our people, we teach them all. *Richard Baxter*

There is a wide difference between preaching *doctrine* and preaching *Christ*.
Andrew Bonar

Preaching is the chariot that carries Christ up and down the world.
Richard Sibbes

We can preach Christ to sinners if we cannot preach sinners to Christ.
C. H. Spurgeon

Preaching and Preachers – Christ the Message

No ministry is worthy of anything that is not first and last and all the time a ministry beneath the cross.
James S. Stewart

PREACHING AND PREACHERS – Dangers

Never put yourself in the position where you have to evacuate the message in order to accommodate the method.

There are three particular temptations that assail Christian leaders: the temptation to shine, the temptation to whine and the temptation to recline.
Anon.

A pleasing preacher is too often an appeasing preacher.
Anon.

There are passages of the Bible that are soiled for ever by the touches of the hands of ministers who delight in the cheap jokes they have left behind them.
Phillips Brooks

A ministry that is college-trained but not Spirit-filled works no miracles.
Samuel Chadwick

A self-serving minister is one of the most loathsome sights in all the world. *Walter J. Chantry*

It has always been a mark of the false prophets and preachers that they preached what people wanted to hear.
Peter De Jong

I had rather be fully understood by ten than admired by ten thousand.
Jonathan Edwards

Popularity has killed more prophets than persecution.
Vance Havner

The false preacher is one who has to say something; the true preacher is one who has something to say.
John Henry Newman

To be always preaching, teaching, speaking, writing, and working public works is unquestionably a sign of zeal. But it is not a sign of zeal according to knowledge. *J. C. Ryle*

A crowd is not an achievement, only an opportunity.
W. E. Sangster

If it is bad to preach over people's heads, not to

preach to their heads at all is worse.
James S. Stewart

No man ought to be in a Christian pulpit who fears man more than God.
William Still

Observance over the years leads one to say that the appeal to the emotions, while often increasing the results, increases the chaff in greater proportion.
F. C. White

PREACHING AND PREACHERS – Divine Calling

None is a Christian minister who has not been ordained by the laying on of unseen hands. *Richard Glover*

A man cannot really preach until preach he must. If he can do something else, he probably should!
Vance Havner

Ministers can never fill the people's hearts unless Christ first fill their hands.
Matthew Henry

A man should only enter the Christian ministry if he cannot stay out of it.
D. Martyn Lloyd-Jones

None but he who made the world can make a minister. *John Newton*

The essence of the minister lies in what God has created him to be rather than in what the church authorized him to do. *John Stacey*

I cannot recall, in any of my reading, a single instance of a prophet who applied for the job.
A. W. Tozer

An ignorant minister is none of God's making, for God gives gifts where he gives a calling.
Henry Wilkinson

He who stations the stars has the disposal of his ministers.
Cornelius Winter

PREACHING AND PREACHERS – Doctrine

Error in the pulpit is like fire in the hayloft.
Anon.

It is not the man who brings the Word that saves the soul, but the Word which the man brings.
Thomas Arthur

Screw the truth into men's minds. *Richard Baxter*

Preaching is truth through personality.
Phillips Brooks

Starched oratory may tickle the brain, but it is plain doctrine that informs the judgement, that convicts the conscience, that bows the will and that wins the heart. *Thomas Brooks*

I should rejoice to hear any one of my congregation saying, 'I forget *who* preached, I felt so much the influence of the *truths* he preached.'
Rowland Hill

Doctrine is only the drawing of the bow; application is hitting the mark.
Thomas Manton

We shall never have great preachers till we have great divines. You cannot build a man-of-war out of a currant-bush.
C. H. Spurgeon

The preacher needs doctrine, to prevent his being a mere barrel-organ, playing over and over again the same tunes.
Augustus H. Strong

If we do not possess a positive appetite for the Word, then we are not meant to be preachers. For it is not anything other than the Word that we are called to preach.
Arthur Skevington Wood

PREACHING AND PREACHERS – Earnestness

Cold preachers make bold sinners. *Thomas Adams*

I preached as never sure to preach again, and as a dying man to dying men.
Richard Baxter

How many souls have been lost for want of earnestness, want of solemnity, want of love in the preacher, even when the words uttered were precious and true!
Horatius Bonar

Preaching is a spending, painful work.
Thomas Brooks

I preached what I did feel, what I smartingly did feel.
John Bunyan

If our preaching fails to catch fire it will hardly warm the hearts of our hearers.
Frank Colquhoun

Preaching is the emission of the soul's energy through speech. *R. L. Dabney*

I go out to preach with two propositions in mind. First, every person ought to give his life to Christ. Second, whether or not anyone else gives him his life, I will give him mine.
Jonathan Edwards

The preaching that comes from the soul most works on the soul.
Thomas Fuller

The God-sent evangelist . . . has nothing in common with the political vote-seeker or entertainer. Nothing is more contemptible than a religious clown who cavorts between serious truth and levity.
James R. Graham

A minister without boldness is like a smooth file.
William Gurnall

The Word of God is too sacred a thing, and preaching too solemn a work, to be toyed and played with. *William Gurnall*

A minister should go to every service as though it were the first, as though it could be the best, and as though it might be the last. *Vance Havner*

If we are not intensely real we shall be but indifferent preachers.
J. A. James

I don't like to hear cut-and-dried sermons. When I hear a man preach I like to see him act as if he were fighting bees.
Abraham Lincoln

Preaching is theology coming through a man who is on fire.
D. Martyn Lloyd-Jones

I preach as though Christ was crucified yesterday, rose from the dead today and was coming back tomorrow. *Martin Luther*

The best way to revive a church is to build a fire in the pulpit.
D. L. Moody

A sermon is not made with an eye upon the sermon, but with both eyes upon the people and all the heart upon God.
John Owen

It is an easier thing to bring our heads to preach than our hearts to preach.
John Owen

True preaching is the sweating of blood. *Joseph Parker*

If you want to warm a church, put a stove in the pulpit. *J. C. Ryle*

We shall never get rid of thorns with ploughs that scratch the surface.
C. H. Spurgeon

That's the best sermon that is digged out of a man's breast. *John Trapp*

I love those that thunder out the Word. The Christian world is in a deep sleep. Nothing but a loud voice can awaken them out of it.
George Whitefield

PREACHING AND PREACHERS – Glory of Preaching

Effective preaching is the dynamic release of a divine word that has gripped the heart and mind of the preacher.

Every time the gospel is preached it is as if God himself came in person solemnly to summon us.
John Calvin

Preaching is the public exposition of Scripture by the man sent from God, in which God himself is present in judgement and in grace. *John Calvin*

Every part of your message rests upon the character of God. *Walter Chantry*

The gift of the ministry is the fruit of Christ's ascension.
Matthew Henry

God knows, I would much rather preach for nothing than not at all.
Philip Henry

To me, the work of preaching is the highest and the greatest and the most glorious calling to which anyone can be called.
D. Martyn Lloyd-Jones

The highest worship of God is the preaching of the Word; because thereby are praised and celebrated the name and the benefits of Christ. *Martin Luther*

Preaching is a manifestation of the incarnate Word, from the written Word, by the spoken word.
Bernard Manning

A holy minister is an awful weapon in the hand of God.
Robert Murray M'Cheyne

The Christian ministry is the worst of all trades, but the best of all professions. *John Newton*

If there be a place under heaven more holy than another, it is the pulpit whence the gospel is preached. *C. H. Spurgeon*

There is more to the ministry than being able to talk.
A. W. Tozer

If we are God's man for the job we should never make apologies for ourselves or for our preaching.
Humphrey Vellacott

PREACHING AND PREACHERS – and the Holy Spirit

Holy eloquence is a gift of the Holy Ghost.
Thomas Brooks

Christian preaching is the preaching of God's grace in Christ, in the power of the Holy Spirit. *Paul Helm*

Effective sermons are the offspring of study, of discipline, of prayer, and especially of the unction of the Holy Ghost.
J. H. Thornwell

PREACHING AND PREACHERS – Humility

No man who is full of himself can ever truly preach the Christ who emptied himself. *J. Sidlow Baxter*

Dispensers of the gospel are the Bridegroom's friends, and they must not speak one word for the Bridegroom and two for themselves. *Thomas Brooks*

No man can give at once the impressions that he himself is clever and that Jesus Christ is mighty to save. *James Denney*

There is not in the universe a more ridiculous nor a more contemptible animal than a proud clergyman.
Henry Fielding

The pulpit can be a shop-window to display our talents; the closet speaks death to display.
Leonard Ravenhill

Make sure it is God's trumpet you are blowing – if it is only yours it won't wake the dead, it will simply disturb the neighbours. *W. Ian Thomas*

Woe be to the church when the pastor comes *up* to the pulpit or comes *into* the pulpit. He must come *down* to the pulpit always. *A. W. Tozer*

Preaching and Preachers – Humility

We are no less sinners than our audience.
Humphrey Vellacott

PREACHING AND PREACHERS – The Preacher's Life

Accuracy in exegesis is no substitute for reality in experience.

We must study as hard how to live well as how to preach well.
Richard Baxter

Study universal holiness of life. Your whole usefulness depends on this. Your sermons last but an hour or two; your life preaches all the week. *E. M. Bounds*

How easy is pen-and-paper piety! I will not say it costs nothing; but it is far cheaper to work one's head than one's heart to goodness. I can write a hundred meditations sooner than subdue the least sin in my soul. *Thomas Fuller*

The ministry will not grace the man; the man may disgrace the ministry.
Joseph Hall

A man might cast a devil out of others and yet have a devil, may be a devil himself.
Matthew Henry

The life of a pious minister is visible rhetoric.
Richard Hooker

An office-bearer who wants something other than to obey his King is unfit to bear his office.
Abraham Kuyper

The man who preaches the cross must be a crucified man.
G. Campbell Morgan

A prepared messenger is more important than a prepared message.
Robert Munger

We do not deal in unfelt truths, but we find ourselves that solid consolation in the gospel which we encourage others to expect from it.
John Newton

If a man teach uprightly and walk crookedly, more will fall down in the night of his life than he built in the day of his doctrine.
John Owen

A man may be a false prophet and yet speak the truth. *Richard Sibbes*

Hell is indeed awful unless its preaching is joined to a life laid down by the preacher. How can a man believe in hell unless he throws away his life to rescue others from its torment? *C. T. Studd*

What a dreadful thing it would be for me if I should be ignorant of the power of the truth which I am preparing to proclaim!
John Wesley

Our ministry is as our heart is. No man rises much above the level of his own habitual godliness.
Thomas Wilson

It takes a lifetime to prepare a sermon because it takes a lifetime to prepare a man of God.
Arthur Skevington Wood

PREACHING AND PREACHERS – Love

Ministers must so speak to the people as if they lived in the very hearts of the people; as if they had been told all their wants, and all their ways, all their sins and all their doubts. *Thomas Brooks*

To love to preach is one thing – to love those to whom we preach, quite another. *Richard Cecil*

The flame of Calvary's love is intense, and should cause a glow in the pulpit.
Christmas Evans

The gospel of a broken heart begins with the ministry of bleeding hearts. As soon as we cease to bleed we cease to bless.
John Henry Jowett

It is not saying hard things that pierces the consciences of our people; it is the voice of divine love amid the thunder.
Robert Murray M'Cheyne

He who preaches to broken hearts always preaches to the times. *Joseph Parker*

More flies are caught with honey than with vinegar. Preach much on the love of God. *C. H. Spurgeon*

PREACHING AND PREACHERS – Prayer

One of the gravest perils which besets the ministry is a restless scattering of energies over an amazing multiplicity of interests

which leaves no margin of time and of strength for receptive and absorbing communion with God.
Andrew Bonar

A prayerless preacher is a misnomer. *E. M. Bounds*

A school to teach preachers how to pray, as God counts praying, would be more beneficial to true piety, true worship and true preaching than all theological schools.
E. M. Bounds

None but praying leaders can have praying followers . . . A praying pulpit will beget praying pews.
E. M. Bounds

Let us, even to the wearing of our tongues to the stumps, preach and pray.
John Bradford

He will make the best divine that studies on his knees. *John Flavel*

To have prayed well is to have studied well.
Martin Luther

He that is more frequent in his pulpit to his people than he is in his closet for his people is but a sorry watchman. *John Owen*

Prayer is the first thing, the second thing, the third thing necessary to a minister. Pray, then, my dear brother, pray, pray, pray.
Edward Payson

We should begin to pray before we kneel down and we should not cease when we rise up.
C. H. Spurgeon

PREACHING AND PREACHERS – Qualifications

Nearness to Christ, intimacy with him, assimilation to his character – these are the elements of a ministry of power. *Horatius Bonar*

The church is looking for better methods; God is looking for better men.
E. M. Bounds

The minister is to be a live man, a real man, a true man, a simple man, great in his love, great in his life, great in his work, great in his simplicity, great in his gentleness.
John Hall

A preacher should have the mind of a scholar, the heart of a child and the hide of a rhinoceros. His biggest problem is how to toughen his hide without hardening his heart.

Vance Havner

Ministers must not be afraid of the rich.

Matthew Henry

Prayer, meditation and temptation make a minister.

Martin Luther

The fundamental qualification for teaching is learning.

Andrew McNab

A preacher should know four things – his times, his Bible, his God and himself.

Joseph Sizzoo

What manner of men should ministers be? They should thunder in preaching, and lighten in conversation. They should be flaming in prayer, shining in life and burning in spirit.

C. H. Spurgeon

You do not need to be eloquent, or clever, or sensational, or skilled in dialectic: you *must* be real.

James S. Stewart

Three things make a preacher – reading, prayer and temptation.

John Trapp

Give me one hundred preachers who fear nothing but sin and desire nothing but God, and I care not a straw whether they be clergymen or laymen; such alone will shake the gates of hell and set up the kingdom of heaven on earth.

John Wesley

What I believe to be absolutely necessary for a guide of souls is a faith unfeigned, the love of God and our neighbour, a burning zeal for the advancement of Christ's kingdom, with a heart and life wholly devoted to God.

John Wesley

PREACHING AND PREACHERS – Results

God sometimes blesses a poor exegesis of a bad translation of a doubtful rendering of an obscure verse of a minor prophet!

Anon.

With me this is a maxim: The sermon that does good is a good sermon.

Adam Clarke

Preaching is not man's work. Neither is its content or consequence at his disposal.

Peter Y. De Jong

Preaching and Preachers – Results

My test of the worth of a preacher is when his congregations go away saying, not, 'What a beautiful sermon!' but, 'I will do something.' *François De Sales*

Application is the life of preaching. *James Durham*

God's grace can do anything without ministers' preaching; but ministers' preaching can do nothing without God's grace.
Matthew Henry

Do not let any conversion astonish you; be astonished rather, that anyone should possibly remain unconverted.
D. Martyn Lloyd-Jones

I would rather beg my bread than preach without success.
Robert Murray M'Cheyne

A faithful ministry will usually be sealed by the conversion of sinners.
Thomas V. Moore

Ministers are seldom honoured with success unless they are continually aiming at the conversion of sinners. *John Owen*

If any minister can be satisfied without conversions, he shall have no conversions.
C. H. Spurgeon

We must reach the point of preferring to die rather than to have a ministry without fruit and without power.
Fernando Vangioni

PREACHING AND PREACHERS – Trials

In the ministry, to keep on keeping on you will find your chief difficulty.
Anon.

It would be a parody on the shrewdness of the devil and a libel on his character and reputation if he did not bring his master influences to adulterate the preacher and the preaching.
E. M. Bounds

Every wise workman takes his tools away from the work from time to time that they may be ground and sharpened; so does the only-wise Jehovah take his ministers oftentimes away into darkness and loneliness and trouble, that he may sharpen and prepare them for harder work in his service.
Robert Murray M'Cheyne

The occupational hazard of the Christian ministry and evangelism is discouragement.

John R. W. Stott

I find it absolutely necessary that gospel ministers should meet with . . . thorns in the flesh, that both ministers and hearers may know themselves to be but men.

George Whitefield

PREACHING AND PREACHERS – Unction

In the pulpit, as elsewhere, education is no substitute for unction.

Preaching ought to be something of an eruption of holy energy and the power of the soul.

John Benton

Unction in the preacher puts God in the gospel.

E. M. Bounds

Unction . . . is heaven's distillation in answer to prayer. *E. M. Bounds*

What is unction? It is the indefinable in preaching which makes it preaching . . . It is the divine in preaching.

E. M. Bounds

All the minister's efforts will be vanity or worse than vanity if he have not unction. *Richard Cecil*

I would sooner expect a frog to sit down and play Beethoven's *Moonlight Sonata* than expect to see some of the slick preachers of this hour preach with an anointing that would cause godly fear among the people.

Leonard Ravenhill

I wonder how long we might beat our brains before we could plainly put into words what is meant by preaching with unction. Yet he who preaches knows its presence, and he who hears soon detects its absence.

C. H. Spurgeon

PREDESTINATION

(See also: Election – and Conversion)

The reason for the predestination of some, and reprobation of others, must be sought for in the goodness of God.

Thomas Aquinas

The predestinating love of God is commended more by those who lead holy and Christ-like lives than by those whose attempts to unravel the mystery partakes of the nature of logic-choppers.

F. F. Bruce

All objections to predestination proceed from the wisdom of the flesh.

Martin Luther

In the wounds of Christ alone is predestination found and understood.

Martin Luther

Instead of shrinking back in horror from the doctrine of predestination, the believer, when he sees this blessed truth as it is unfolded in the Word, discovers a ground for gratitude and thanksgiving such as nothing else affords, save the unspeakable gift of the Redeemer himself.

A. W. Pink

It is well to fall back every now and then upon the great truth of predestination . . . It should be a couch for our refreshment. *C. H. Spurgeon*

The difficulties we feel with regard to predestination are not derived from the Word. The Word is full of it, because it is full of God, and when we say God and mean God – God in all that God is – we have said Predestination.

Benjamin B. Warfield

To get rid of predestination we have been willing to degrade our God into a godling.

Benjamin B. Warfield

Let a man go to the grammar school of faith and repentance before he goes to the university of election and predestination.

George Whitefield

PREJUDICE

A little prejudice goes a long way.

Prejudice is a great time saver. It enables you to form opinions without bothering to get the facts.

Anon.

Prejudice is a loose idea, firmly held. *Anon.*

A prejudice is a vagrant opinion without visible means of support.

Ambrose Bierce

The prejudiced and obstinate man does not so much hold opinions, as his opinions hold him.
Tryon Edwards

A great many people think they are thinking when they are merely rearranging their prejudices.
William Jones

PRIDE – Characteristics

Most of us have too big an appetite for appreciation.

A proud soul is content with nothing.
Thomas Brooks

There is nothing that human pride resents so much as to be rebuked.
G. B. Duncan

The proud hate pride – in others.
Benjamin Franklin

It is difficult to be high and not to be high-minded.
William Jenkyn

The devil is content that people should excel in good works, provided he can but make them proud of them. *William Law*

Pride not only withdraws the heart from God, but lifts it up against God.
Thomas Manton

Every breathing of pride in its first stirrings, if it had its way, would run and tear the crown off God's head. *Al Martin*

Pride is intolerable to pride. *Richard Sibbes*

PRIDE – Description

Pride is the oldest sin in the universe, and shows no signs of growing weaker with age.

Pride is the perverse desire of height. *Augustine*

Pride is the very image of the devil.
Thomas Boston

As death is the last enemy, so pride the last sin that shall be destroyed in us.
John Boys

Pride is the master sin of the devil. *E. H. Chapin*

The man who thinks he is too big for a little place is too little for a big place.
Vance Havner

Pride – Description

Pride is the idolatrous worship of ourselves, and that is the national religion of hell. *Alan Redpath*

Pride . . . that filthy spirit gotten into the midst of men. *John Trapp*

When pride begins, love ceases.
Johann C. Lavater

Pride is the cause of all other sins.
Thomas Manton

As the first step heavenward is humility, the first step hellward is pride.
John Mason

PRIDE – Effects

Pride thrust proud Nebuchadnezzar out of men's society, proud Saul out of his kingdom, proud Adam out of paradise, proud Haman out of the court and proud Lucifer out of heaven.
Thomas Adams

Pride is such a choking weed that nothing will prosper near it.
Joseph Alleine

There is no room for God in him who is full of himself. *Anon.*

It was pride that changed angels into devils; it is humility that makes men as angels. *Augustine*

Pride and grace dwell never in one place.
Thomas Fuller

A proud heart and a lofty mountain are always barren. *William Gurnall*

All the sin of heathendom, all the sin of Christendom, is but the outgrowth of the one root – God dethroned, self enthroned in the heart of man.
Andrew Murray

The Christ we manifest is too small because in ourselves we have grown too big. *Watchman Nee*

The pride of others offends me, and makes me studious to hide my own.
John Newton

God can do little with those who love their lives or reputations.
C. T. Studd

Discontent is the daughter of pride.
Augustus M. Toplady

The greatest hindrance to revival is pride amongst the Lord's people.
Arthur Skevington Wood

Just as you find it impossible to tear away your shadow so that it may not haunt your body, so you will find it impossible to prevent shame and destruction from dogging the steps of pride.
Spiros Zodhiates

PRIDE – Essence
(See also: Conceit; Egotism)

There is no spirit in man more opposed to the Spirit of God than the spirit of pride.

It is the devil's masterpiece to make us think well of ourselves. *Anon.*

Pride, in the religious sense, is the attitude of autonomy, of self-determination, of independence of God.
J. C. P. Cockerton

Pride is to character like the attic to the house, the highest part and generally the most empty.
Sydney H. Gay

Nothing is as hard to do gracefully as getting down off your high horse.
Franklin P. Jones

Other sins are against God's law, but pride is against God's sovereignty.
Thomas Manton

The essence of sin is arrogance; the essence of salvation is submission.
Alan Redpath

To be proud of learning is the greatest ignorance.
Jeremy Taylor

All pride is idolatry.
John Wesley

PRIDE – Folly

A mirror never calls attention to itself unless there are flaws in it. *Anon.*

Man ought to be ashamed of being proud, seeing that God was humbled for his sake. *Augustine*

Those who think too much of themselves don't think enough. *Amy Carmichael*

A proud faith is as much a contradiction as a humble devil. *Stephen Charnock*

I know of no case where a man added to his dignity by standing on it.
Winston Churchill

If a man must boast of anything as his own, he must boast of his misery and sin, for there is nothing else but this that is his own property.
William Law

Pride – Folly

No man is weaker than a proud man. For a proud man rests on nothing.
Richard Sibbes

PRIDE – Opposed by God

God assists the humble but resists the proud.

God deliberately sets himself in array against arrogance.

If we insist on our glory, God will withdraw his.

Pride is God's greatest enemy. *Harry Foster*

God sends no one away empty except those who are full of themselves.
D. L. Moody

God is not out to hurt our pride; he is out to kill it.
Donald Pfotenhauer

God abhors them worst who adore themselves most.
William Secker

God will not go forth with that man who marches in his own strength.
C. H. Spurgeon

If we think we can do anything of ourselves, all we shall get from God is the opportunity to try.
C. H. Spurgeon

PRINCIPLES

Better be poisoned in one's blood, than to be poisoned in one's principles.
Anon.

The only standards some people have known are expediency and inclination.
Anon.

I will stay in prison till the moss grows on my eyebrows rather than make a slaughterhouse of my principles. *John Bunyan*

Man's practices are the best indexes of his principles.
Stephen Charnock

Corrupt practices are the genuine end product of corrupt principles.
Matthew Henry

Principles are primers to point to the pathway of power. *F. E. Marsh*

Right is right, even if everyone is against it; and wrong is wrong, even if everyone is for it.
William Penn

Principles are not like skirts which vary in length and width from one season to another. *Mary S. Wood*

PRIVILEGE

Every responsibility is a privilege, and every privilege a responsibility.

Never did the holy God give a privilege where he did not expect a duty.
Joseph Hall

PROCRASTINATION

Duties delayed are the devil's delight. *Anon.*

Procrastination is not only the thief of time, it is also the grave of opportunity. *Anon.*

Tomorrow is often the busiest day of the week.
Anon.

God has promised forgiveness to your repentance; but he has not promised tomorrow to your procrastination. *Augustine*

Faith in tomorrow instead of Christ is Satan's nurse for man's perdition.
G. B. Cheever

He that saith he will be good tomorrow, he saith he will be wicked today.
James Janeway

Many think not of living any holier till they can live no longer.
William Secker

PROMISES OF GOD

(See also: Prayer – and the Promises of God)

God's providence will fulfil all his promises.

If God gives himself to us in promises, we must give ourselves to him in duties. *Anon.*

You cannot starve a man who is feeding on God's promises. *Anon.*

The promises of God are just as good as ready money any day.
Billy Bray

Men many times eat their words, but God will never eat his. *Thomas Brooks*

The possibilities of prayer run parallel with the promises of God.
E. M. Bounds

The resurrection of Christ is the Amen of all his promises. *John Boys*

We cannot rely on God's promises without obeying his commandments.
John Calvin

God has never promised to solve our problems. He has not promised to answer our questions . . . He has promised to go with us.
Elisabeth Elliot

It is better to be as low as hell with a promise than in paradise without one.
John Flavel

Mercy in the promise is as the apple in the seed.
William Gurnall

The promises are not a common for swine to root in; but Christ's sheep-walk for his flock to feed in.
William Gurnall

We must never promise ourselves more than God has promised us.
Matthew Henry

The purposes of God are his concealed promises; the promises – his revealed purposes! *Philip Henry*

My future is as bright as the promises of God.
Adoniram Judson

It is because God has promised certain things that we can ask for them with the full assurance of faith.
A. W. Pink

The promises of God have never borrowed help from moral probabilities.
Thomas Sherlock

If you appropriate a promise it will not be pilfering: you may take it boldly and say, 'This is mine.' *C. H. Spurgeon*

Faith in the promises works obedience to the precepts.
George Swinnock

The Bible is bespangled with promises made to prayer. *Thomas Watson*

His every word of grace is strong
As that which built the skies;
The voice that rolls the stars along
Speaks all the promises.
Isaac Watts

You never pray with greater power than when you plead the promises of God.
William J. C. White

PROPHECY

Nothing is so damaging in the study of New Testament

prophecy as to imagine that the eternal God who stands outside and above time is bound by the clocks and calendars of men. *E. M. Blaiklock*

Prophesying is a dangerous business for those who are not inspired.

R. L. Dabney

Prophecy takes up approximately one-fourth of all Scripture. And yet we have soft-pedalled what the Bible says about future history... A tremendously relevant and gripping part of the Christian [hope] has been left out.

Leighton Ford

I know that some are always studying the meaning of the fourth toe of the right foot of some beast in prophecy and have never used either foot to go and bring men to Christ.

Vance Havner

Words of prophecy in the mouth are no infallible evidence of a principle of grace in the heart.

Matthew Henry

Prophecy is not given to make men prophets, but as a witness to God when it is fulfilled.

Isaac Newton

I would not give much for prophetic intelligence if it does not begin, continue and end with the person, work and glory of Christ.

H. H. Snell

Prophecy is like the German sentence – it can be understood only when we have read its last word.

Augustus H. Strong

PROSPERITY

(See also: Luxury; Materialism; Money; Possessions; Riches; Wealth)

Fewer men survive the test of prosperity than the pressure of poverty. *Anon.*

We do not realize how much we are attached to the good things of this world until they are taken from us. *Augustine*

In the day of prosperity we have many refuges to resort to; in the day of adversity, only one.

Horatius Bonar

The snow covers many a dunghill; so doth prosperity many a rotten heart.

Thomas Brooks

In prosperity, our friends know us; in adversity we know our friends.

Churton Collins

The saints' spots are most got in peace, plenty and prosperity.
William Gurnall

Let prosperity be as oil to the wheels of obedience and affliction as wind to the sails of prayer.
Philip Henry

Material abundance without character is the surest way to destruction.
Thomas Jefferson

Prosperity is good campaigning weather for the devil. *C. S. Lewis*

If a man will make his nest below, God will put a thorn in it; and if that will not do, he will set it on fire. *John Newton*

I am never afraid for my brethren who have many troubles, but I often tremble for those whose career is prosperous.
C. H. Spurgeon

If you want to destroy a nation give it too much – make it greedy, miserable and sick.
John Steinback

PROVIDENCE

(See also: Will of God)

All the world's thrones are occupied by rulers under God's authority.

God's providence will fulfil all his promises.

The same God who controls the sun cares for the sparrow.

There are no accidents in the life of a Christian.
Rowland Bingham

We cannot be robbed of God's providence.
Jane Welsh Carlyle

Happy the man who sees a God employed in all the good and ill that chequers life.
William Cowper

What God *intends*, he decrees; what God *permits*, he has foreseen.
Arthur C. Custance

While providence supports,
Let saints securely dwell;
That hand which bears all
  nature up
Shall guide his children
  well.
Philip Doddridge

God's providence is like the Hebrew Bible; we must

begin at the end and read backward in order to understand it. *A. J. Gordon*

God's providence leaves room for the use of our prudence.
Matthew Henry

God is in the facts of history as truly as he is in the march of the seasons, the revolutions of the planets, or the architecture of the worlds.
John Lanahan

If our circumstances find us in God, we shall find God in our circumstances.
George Muller

If you think you see the ark of God falling you can be sure it is due to a swimming in your head.
John Newton

All real evil is averted from the people of God, or is so controlled as in the end to do them good.
William S. Plumer

There's a Divinity that shapes our ends, rough-hew them how we will.
William Shakespeare

Providence is the perpetuity and continuance of creation. *Richard Sibbes*

In the working of God's providence the unseen is prop enough for the seen.
Augustus H. Strong

God has plans for this world, not problems. There is never a panic in heaven.
W. Ian Thomas

Not a drop of rain falls in vain. *John Trapp*

A firm faith in the universal providence of God is the solution of all earthly problems. It is almost equally true that a clear and full apprehension of the universal providence of God is the solution of most theological problems.
Benjamin B. Warfield

God is to be trusted when his providences seem to run contrary to his promises.
Thomas Watson

We turn to God when our foundations are shaking, only to learn that it is God who is shaking them.
Charles C. West

God is not defeated by human failure.
William J. C. White

PUNISHMENT

(See also: Judgement)

Righteous punishment is a thousand light years away from revenge. *Anon.*

Punishment, that is the justice of the unjust.
Augustine

If men refuse to be taught by precept they must be taught by punishment.
Thomas V. Moore

PURITY

The price of purity is high; but impurity is dirt cheap.

Purity lives and derives its life solely from the Spirit of God.
Julius Charles Hare

Genuine purity is internal.
William S. Plumer

PURPOSE

The two greatest days in a person's life are the day he was born and the day he finds out why he was born. *Anon.*

All who are ignorant of the purpose for which they live are fools and madmen.
John Calvin

Here is what frightens me: to see the sense of this life dissipated; to see the reason for our existence disappear. That is what is intolerable. Man cannot live without meaning.
Albert Camus

The man without purpose is like a ship without a rudder. *Thomas Carlyle*

What makes life dreary is absence of motive. What makes life complicated is multiplicity of motive. What makes life victorious is singleness of motive.
George Eliot

Those who have a 'why' to live can bear with almost any 'how'.
Victor E. Frankl

You must have an aim in life if you want to make a hit. *Nora Grey*

God does nothing in time which he did not design to do from eternity.
William Jay

If a man has a *why* for his life he can bear with almost any *how*.
Friedrich Nietzsche

Who shoots at the midday sun, though he be sure he shall never hit the mark, yet as sure as he is he shall shoot higher than who aims but at a bush.

Philip Sidney

Spiritual life depends on the purposes we cherish.

C. H. Spurgeon

REASON

(See also: Education; Knowledge; Mind)

God does not expect us to submit our faith to him without reason, but the very limits of our reason make faith a necessity. *Augustine*

It is no more possible for finite man to comprehend the infinite God than for a child to dip the ocean into a hole he has made in the sand.

Augustine

No man can understand spiritual mysteries by carnal reason. *Thomas Brooks*

Water cannot rise higher than its source, neither can human reason.

Samuel Taylor Coleridge

He that will believe only what he can fully comprehend must have a very long head or a very short creed. *C. C. Colton*

Reason can never show itself more reasonable than in ceasing to reason about things which are above reason. *John Flavel*

The faith that does not come from reason is to be doubted, and the reason that does not lead to faith is to be feared.

G. Campbell Morgan

Nothing but faith will ever rectify the mistakes of reason on divine things.

William S. Plumer

Where reason cannot wade, there faith may swim.

Thomas Watson

REDEMPTION

(See also: Atonement; Salvation)

By Christ's purchasing redemption, two things are intended: his satisfaction and his merit; the one pays our debt, and so satisfies; the other procures our title, and so merits. The satisfaction of Christ is to free us from misery; the merit of Christ is to purchase happiness for us.

Jonathan Edwards

As a race we are not even stray sheep, or wandering prodigals merely, we are rebels with weapons in our hands. Our supreme need from God, therefore, is not the education of our conscience . . . but our redemption.

P. T. Forsyth

No creature that deserved redemption would need to be redeemed. *C. S. Lewis*

The believer is not redeemed by obedience to the law but he is redeemed unto it.

John Murray

Justification and sanctification are two aspects or the two sides of the one coin of divine redemption.

W. Stanford Reid

The only thing that a man can contribute to his own redemption is the sin from which he needs to be redeemed.

William Temple

REGENERATION

(See also Conversion; Faith – Saving)

Becoming a Christian is not making a new start in life; it is receiving a new life to start with.

Take away the mystery from the new birth and you have taken away its majesty.

Repentance is a change of the mind and regeneration is a change of the man.

Thomas Adams

Regeneration is the fountain; sanctification is the river. *J. Sidlow Baxter*

Adoption gives us the *privilege* of sons, regeneration the *nature* of sons.

Stephen Charnock

Regeneration is a spiritual change; conversion is a spiritual motion.

Stephen Charnock

If the second birth hath no place in you, the second death shall have power over you. *William Dyer*

Regeneration is a single act, complete in itself, and never repeated; conversion, as the beginning of holy living, is the commencement of a series, constant, endless and progressive. *A. A. Hodge*

Spiritual life is the consequence of spiritual quickening. The baby cries because it is born; it is not born because it cries.

Erroll Hulse

When God works in us, the will, being changed and sweetly breathed upon by the Spirit of God, desires

and acts, not from *compulsion,* but *responsively.*
Martin Luther

Just as in the beginning 'God said, "Let there be light"; and there was light' so, at the moment he appointed for our new birth, he said, 'Let there be life' and there was life.
J. A. Motyer

We are helpless to co-operate in our regeneration as we are to co-operate in the work of Calvary.
Iain H. Murray

Let them pretend what they please, the true reason why any despise the *new birth* is because they hate a *new life.* *John Owen*

Sinners cannot obey the gospel, any more than the law, without renewal of heart. *J. I. Packer*

If you are never born again, you will wish you had never been born at all. *J. C. Ryle*

There are no still-born children in the family of grace. *William Secker*

A dead man cannot assist in his own resurrection.
W. G. T. Shedd

Regeneration is essentially a changing of the fundamental taste of the soul. By taste we mean the direction of man's love, the bent of his affections, the trend of his will.
Augustus H. Strong

Mere outward reformation differs as much from regeneration as white-washing an old rotten house differs from pulling it down and building a new one in its place. *Augustus M. Toplady*

RELIGION

(See also: Man a Religious Being)

It is possible to be diligent in our religion yet distant in our relationship.

It is religion without love that has been responsible for most of the misery of the world. *Anon.*

Some people's religion is just like a wooden leg. There is neither warmth nor life in it and although it helps you to hobble along it never becomes part of you, but must be strapped on every morning.
Anon.

Nothing so tends to mask the face of God as religion;

it can be a substitute for God himself. *Martin Buber*

If men are so wicked with religion, what would they be without it?
Benjamin Franklin

Many Christians have enough religion to make them decent, but not enough to make them dynamic. *Kenneth Grider*

God calls people to worship him with their obedience, and instead they try to fob him off with their religion.
John Hercus

Religion is what keeps a nation from chaos – from falling asunder like uncemented sand.
A. A. Hodge

Religion's in the heart, not in the knee.
Douglas Jerrold

A life that will bear the inspection of men and of God is the only certificate of true religion.
Samuel Johnson

Formal religion always makes fertile soil for false religion. *Gilbert W. Kirby*

The heart of religion lies in its personal pronouns.
Martin Luther

A cheap religion is always a cheat religion.
Thomas V. Moore

There is nothing more irreligious than self-absorbed religion. *J. I. Packer*

Religion is union between God and the soul.
Paul Sabatier

The heart of religion is not an opinion about God, but a personal relationship with him. *W. E. Sangster*

People can be inoculated against religion by small injections of it.
W. E. Sangster

No man's religion ever survives his morals.
Robert South

I would not give much for your religion unless it can be seen. Lamps do not talk, but they do shine. *C. H. Spurgeon*

Religion is nothing if it is not the foundation of our whole life.
Robert Thornton

No religion has ever been greater than its idea of God. *A. W. Tozer*

You can find more carnal, unregenerate, self-centred characters who have religion and are sensitive toward it than you can bury in the Grand Canyon.

A. W. Tozer

Religion is the first and the last thing, and until a man has found God, and been found by God, he begins at no beginning and works to no end.

H. G. Wells

REPENTANCE – Blessings

If sin and thy heart be two, Christ and thy heart are one. *Thomas Brooks*

Nothing will make the faces of God's children more fair than for them to wash themselves every morning in their tears.

Samuel Clark

Repentance, if it be true, strikes at the root and washes the heart from wickedness.

Matthew Henry

Repentance is the next happiest state to that of sinlessness. *Lorinus*

The sunshine is always sweeter after we have been in the shade; so you will find Jesus in returning to him.

Robert Murray M'Cheyne

REPENTANCE – Essence

(See also: Confession; Contrition; Conviction of Sin; Penitence)

Obedience is the positive side of repentance.

Repentance is a change of the mind and regeneration is a change of the man.

Thomas Adams

Repentance is a continual spring, where the waters of godly sorrow are always flowing. *Thomas Brooks*

To forsake sin is to leave it without any thought reserved of returning to it again. *William Gurnall*

Repentance is the tear in the eye of faith.

D. L. Moody

Repentance is a thorough change of man's natural heart on the subject of sin.

J. C. Ryle

When the Word of God converts a man, it takes away from him his despair, but it does not take from him his repentance.

C. H. Spurgeon

Man truly repents only when he learns that his sin has made him unable

to repent without the renewing grace of God.
Augustus H. Strong

The true holy water is not that which the pope sprinkles, but is distilled from the penitent eye.
Thomas Watson

O Jesus, full of truth and
grace,
More full of grace than
I of sin,
Yet once again I seek thy
face;
Open thine arms, and take
me in,
And freely my backslidings
heal,
And love the faithless sinner
still.
Charles Wesley

REPENTANCE – False

Many persons who appear to repent are like sailors who throw their goods overboard in a storm, and wish for them again in a calm. *Anon.*

He who beats his heart, but does not mend his ways, does not remove his sins but hardens them.
Augustine

Our pride is disgusted at our faults and we mistake this disgust for true repentance. *François Fenelon*

Sin may be the occasion of great sorrow, when there is no sorrow for sin.
John Owen

The eye may be watery and the heart flinty. An apricot may be soft without, but it has a hard stone within.
Thomas Watson

REPENTANCE – and Holiness

God has nowhere undertaken to forgive a sin that man is not prepared to forsake.

Repentance is not an idea; it is action.

Repentance is the relinquishment of any practice from the conviction that it has offended God.
Joseph Addison

True repentance is to cease from sin. *Ambrose*

He never truly repented of any sin whose heart is not turned against every sin. *Thomas Brooks*

You must fall out with sin if ever you fall in with God. *Thomas Brooks*

Repentance without amendment is like continually pumping without mending the leak.
Lewis W. Dillwyn

Purity as well as pardon is desired by all true penitents. *Andrew Fausset*

Those that profess repentance must practise it.
Matthew Henry

You should never think of sin without repenting.
Philip Henry

To do so no more is the truest repentance.
Martin Luther

Repentance begins in the humiliation of the heart and ends in the reformation of the life.
John Mason

Real repentance consists in the heart being broken for sin and from sin.
William Nevins

I charge you that you do not escape hell if you have no inclination to escape from the things that make it.
David Shepherd

The faith which receives Christ must be accompanied by the repentance which rejects sin.
John R. W. Stott

The idea that God will pardon a rebel who has not given up his rebellion is contrary both to Scripture and to common sense.
A. W. Tozer

REPENTANCE – Importance

Repentance and faith are graces we have received, not goals we have achieved.

Repentance and faith are twins.

The Christian who has stopped repenting has stopped growing.

There is no going to the fair haven of glory without sailing through the narrow strait of repentance.
William Dyer

Wherever God designs to give life he gives repentance. *Matthew Henry*

Repentance is the only gate through which the gospel is received.
Basilea Schlink

Many have the *space* of repentance who have not the *grace* of repentance.
William Secker

Exhalation is as necessary to life as inhalation. To accept Christ it is necessary that we reject whatever is contrary to him.
A. W. Tozer

Our repentance needs to be repented of, and our tears washed in the blood of Christ.
George Whitefield

You cannot repent too soon, because you do not know how soon it may be too late.
Thomas Fuller

If God's today be too soon for thy repentance, thy tomorrow may be too late for his acceptance.
William Secker

Sin and hell are married unless repentance proclaims the divorce.
C. H. Spurgeon

He who promised forgiveness to them that repent has not promised repentance to them that sin.
Ralph Venning

REPENTANCE – Urgency

If we lose our time to repent, we shall repent for ever that we once lost our time. *Thomas Adams*

None can be too young to amend that is old enough to die. *Thomas Adams*

A religion that does not begin with repentance is certain to end there – perhaps too late. *Anon.*

Though after this life repentance be perpetual, it is in vain. *Augustine*

RESPONSIBILITY

(See also: Duty; Service)

Every responsibility is a privilege, and every privilege a responsibility.

We must never let our theology rob us of our responsibility.

We are morally responsible to God because we are made in the image of a moral Deity.
E. H. Andrews

There are too many people ready to assert their rights

who are not ready to assume their responsibilities.
Vance Havner

Responsibility brings accountability.
Ken Robins

My dear friends, you may take it as a rule that the Spirit of God does not usually do for us what we can do for ourselves.
C. H. Spurgeon

Men are free to decide their own moral choices, but they are also under the necessity to account to God for those choices.
A. W. Tozer

The most important thought I ever had was that of my individual responsibility to God.
Daniel Webster

RESURRECTION OF CHRIST

The Easter story ends not with a funeral but with a festival.

The resurrection of Jesus demands not our applause but our allegiance, not our compliments but our capitulation.

The best news the world ever had came from a graveyard. *Anon.*

The resurrection of Christ is the Amen of all his promises. *John Boys*

The New Testament preaches a Christ who was dead and is alive, not a Christ who was alive and is dead. *James Denney*

Jesus has forced open a door that had been locked since the death of the first man. He has met, fought and beaten the King of Death. Everything is different because he has done so.
C. S. Lewis

Our Lord has written the promise of the resurrection, not in books alone, but in every leaf in springtime.
Martin Luther

The empty tomb of Christ has been the cradle of the church.
W. Robertson Nicoll

The victim of Calvary is now . . . loose and at large.
J. I. Packer

The Christian church has the resurrection written all over it. *E. G. Robinson*

Christianity is essentially a religion of resurrection.
James S. Stewart

The resurrection of Jesus is the Gibraltar of the Christian faith and the Waterloo of infidelity and rationalism. *R. A. Torrey*

Christ did not rise from the dead as a private person, but as the public Head of the church.
Thomas Watson

Our Lord is risen from the dead,
Our Jesus is gone up on high.
The powers of hell are captive led,
Dragged to the portals of the sky.
Charles Wesley

RESURRECTION OF CHRISTIANS

Our friends bring us to the grave and leave us there, but God will not.
Anon.

Bless God that there is *in* us resurrection life, and that there *awaits* us a resurrection. *J. J. Bonar*

Christians out-die pagans and the resurrection of Christ is the reason.
T. R. Glover

God fits our souls here to possess a glorious body after; and he will fit the body for a glorious soul.
Richard Sibbes

We are more sure to arise out of our graves than out of our beds.
Thomas Watson

REVELATION

(See also: Bible — Divine Authorship; Knowledge of God)

Only God can interpret his own handwriting.

To know God without God is impossible; as he is the source of all knowledge, he must be the source of knowledge about himself.

Man cannot cover what God would reveal.
Thomas Campbell

God frames his language to our dullness, not to his own state.
Stephen Charnock

The message of the gospel is a noise, not a communi-

cation, until God tunes the set of man's heart.
Arthur C. Custance

The need of the world is to listen to God.
Albert Einstein

Nature is a first volume, in itself incomplete, and demanding a second volume, which is Christ.
Charles Gore

Revelation is from the Father, through the Son, by the Spirit. Redemption is to the Father, by the Son, through the Spirit.
A. A. Hodge

Our need of revelation is like our need of redemption: it is total. *Robert Horn*

Apart from special, saving revelation – the revelation that centres upon the Lord Jesus Christ – we do not and cannot know God.
J. I. Packer

It is not for us to imagine that we can prove the truth of Christianity by our own arguments; nobody can prove the truth of Christianity save the Holy Spirit.
J. I. Packer

The real view of the world is that which revelation presents us.
Hans Rohrbach

Every genuine revelation of God has this mark upon it, that it makes him appear more glorious.
C. H. Spurgeon

Christianity . . . is the revelation of God, not the research of man.
James A. Stewart

Christianity is the one revealed religion.
Benjamin B. Warfield

Scriptural revelation terminates on the heart.
Benjamin B. Warfield

REVENGE

(See also: Anger; Hatred)

Injuries cost more to avenge than to bear.

Revenge is a dish that should be eaten cold.
Anon.

The smallest revenge will poison the soul. *Anon.*

Revenge is the most worthless weapon in the world.
David Augsburger

The only people with whom you should try to

get even are those who have helped you.
John E. Southard

REVERENCE

(See also: Awe; Worship)

Reverence is essential to worship. *Frank Gabelein*

We must rejoice in God, but still with a holy trembling.
Matthew Henry

The spirit which loses reverence for God turns naturally to sinning.
John Hercus

Reverence is the very first element of religion; it cannot but be felt by everyone who has right views of the divine greatness and holiness, and of his own character in the sight of God. *Charles Simmons*

REVIVAL

A revival may produce noise, but it does not consist of it. The real thing is whole-hearted obedience. *Ernest Baker*

It is easier to speak about revival than to set about it. *Horatius Bonar*

Revival is the exchange of the form of godliness for its living power.
John Bonar

Revival is not the top blowing off but the bottom falling out.
Darrell Bridges

A revival of religion . . . consists in new spiritual life imparted to the dead and in new spiritual health imparted to the living.
James Buchanan

In our biblical desire for revival, we must refuse to seek any experience which proposes to eliminate our natural weakness.
Walter Chantry

When God visits his church according to his promises, effects follow that make people shout, 'This is the finger of God!'
John Elias

All ministers should be revival ministers, and all preaching should be revival preaching.
Charles G. Finney

Every revival that ever came in the history of the world, or in the history of the church, laid great emphasis on the holiness of God.
Billy Graham

Revival is not going down the street with a big drum; it is going back to Calvary with a big sob.

Roy Hession

Revival is a series of new beginnings. *David McKee*

We ought to be so living that when God begins his great triumphant march we shall fall in with the first battalion, and have part in the first victories.

G. Campbell Morgan

In any biblical revival the norm is heightened; it is not suspended while another type of Christianity is introduced.

Iain H. Murray

Waiting for general revival is no excuse for not enjoying personal revival.

Stephen Olford

The best definition of revival is 'times of refreshing . . . from the presence of the Lord'.

J. Edwin Orr

Revival means the work of God restoring to a . . . church, in a manner out of the ordinary, those standards which the New Testament sets forth as being entirely ordinary.

J. I. Packer

True revival has always begun with and resulted in separation.

Vernon Patterson

A revival is from God or it is no revival at all.

Wilbur M. Smith

God is more willing to give revival than we are to receive it.

Erlo Stegan

The true spirit of revival eludes the grasp of the organizer and the advertiser. It cannot be created by machinery nor promoted by printer's ink.

James A. Stewart

It is useless for large companies of believers to spend long hours begging God to send revival. Unless we intend to reform we may as well not pray.

A. W. Tozer

In one sense, Pentecost can never happen again. In another sense, it may always be happening, since we live in the age of the Spirit.

Arthur Skevington Wood

Revival is not an earthly concoction; it is a heavenly creation.

Arthur Skevington Wood

RICHES

(See also: Luxury; Materialism; Money; Possessions; Prosperity; Wealth)

If your treasure is on earth, you are going from it; if it is in heaven, you are going to it. *Anon.*

No amount of riches can atone for poverty of character. *Anon.*

Earthly riches are full of poverty. *Augustine*

Of all the riches that we hug . . . we can carry no more out of this world than out of a dream.
James Bonnell

The fulness of the earth can never satisfy the soul.
William Bridge

If the whole world were changed into a globe of gold it could not fill thy heart. *Thomas Brooks*

It is not the fact that a man has riches which keeps him from the kingdom of heaven, but the fact that riches have him. *J. Caird*

Riches may leave us while we live; we must leave them when we die.
Thomas Fuller

Man takes great pains to heap up riches, and they are like heaps of manure in the furrows of the field, good for nothing unless they be spread.
Matthew Henry

It ill disposes the servant to seek to be rich and great and honoured in this world where his Lord was poor and mean and despised. *George Muller*

While riches are they are not. *William Secker*

What good is there in having a fine suit with the plague in it? *John Trapp*

The world's golden sands are quicksands.
Thomas Watson

To lay up treasure on earth is as plainly forbidden by our Master as adultery and murder.
John Wesley

RITUALISM

(See also: Formalism)

Ritualism has always been the rival of true religion.
Richard Glover

The path of piety avoids ritualism and rationalism.
Richard Glover

Ritualism, like eczema in the human body, is generally a symptom of a low state of the blood.

A. J. Gordon

RUMOUR

(See also: Gossip; Slander; Speech)

It is said that where there's smoke there's fire; but the smoke may be no more than dust and hot air.

A rumour is about as hard to unspread as butter.

Anon.

Believe not half you hear; repeat not half you believe; when you hear an evil report, halve it, then quarter it, and say nothing about the rest of it.

C. H. Spurgeon

SACRIFICE

Sacrifice is the ecstasy of giving the best we have to the one we love the most.

Anon.

He is no fool who gives what he cannot keep to gain what he cannot lose.

Jim Elliot

Too much of our Christianity today is drenched with sentiment, but devoid of sacrifice.

Frank Farley

Sacrifice without obedience is sacrilege.

William Gurnall

The sign of our professed love for the gospel is the measure of sacrifice we are prepared to make in order to help its progress.

Ralph P. Martin

Nothing less than a living sacrifice is demanded. Not a loan, but a gift; not a compromise, but a sacrifice; not our poorest, but our best; not a dead but a living offering. Each drop of our blood, each ounce of our energy, each throb of our heart, we must offer to God.

Joseph Pearce

If Jesus Christ be God and died for me, then no sacrifice can be too great for me to make for him.

C. T. Studd

God is looking for some wicks to burn. The oil and the fire are free.

J. Hudson Taylor

The only life that counts is the life that costs.

Frederick P. Wood

SALVATION

(See also: Atonement; Redemption)

God's plan and purpose of

salvation is like himself, it is eternal.
Eric Alexander

In creation, God shows us his hand; in salvation, his heart. *Anon.*

Salvation, the salvation of man, is the final purpose of the whole Bible.
J. H. Bernard

God never saves a spectator.
Robert Brown

There are as many paths to Christ as there are feet to tread them, but there is only one way to God.
A. Lindsay Glegg

Salvation is a helmet, not a nightcap! *Vance Havner*

Christ is not only the Saviour but the salvation itself. *Matthew Henry*

Our salvation is so well contrived, so well concerted, that God may have mercy upon poor sinners, and be at peace with them, without any wrong to his truth and righteousness. *Matthew Henry*

All our salvation consists in the manifestation of the nature, life and Spirit of Jesus in our inward new man. *William Law*

The salvation of a single soul is more important than the production or preservation of all the epics and tragedies in the world. *C. S. Lewis*

God's plan of salvation is not an afterthought; it antedates the work of creation. *J. A. Motyer*

No sinner was ever saved by giving his heart to God. We are not saved by our giving, we are saved by God's giving.
A. W. Pink

Except the names given to God and our Saviour, there is no sweeter word than salvation.
William S. Plumer

The essence of sin is arrogance; the essence of salvation is submission.
Alan Redpath

I have no rights to work out my own salvation in the way I choose.
Helen Roseveare

God gets more out of your salvation than you ever will. *David Shepherd*

Salvation is not deliverance from hell alone, it is deliverance from sin.
C. H. Spurgeon

There are two hopeless things, salvation without Christ and salvation without holiness. *C. T. Studd*

Our salvation is a pure gratuity from God.
Benjamin B. Warfield

Not for our duties or deserts,
But of his own abounding grace
He works salvation in our hearts,
And forms a people for his praise.
Isaac Watts

SATAN

(See also: Temptation – and Satan; Hell)

The devil has no difficulty in making sin look innocent.

The devil is usually good-looking.

Satan promises the best, but pays with the worst; he promises honour and pays with disgrace; he promises pleasure and pays with pain; he promises profit and pays with loss; he promises life and pays with death.
Thomas Brooks

Satan is an acute theologian.
John Calvin

Satan is God's ape.
Stephen Charnock

Satan does not work haphazardly but attacks systematically.
Thomas Cosmades

If you don't believe in the devil's existence, just try resisting him for a while. *Charles G. Finney*

Our arch-enemy is to be cast into hell – and it will take only *one* angel to bind him!
A. Lindsay Glegg

No player hath so many dresses to come in upon the stage with as the devil hath forms of temptation.
William Gurnall

Satan commonly stops the ear from hearing sound doctrine before he opens it to embrace corrupt.
William Gurnall

The devil sometimes . . . borrows God's bow to shoot his arrows from.
William Gurnall

Satan is not fighting churches; he is joining them. He does more harm by sowing tares than by pulling up wheat. He accomplishes more by imitation than by outright opposition.

Vance Havner

The devil's image complete is a complication of malice and falsehood.

Matthew Henry

No sooner is a temple built to God, but the devil builds a chapel hard by.

George Herbert

The devil makes little of sin, that he may retain the sinner. *Rowland Hill*

The devil shapes himself to the fashions of all men.

William Jenkyn

As an angel of light the devil is utterly self-effacing, so that you would never think to charge him with the sudden trouble that has emerged.

R. T. Kendall

When Satan fell he may have lost his innocence but he did not lose his intelligence. *Trevor Knight*

The devil is the most diligent of preachers.

Hugh Latimer

Satan's might is such that Almightiness alone exceeds.

Henry Law

If Satan dared to use Scripture for the temptation of our Lord he will not scruple to use it for the delusion of men.

Donald MacLeod

I believe Satan to exist for two reasons: first, the Bible says so; and second, I've done business with him. *D. L. Moody*

Even as great an angel as Michael the archangel did not dare take on Satan alone but called on the Lord to rebuke him. No Christian, then, should ever feel that he is wise enough or powerful enough to engage Satan apart from complete dependence on the Lord.

Charles Caldwell Ryrie

The use of a counterfeit is Satan's most natural method of resisting the purposes of God.

Stephen Slocum

Certain theologians, nowadays, do not believe in the existence of Satan. It is singular when children do not believe in the existence of their own father. *C. H. Spurgeon*

Let us learn not to fondle Satan.

Augustus H. Strong

The devil is a better theologian than any of us and is a devil still.

A. W. Tozer

There are references in the Bible to the devil's wiles and his shrewdness. But when he gambled on his ability to unseat the Almighty he was guilty of an act of judgement so bad as to be imbecilic.

A. W. Tozer

Have the devil for your taskmaster and you will have him also for your paymaster. *John Trapp*

SCIENCE

Science can add years to your life, but only Christ can add life to your years.

Anon.

A God proved by science would not be God. For I can prove only that which is by creation lower than I, that which is at my disposal.

Gerhard Bergmann

The very sciences from which objections have been brought against religion have, by their own progress, removed those objections, and in the end furnished full confirmation of the inspired Word of God.

Tryon Edwards

I only trace the lines that flow from God.

Albert Einstein

I have never seen anything incompatible between those things of man which can be known by the spirit of man which is within him and those higher things concerning his future which cannot be known by that spirit. *Michael Faraday*

In point of fact, there is no battle between an informed belief in God and the assured results of science. *Michael Green*

Science knows nothing of rationality and consciousness, of personality and sociability.

Michael Green

Sin has got man into more trouble than science can get him out of.

Vance Havner

Science can give us the 'know-how', but it cannot give us the 'know-why'.

J. N. Hawthorne

The person who thinks there can be any real conflict between science and

religion must be either very young in science or very ignorant in religion.
Philip Henry

Science cannot solve man's moral problems.
Carl Gustav Jung

Men became scientific because they expected law in nature, and they expected law in nature because they believed in a Legislator. *C. S. Lewis*

No sciences are better attested than the religion of the Bible.
Isaac Newton

Unfortunately for the scientifically-minded, God is not discoverable or demonstrable by purely scientific means. But that really proves nothing; it simply means that the wrong instruments are being used for the job.
J. B. Phillips

If God said that Jonah was swallowed by a whale, then the whale swallowed Jonah, and we do not need a scientist to measure the gullet of a whale.
A. W. Tozer

The modern vogue of bringing science to the support of Christianity proves not the truth of the Christian faith but the gnawing uncertainty in the hearts of those who must look to science to give respectability to their faith.
A. W. Tozer

The scientific way of looking at the world is not wrong any more than the glass-manufacturer's way of looking at the window. This way of looking at things has its very important uses. Nevertheless the window was placed there not to be looked at but to be looked through; and the world has failed of its purpose unless it too is looked through and the eye rests not on it but on its God.
Benjamin B. Warfield

SECOND COMING OF CHRIST

Many people will be surprised when Jesus comes again – but nobody will be mistaken.

The certainty of the Second Coming of Christ should touch and tincture every part of our daily behaviour.

He that rose from the clods we expect from the clouds. *Thomas Adams*

He who loves the coming of the Lord is not he who affirms it is far off, nor is it he who says it is near. It is he who, whether it be far or near, awaits it with sincere faith, steadfast hope and fervent love.
Augustine

That day lies hid that every day we be on the watch. *Augustine*

In the first advent God veiled his divinity to prove the faithful; in the second advent he will manifest his glory to reward their faith. *Chrysostom*

As Christians, we should not be exitists, looking for our going, but adventists, looking for his coming. *William Freel*

Christ hath told us he will come, but not when, that we might never put off our clothes, or put out the candle.
William Gurnall

I never preach a sermon without thinking that possibly the Lord may come before I preach another.
D. L. Moody

I never begin my work in the morning without thinking that perhaps *he* may interrupt my work and begin his own. I am not looking for death, I am looking for *him*.
G. Campbell Morgan

Oh, that Christ would make long strides! Oh, that he would fold up the heavens as a cloak, and shovel time and days out of the way! *Samuel Rutherford*

The fact that Jesus Christ is to come again is not a reason for star-gazing, but for working in the power of the Holy Ghost.
C. H. Spurgeon

The Christian hope is not a matter for tickling our minds, but for changing our minds and influencing society. *Stephen Travis*

I am daily waiting for the coming of the Son of God.
George Whitefield

SECURITY

Security is not the absence of danger, but the presence of God, no matter what the danger. *Anon.*

They are well kept whom God keeps. *Anon.*

Should storms of sevenfold
thunder roll,
And shake the globe from
pole to pole;
No flaming bolt could
daunt my face,
For Jesus is my hiding-
place.

Jehoiada Brewer

Nothing is more foolish than a security built upon the world and its promises, for they are all vanity and a lie. *Matthew Henry*

A sovereign Protector I have,
Unseen, yet for ever at hand,
Unchangeably faithful to
save,
Almighty to rule and com-
mand.
He smiles, and my comforts
abound;
His grace as the dew shall
descend;
And walls of salvation sur-
round
The soul he delights to
defend.

Augustus M. Toplady

SELF

(See also: Conceit; Egotism; Pride)

A self-made man has no one to blame but himself.

Anon.

Far too frequently in this life we are interested in only three persons: me, myself and I. *Anon.*

The man who lives only for himself runs a very small business. *Anon.*

The most common disease in the world is 'I' trouble.

Anon.

No man can really at one and the same time call attention to himself and glorify God. *Louis Benes*

Deliver me, O Lord, from that evil man, myself.

Thomas Brooks

Self is the chief end of every natural man.

Stephen Charnock

Self-interest, of course, is the lowest form of motivation for doing what is morally right. *Mort Crim*

Talk to a man about himself and he will listen for hours. *Benjamin Disraeli*

If you must talk of yourself, let it be behind your own back. *George Eliot*

Self is the destruction of safety and sanctity alike.

Richard Glover

Self often stands concealed in the shadows of the unconscious.

E. Stanley Jones

The self-centred are the self-disrupted.
E. Stanley Jones

We never say that self is dead; were we to do so, self would be laughing at us round the corner.
F. B. Meyer

I have more trouble with D. L. Moody than with any man I ever met.
D. L. Moody

I have read of many wicked popes, but the worst pope I ever met with is Pope *Self.* *John Newton*

The man who lives by himself and for himself is apt to be corrupted by the company he keeps.
Charles H. Parkhurst

The personal pronoun 'I', might well be the coat of arms of some individuals.
Antoine Rivarol

Beware of no man more than yourself; we carry our worst enemies within us. *C. H. Spurgeon*

So subtle is self that scarcely anyone is aware of its presence.
A. W. Tozer

SELF-CRUCIFIXION

(See also: Humility; Meekness)

To die to our own comforts, ambitions and plans is of the very essence of Christianity.

Life offers only two alternatives: crucifixion with Christ or self-destruction without him. *Anon.*

The concept of resurrection is welcomed by all, but the prior concern of self-crucifixion is a higher price than most men are willing to pay. *Anon.*

Kill sin before it kills you.
Richard Baxter

The cross must be borne, carried; we are not at liberty to step over it, or go round to avoid it.
Richard Baxter

The mortification of the flesh is the quickening of the spirit. *John Calvin*

Taking up the cross is the conscious choice of a painful alternative motivated by love for Christ.
Walter J. Chantry

Without a cross there is no following Christ.
Walter J. Chantry

All Christians lead a dying life; it is the secret of their strange vitality.

John Cordelier

Crucifixion is something that is done *to* us; it is not something that we do to ourselves. We can only initiate it by picking up the crossbar, that is, by a complete honest determination.

Arthur C. Custance

The believer mortifies because God is pacified towards him; the legalist mortifies that he may pacify God by his mortification . . . that he may have whereof to glory.

Ralph Erskine

There is no other way to live this Christian life than by a continual death to self.

François Fenelon

No man has a velvet cross.

John Flavel

We are bid to take, not to make our cross. God in his providence will provide one for us.

William Gurnall

God creates out of nothing. Therefore until a man is nothing, God can make nothing out of him.

Martin Luther

Mortified Christians are the glory of Christ.

Thomas Manton

'Crucified' is the only definitive adjective by which to describe the Christian life.

J. Furman Miller

There was a day when I died to George Muller; his opinions and preferences, taste and will; died to the world, its approval or censure; died to the approval or blame even of my brethren or friends; and since then I have striven only to show myself approved unto God.

George Muller

What does it mean for me to be 'crucified'? I think the answer is best summed up in the words the crowd used of Jesus: 'Away with him!'

Watchman Nee

Be killing sin or it will be killing you.

John Owen

He who ceases from mortification lets go all endeavours after holiness.

John Owen

Christ's cross is the sweetest burden that ever I bare; it is such a burden as wings are to a bird or sails to a ship.

Samuel Rutherford

Christianity has a secret unknown to communists or capitalists . . . *how to die to self*. This secret makes us invincible.
W. E. Sangster

Prepare yourselves, my younger brethren, to become weaker and weaker; prepare yourselves for sinking lower and lower in self-esteem; prepare yourselves for self-annihilation – and pray God to expedite the process. *C. H. Spurgeon*

To be sweet-smelling to God, we must be broken and poured out, not merely containers of a sweet smell.
C. T. Studd

When you put your life on the altar, when you make ready and accept to die, you are invincible. You have nothing any more to lose. *Josif Ton*

Among the plastic saints of our times Jesus has to do all the dying and all we want to hear is another sermon about his dying.
A. W. Tozer

The cross is easier to him who takes it up than to him who drags it along.
J. E. Vaux

SELF-DENIAL

It is easier to give anything we have than to give ourselves.

When self is not negated, it is necessarily worshipped.
Anon.

Death is half disarmed when the pleasures and interests of the flesh are first denied.
Richard Baxter

All great virtues bear the imprint of self-denial.
William E. Channing

As a man goes down in self he goes up in God.
G. B. Cheever

Surely those who know the great passionate heart of Jehovah must deny their own loves to share in the expression of his!
Jim Elliot

The first lesson in Christ's school is self-denial.
Matthew Henry

They that deny themselves for Christ shall enjoy themselves in Christ.
J. M. Mason

There is a great difference between denying yourself things and denying yourself. *Adrian Rogers*

Self-emptiness prepares for spiritual fulness.

Richard Sibbes

Self-denial is indispensable to the enjoyment of religious peace and comfort.

J. H. Thornwell

There is a sweet theology of the heart that is only learned in the school of renunciation.

A. W. Tozer

SELF-EXAMINATION

An humble knowledge of thyself is a surer way to God than a deep search after learning.

Thomas à Kempis

Self-inspection is the best cure for self-esteem.

Anon.

Christ, the Scripture, your own hearts and Satan's devices are the four prime things that should be first and most studied and searched. *Thomas Brooks*

When I look into my heart, and take a view of my wickedness, it looks like an abyss infinitely deeper than hell.

Jonathan Edwards

The way to test yourself, the way to test any man, is to look below the surface.

D. Martyn Lloyd-Jones

We cannot too often or too earnestly ask God to make us honest with ourselves. *William S. Plumer*

Self-examination is the beaten path to perfection.

William Secker

An unexamined life is not worth living. *Socrates*

Secret sins, like secret conspirators, must be hunted out. *C. H. Spurgeon*

The man who does not like self-examination may be pretty certain that things need examining.

C. H. Spurgeon

It is good to find out our sins, lest they find us out.

Thomas Watson

Though not always called upon to condemn ourselves, it is always safe to suspect ourselves.

Richard Whately

SELFISHNESS

A selfish spirit is unworthy of a Christian.

Joseph Alleine

Selfishness is a very little world inhabited by one man. *Anon.*

Selfishness tarnishes everything it touches. *Anon.*

Selfishness is not only sin but lies at the root of all sin. *R. B. Kuyper*

SEPARATION

Christians should penetrate the world without ever becoming part of it.

When a sin is fashionable, Christians should be out of fashion.

For all the world forsake not Christ, but all the world forsake for Christ.
Anon.

I have nothing to do with earth, but only to labour in it honestly for God. I do not desire to live one minute for anything which earth can afford.
David Brainerd

I am sure that you understand that it is not enough to be merely separated from the world. For we can be separated and be quite proud about it.
François Fenelon

Beware of separation which leads only to isolation and insulation.
Eric Hutchings

The measure of our discord with the world is the measure of our accord with the Saviour.
Alexander MacLaren

The world hates Christian people if they can see Christ in them.
G. Campbell Morgan

True revival has always begun with and resulted in separation.
Vernon Patterson

If you are in with God you are out with the world.
Rodney ('Gipsy') Smith

SERVICE – Dignity

God is not greater if you reverence him, but you are greater if you serve him. *Augustine*

We shall never be fit for the service of God if we look not beyond this fleeting life. *John Calvin*

There is nothing small in the service of God.
François De Sales

What dignity the service of God brings to the servants of God! *Frank Farley*

Man is immortal till his work is done.
Thomas Fuller

All Christ's commands are acts of grace; it is a favour to be employed about them. *William Gurnall*

If the work be done *in* Christ's name, the honour is due *to* his name.
Matthew Henry

The meanest work for Jesus is a grander thing than the dignity of an emperor. *C. H. Spurgeon*

SERVICE – God's Part

When God wants a worker he calls a worker. *Anon.*

We do the works, but God works in us the doing of the works. *Augustine*

God does not need your talents, wisdom, holiness and strength. But rather you, in weakness, desperately need the power of his Spirit in your labours.
Walter J. Chantry

God will not thank thee for doing that which he did not set thee about.
William Gurnall

Our efficiency without God's sufficiency is only a deficiency.
Vance Havner

None are allowed to go for God but those who are sent by him.
Matthew Henry

You never test the resources of God until you attempt the impossible.
F. B. Meyer

Divine work must be divinely initiated.
Watchman Nee

God hath work to do in this world; and to desert it because of its difficulties and entanglements is to cast off his authority.
John Owen

Whom God calls he qualifies. *Richard Sibbes*

Depend upon it – God's work done in God's way will never lack supplies.
J. Hudson Taylor

All God's giants have been weak men who did great things for God because they reckoned on his being with them.
J. Hudson Taylor

A master gives his servant work to do, but he cannot give him strength to work; but God, as he cuts us out work, so he gives us strength. *Thomas Watson*

SERVICE – Prayer

To attempt any work for God without prayer is as futile as trying to launch a space probe with a pea-shooter.

Do not pray for easy lives. Pray to be stronger men. Do not pray for tasks equal to your powers. Pray for powers equal to your tasks.
Phillips Brooks

To pray without labouring is to mock God: to labour without prayer is to rob God of his glory.
Robert Haldane

Never undertake more Christian service than you can cover by believing prayer. *Alan Redpath*

SERVICE – Responsibility

Christians should be springs, not sponges.

Morally, a Christian is called to holiness; dynamically, he is called to service.

You can't be reconciled to God without being recruited. *Stuart Briscoe*

It is almost as presumptuous to think you can do nothing as to think you can do everything.
Phillips Brooks

Your salvation is God's business; his service your business. *Thomas Fuller*

The vision must be followed by the venture. It is not enough to stare up the steps – we must step up the stairs. *Vance Havner*

Whom God sends he employs, for he sends none to be idle.
Matthew Henry

What were candles made for but to burn?
Matthew Henry

Faithfulness to God is our *first* obligation in all that we are called to do in the service of the gospel.
Iain H. Murray

It is a truth that stands out with startling distinctness on the pages of the New Testament that God has no sons who are not servants. *H. D. Ward*

Our humility serves us falsely when it leads us to shrink from any duty. The plea of unfitness or inability is utterly insufficient to excuse us.

Spiros Zodhiates

Oh, how sweet to work all day for God, and then lie down at night beneath his smile!

Robert Murray M'Cheyne

SERVICE – Rewards

If the love of God sets us to work, the God of love will find us the wages.

Anon.

Christians that would hold on in the service of the Lord must look more upon the crown than upon the cross. *Thomas Brooks*

Today, let us rise and go to our work. Tomorrow, we shall rise and go to our reward.

Richard Fuller

If you read history you will find that the Christians who did most for the present were just those who did most for the next.

C. S. Lewis

I have had many things in my hands and have lost them all. But whatever I have been able to place in God's hands I still possess. *Martin Luther*

SERVICE – Wholeheartedness (See also: Zeal)

God does not ask about our ability or our inability, but our availability.

Anon.

God only asks you to do your best.

Robert H. Benson

Service is the overflow of superabounding devotion.

Oswald Chambers

Since my heart was touched at seventeen, I believe I have never awakened from sleep, in sickness or in health, by day or by night, without my first waking thought being how best I might serve my Lord.

Elizabeth Fry

No duty can be performed without wrestling. The Christian needs his sword as well as his trowel.

William Gurnall

Ministry that costs nothing accomplishes nothing.

John Henry Jowett

You will certainly carry out God's purpose, however you act, but it makes a difference to you whether you serve like Judas or John. *C. S. Lewis*

No divinely sent opportunity must elude us.
Watchman Nee

There is no service like his who serves because he loves. *Philip Sidney*

SEX

(See also: Lust)

God thought of sex before man did, and when man leaves God out of his sexual thinking he is in trouble.

What would you not give to have the word 'sex' set free from every trace of fear, guilt, shame and impurity?

All healthy men, ancient and modern, Eastern and Western, know that there is a certain fury in sex that we cannot afford to inflame, and that a certain mystery and awe must ever surround it if we are to remain sane.
G. K. Chesterton

Sex without love is a dead end. *Fred Catherwood*

What happens when sex is liberated is not equality but a vast intensification of sexual competition from which there is no sure haven except impotence and defeat. *George Gilder*

The battle of life will probably not rise above the sex battle.
E. Stanley Jones

Sexual desire is not love. Desire is quite compatible with personal hatred, or contempt, or indifference.
John MacMurray

God never intended that man could find the true meaning of his sexuality in any other relationship than that of the total self-giving involved in marriage. *Al Martin*

Whereas the charge levelled at the Victorians was 'love without sex', today it is 'sex without love'.
David Watson

Sex involves the entire life and personality, and to misuse sex is to abuse oneself as well as one's partner. *Harold P. Wells*

SICKNESS

(See also: Pain; Suffering; Trials)

All disease is primarily the result of sin, but not always directly so.

Sickness shows us what we are. *Anon.*

Sickness, when sanctified, teaches us four things: the vanity of the world, the vileness of sin, the helplessness of man and the preciousness of Christ.
Anon.

Sometimes Christ sees that we need the *sickness* for the good of our souls more than the *healing* for the ease of our bodies.
Matthew Henry

Medical science recognizes that emotions such as fear, sorrow, envy, resentment and hatred are responsible for the majority of our sicknesses. Estimates vary from 60% to nearly 100%.
S. I. McMillen

The time of sickness is a time of purging from that defilement we gathered in our health . . . That is a good sickness which tends to the health of the soul.
Richard Sibbes

I venture to say that the greatest earthly blessing that God can give to any of us is health, with the exception of sickness. Sickness has frequently been of more use to the saints of God than health has.
C. H. Spurgeon

I am mended by my sickness, enriched by my poverty, and strengthened by my weakness.
Abraham Wright

SILENCE

A closed mouth gathers no foot. *Anon.*

It often shows a fine command of language to say nothing. *Anon.*

There are two sciences which every person ought to learn: the science of speech and the more difficult one of silence.
Anon.

Silence is so rare a virtue where wisdom regulates it, that it is accounted a virtue where folly imposes it. *Thomas Brooks*

God still comes where he can find someone quiet enough to listen and alone enough to heed.
G. B. Duncan

Speech is . . . only good when it is better than silence. *Richard Sibbes*

Either keep silence, or speak that which is better than silence. *John Trapp*

A man may wrong another as well by silence as by slander. *Thomas Watson*

SIN – and the Christian

Two sorts of peace are more to be dreaded than all the troubles in the world – peace with sin, and peace in sin.
Joseph Alleine

If hell were on one side and sin on the other, I would rather leap into hell than willingly sin against my God. *Anselm*

Our sense of sin is in proportion to our nearness to God.
Thomas D. Bernard

It is our duty to feel sin, to fear sin, and to fly sin as far as we can.
John Boys

Sin may rebel in a saint, but it shall never reign in a saint.
Thomas Brooks

Whenever a godly man sins, he sins against the general purpose of his soul.
Thomas Brooks

I preach and think that it is more bitter to sin against Christ than to suffer the torments of hell.
Chrysostom

I do not understand how a man can be a true believer in whom sin is not the greatest burden, sorrow and trouble. *John Owen*

Never was anything more futile than the war against the Lamb.
William S. Plumer

I am convinced that the first step towards attaining a higher standard of holiness is to realize more fully the amazing sinfulness of sin. *J. C. Ryle*

There is no sin so great but a great saint may fall into it. There is no saint so great but he may fall into a great sin.
J. C. Ryle

Do believe it, Christian, that your sin is a condemned thing. It may kick and struggle, but it is doomed to die.
C. H. Spurgeon

Sin – and the Christian

For the Christian, sin is not the done thing!
Mary S. Wood

SIN – Deceitfulness

If sin was not such a pleasure it would not be such a problem.

The most deadly sins do not *leap* upon us; they *creep* upon us.
Stephen Olford

Sin is never less quiet than when it seems to be most quiet. *John Owen*

Sin may be clasped so close we cannot see its face. *Richard C. Trench*

The most stupendous blunder a man ever made was to think that anything could be made out of sinning.
Frederick P. Wood

SIN – Effects

Sin has scarred the ecology of the whole universe.

There is a high cost in low living.

Were it not for sin, death would never have had a beginning. Were it not for death, sin would never have an ending. *Anon.*

Each man's sin is the instrument of his punishment, and his iniquity is turned into his torment.
Augustine

Sin is the great punishment of sin. *John Boys*

Vices are more costly than virtues. *Thomas Brooks*

The pleasure of sin never survives this world.
William Gurnall

If we be *ruled* by sin we shall inevitably be *ruined* by it.
Matthew Henry

Sinners wilfully lose God for a friend.
Matthew Henry

Sin carrieth two rods about it: shame and fear.
Edward Marbury

We cannot think lightly of sin if we think honestly of its results.
David C. Potter

All the sorrows of faith put together do not equal in bitterness one drop of the sorrows of sin.
C. H. Spurgeon

Guilt is related to sin as the burnt spot to the blaze.
Augustus H. Strong

Sin is the womb of our sorrows and the grave of our comforts.
Thomas Watson

SIN – Essence

Sin defiles man and defies God.

There is no such thing as a little sin because there is no such person as a little God to sin against.

Sin is not only an offence which needs forgiving, it is a pollution which needs cleansing. *Eric Alexander*

Sin is God's would-be murderer. *Anon.*

Sin is man's declaration of independence of God.
Anon.

Sin is so big that it takes a Christ with a cross to measure it. *Anon.*

Any departure by man from what he knows he ought to do, however small his offence may be, slaps the very face of God.
Saphir R. Athyal

It is of the heart of sin that men use what they ought to enjoy and enjoy what they ought to use.
Augustine

Sin is the refusal of divine lordship and disobedience to God's will.
Samuel A. Benetreau

A will to sin is sin in God's account. *Thomas Brooks*

Every yielding to sin is a welcoming of Satan into our very bosoms.
Thomas Brooks

Sin is the dare of God's justice, the rape of his mercy, the jeer of his patience, the slight of his power and the contempt of his love. *John Bunyan*

Never think to find honey in the pot when God writes poison on its cover.
William Gurnall

Forgetfulness of God is the cause of all the wickedness of the wicked.
Matthew Henry

Sin is the most unmanly thing in God's world. You never were made for sin and selfishness. You were made for love and obedience. *John G. Holland*

Sin is essentially a departure from God. *Martin Luther*

Sin is that abominable thing which God hates.
Thomas V. Moore

Sin is a clenched fist and a blow in the face of God.
Joseph Parker

All sin is a *lie.* By it we attempt to cheat God; by it we actually cheat our souls.
William S. Plumer

If sin had its way it would both dethrone and annihilate God.
William S. Plumer

Sin is God's one intolerance. *W. E. Sangster*

Sin is self-coronation.
Vincent Taylor

We hate sin not merely because its consequences are disastrous, or its forms repugnant to our tastes and sensibilities, but because it is a reflection upon God.
J. H. Thornwell

Sin is basically an act of moral folly, and the greater the folly, the greater the fool. *A. W. Tozer*

Sin is a little word with only three letters, but the biggest is I.
Arthur Skevington Wood

SIN – Fact

Every sin is reprehensible, because the sinner is responsible.

People used to argue as to whether the world was square or round – but the Bible says it is crooked!

We are born in sin and spend our lives coping with the consequences.

Sin is like seed – to cover it is to cultivate it. *Anon.*

The only dreadful thing is sin. *Elisha Coles*

There is in truth only one religious problem in the world – the existence of sin. Similarly there is only one religious solution to it – the atonement.
James Denney

Christianity begins with the doctrine of sin.
Soren Kierkegaard

The alienation of man from God is a fact. It is our business not to deny it but to end it. *William Temple*

If the best man's faults were written in his forehead, it would make him pull his hat over his eyes.
John Trapp

SIN – Power

Sin has two great powers; it reigns and it ruins.

Sin is not a toy, it is a tyrant.

Sin is the strength of death and the death of strength. *Thomas Adams*

A swarm of locusts can do more damage to a field than a full-grown cow. *Anon.*

There is no sin so little as not to kindle an eternal fire. *Anon.*

A man may die as well by a fly choking him as by a lion devouring him . . . so likewise, little sins will sink a man to hell as soon as great sins.
Daniel Cawdray

How deep is the pollution of sin that nothing but the blood of Christ can cleanse it! *John Flavel*

We must deal with the seeds of sin in our hearts. If neglected the seeds soon become weeds.
Vance Havner

A slight sore, neglected, may prove of fatal consequence, and so may a slight sin slighted and left unrepented of.
Matthew Henry

All sin hardens the heart, stupefies the conscience and shuts out the light of truth.
William S. Plumer

Sin has digged every grave.
William S. Plumer

Sins begin like cobwebs, but become iron clamps.
J. C. Ryle

Men hate their sins but cannot leave them.
Seneca

Sin and death are an adamantine chain and link that none can sever. Who shall separate that which God in his justice hath put together?
Richard Sibbes

The least sin is damnable . . . A pistol will kill as dead as a cannon.
George Swinnock

No place can be so pleasant but sin will lay it waste.
John Trapp

There is in sin a commanding and a condemning power. *Thomas Watson*

As a very little dust will disorder a clock, and the least grain of sand will obscure our sight, so the least grain of sin which is upon the heart will hinder its right motion toward God. *John Wesley*

SIN – and Satan

Sin is an odious thing, the devil's drivel or vomit.
John Trapp

Sin stamps the devil's image on a man.
Thomas Watson

The sinner's heart is the devil's mansion house.
Thomas Watson

SINCERITY

(See also: Honesty; Integrity)

It is better to be ingenuous than ingenious.

We are not saved by sincerity, but we may certainly be lost through insincerity.
Robert Black

Sincerity is the very queen of virtues.
Thomas Brooks

Sincerity . . . keeps the soul pure in the face of temptation. *William Gurnall*

I know no religion but sincerity. *Matthew Henry*

There is no substitute for godly sincerity.
William S. Plumer

Sincerity is the truth of all grace. *William Secker*

He that is sincere is sincere in all places and at all times. *Richard Sibbes*

SINFUL NATURE

(See also: Depravity; Guilt; Man – a Sinner; Sin)

We all carry about with us material that Satan can work upon. *Anon.*

The greatest struggles that life can know are not within the unsaved, but within the saved.
Donald Grey Barnhouse

Ourselves are the greatest snares to ourselves.
Richard Baxter

Sin in a wicked man is like poison in a serpent; it is in its natural place.
Thomas Brooks

The man without a navel still lives in me.
Thomas Browne

The procuring cause of our misery is in ourselves.
John Calvin

Nothing leads to self-repudiation so much as spiritual meditation on the corruption and wickedness of your heart.
Walter J. Chantry

All the old primitive sins are not dead, but are crouching in the dark corners of our modern hearts. *Carl Gustav Jung*

In youth, mid-age, and now after many battles, I find nothing in me but vanity and corruption.
John Knox

I more fear what is within me than what comes from without. *Martin Luther*

Whosoever contends against indwelling sin shall know and find that it is present with them, that it is powerful in them. *John Owen*

Impress the young convert from the very beginning with the conviction that God has called him into his kingdom to struggle with the corruptions of his heart.
William B. Sprague

There may be persons who can always glide along like a tramcar on rails without a solitary jerk, but I find that I have a vile nature to contend with, and spiritual life is a struggle with me. I have to fight from day to day with inbred corruption, coldness, deadness, barrenness, and if it were not for my Lord Jesus Christ my heart would be as dry as the heart of the damned. *C. H. Spurgeon*

Our old nature is no more extinct than the devil; but God's will is that the dominion of both should be broken.
John R. W. Stott

Sins are because sin is.
A. W. Tozer

I see no fault that I might not have committed myself.
Johannes Von Goethe

Original sin is a sea that will not, in this life, be dried up. *Thomas Watson*

Believers are no more able now *of themselves* to think one good thought, to form one good desire, to speak one good word, or to do one good work, than before they were justified.
John Wesley

Worst of all my foes, I fear the enemy within.
John Wesley

SLANDER

(See also: Gossip; Rumour; Speech)

No greater injury can be inflicted upon men than to wound their reputation.

John Calvin

Slander has a marvellous way of driving us into the arms of our heavenly Father. *Stuart Olyott*

Slander is a vice that strikes a double blow, wounding both him that commits and him against whom it is committed.

Jacques Saurin

SOCIAL RESPONSIBILITY

A man ought to carry himself in the world as an orange-tree would if it could walk up and down in the garden – swinging perfume from every little censer it holds up to the air. *Chrysostom*

Social service need not be the 'social gospel' . . . It means doing something about . . . pain and suffering, for the sake of Christian love, and not insinuating at every turn that what we do is in order to get people into our churches and to take up our form of creed. *Jose D. Fajardo*

If God is God and man is made in his image, then *each* man is significant.

Os Guinness

The Christian with social concern must champion all those who need champions, not just those whose championing is currently popular.

Os Guinness

The church cannot be concerned with the redemption of men in such a way that their becoming Christians means that they must withdraw from God's creation.

Paul Helm

To live as contemporary Christians means at least this – to take account of the fact that our neighbours are made in the image of God. *Paul Helm*

Church members who deny in fact their responsibility for the needy in any part of the world are just as much guilty of heresy as those who deny this or that article of the faith.

W. A. Visser't Hooft

We have no liberty to say that our sole responsibility as Christians is to preach the gospel of salvation, since moral and social righteousness will then follow normally. *John R. W. Stott*

It's a mistake to assume that God is only interested in religion.
William Temple

The New Testament churches did not have specific programmes of social reform in their community action, but they did have Christ and the gospel so that social reform in the community inevitably came, and with awful and positive power.
Foy Valentine

The gospel of Christ knows of no religion but social, no holiness but social holiness. *John Wesley*

SORROW

Sorrow commonly comes on horseback but goes away on foot. *Thomas Adams*

How amazing it is that we have so few tears these days when there is so much to weep about!
Isaac H. A. Ababio

Godly sorrow is better than worldly joy. *Anon.*

Night brings out stars as sorrow shows us truths.
Gamaliel Bailey

The soul would have no rainbow had the eyes no tears.
John Vance Cheney

If one man should suffer all the sorrows of all the saints in the world, yet they are not worth one hour's glory in heaven.
Chrysostom

The finest flowers are often found growing in the soil of sorrow. *G. B. Duncan*

You learn your theology most where your sorrows take you. *Martin Luther*

Earth has no sorrow that heaven cannot heal.
Thomas Moore

One Son God hath without sin, but none without sorrow. *John Trapp*

SOUL-WINNING

(See also: Evangelism; Witnessing)

If we would win some we must be winsome.
Anon.

I remember no one sin that my conscience doth so accuse me and judge me as for doing so little for the saving of men's souls and for dealing no more fervently and earnestly for their conversion.

Richard Baxter

You do not choose to be in the business of bringing men to Christ; you choose Christ and you are at once in the business.

Joe Blinco

Some like to live within the sound of church or chapel bell; I'd rather run a rescue shop within a yard of hell.

William Booth

I cared not where or how I lived, or what hardships I went through, so that I could but gain souls for Christ.

David Brainerd

The longing of my heart would be to go all round the world before I die, and preach one gospel invitation in the ear of every creature. *William Burns*

The solemn one thing of my life shall be to save souls. *Thomas Collins*

I long for the conversion of souls more sensibly than anything else besides.

Philip Doddridge

No man can be a Christian who is unconcerned for the salvation of others.

Richard Haldane

Lord, speak to me, that I may speak
In living echoes of thy tone;
As thou hast sought, so let me seek
Thy erring children lost and lone.

Frances Ridley Havergal

I would think it a greater happiness to gain one soul for Christ than mountains of silver and gold for myself. *Matthew Henry*

The joy of catching a soul is unspeakable. When we have got one soul we become possessed by the passion for souls. Get one and you will want a crowd.

John Henry Jowett

The salvation of a single soul is more important than the production or preservation of all the epics and tragedies in the world.

C. S. Lewis

Ere the sun goes down think of some one action which may tend to the conversion of some one person, and do it with all your might.

C. H. Spurgeon

If anybody had told me, 'Somebody has left you £20,000,' I should not have given a snap of my fingers for it, compared with the joy which I felt when I was told that God had saved a soul through my ministry.
C. H. Spurgeon

Winners of souls must first be weepers for souls.
C. H. Spurgeon

Our joy until we die is to win men for the Lord.
Nicolaus Ludwig Von Zinzendorf

We have one business on earth – to save souls.
John Wesley

Give me souls or take away my soul!
George Whitefield

SPEECH

(See also: Eloquence; Gossip; Rumour; Slander)

His heart cannot be pure whose tongue is not clean.
Anon.

In company, guard your tongue – in solitude, your thoughts. *Anon.*

Lord, make my words gracious and tender, for tomorrow I may have to eat them! *Anon.*

Nothing is so opened more by mistake than the mouth.
Anon.

There are two sciences which every person ought to learn: the science of speech and the more difficult one of silence. *Anon.*

What is in the well of your heart will show up in the bucket of your speech.
Anon.

One of the first things that happens when a man is really filled with the Spirit is not that he speaks with tongues, but that he learns to hold the one tongue he already has.
J. Sidlow Baxter

A sanctified heart is better than a silver tongue.
Thomas Brooks

Of all the members in the body, there is none so serviceable to Satan as the tongue. *Thomas Brooks*

We know metals by their tinkling and men by their talking. *Thomas Brooks*

There is nothing more slippery or loose than the tongue. *John Calvin*

During a long life I have had to eat my own words many times and I have found it a very nourishing diet.
Winston Churchill

Think all you speak but speak not all you think.
Patrick Delaney

If I speak what is false, I must answer for it; if truth, it will answer for me. *Thomas Fuller*

The jawbone of an ass was a killer in Samson's time. It still is.
Morris Gilber

It is bad to think ill, but it is worse to speak it.
Matthew Henry

A sharp tongue is the only edged tool that grows keener with constant use.
Washington Irving

A fool is hardly discerned when silent; his picture is best taken when he is speaking. *William Jenkyn*

Sharp tongues have a way of sharpening other tongues.
E. Stanley Jones

Blessed are they who have nothing to say and who cannot be persuaded to say it.
James Russell Lowell

Most of a man's sins are in his words.
Thomas Manton

If you think twice before you talk once, you will speak twice the better for it. *William Penn*

Speech is the index of the mind. *Seneca*

Speech is . . . only good when it is better than silence. *Richard Sibbes*

Some men's tongues bite more than their teeth.
C. H. Spurgeon

Whatever moves the heart wags the tongue.
C. T. Studd

Evil tongues are the devil's bellows. *John Trapp*

How can Christ be in the heart when the devil has taken possession of the tongue? *Thomas Watson*

Words are the looking-glass of the mind.
Thomas Watson

SPIRITUAL GIFTS

All Christ's gifts are like himself, spiritual and heavenly. *Thomas Brooks*

There is none so poor in the church of Christ who may not impart to us something of value.
John Calvin

Spiritual gifts are not toys with which to play; they are tools of the Spirit with which to do the Lord's work effectively.
G. Raymond Carlson

Spiritual gifts are no proof of spirituality.
Samuel Chadwick

You cannot have the *gifts* of Christ apart from the *government* of Christ.
A. Lindsay Glegg

Pride of gifts robs us of God's blessing in the use of them.
William Gurnall

A drop of grace is worth a sea of gifts.
William Jenkyn

The best gifts are those which benefit the whole body. You don't find many people asking for the gift of liberality.
Harry Kilbride

To consider the charismata as intended merely to adorn and benefit the person endowed would be just as absurd as to say, 'I light the fire to warm not the *room* but the *stove*.'
Abraham Kuyper

Gifts are but as dead graces, but graces are living gifts.
Christopher Nesse

SPIRITUAL HUNGER

It is easy to mistake intellectual curiosity for spiritual hunger.
François Fenelon

If there is a man anywhere who is hungering after God and is not filled, then the Word of God is broken. We are as full as we want to be.
A. W. Tozer

If there is anything in your life more demanding than your longing after God, then you will never be a Spirit-filled Christian.
A. W. Tozer

SPIRITUALITY

A man's true spiritual quality is to be judged by his graces, not his gifts.

You are only as spiritual as you are scriptural.
Myron Augsburger

The best measure of a spiritual life is not its ecstasies but its obedience.
Oswald Chambers

Prayer is conditioned by one thing alone and that is spirituality.
Leonard Ravenhill

Spiritual things are against the stream; heaven is up the hill. *Richard Sibbes*

Real spirituality always has an outcome.
Oswald J. Smith

Our estimate of Christ is the best gauge of our spiritual condition.
C. H. Spurgeon

SPIRITUAL RICHES

God's purposes always have God's provision.

Treasures in heaven are laid up only as treasures on earth are laid down.
Anon.

Shame on us for being paupers when we were meant to be princes.
D. Martyn Lloyd-Jones

How vast the treasures we possess!
How rich thy bounty, King of grace!
This world is ours, and worlds to come;
Earth is our lodge, and heaven our home.
Isaac Watts

SPIRITUAL WARFARE

The call to Christian commitment is not basically a call to enjoy happiness but to endure hardness.

For the Christian, this world is an arena, not an armchair.

No duty can be performed without wrestling. The Christian needs his sword as well as his trowel.
William Gurnall

Our journey is uphill, with a dead body upon our backs, the devil doing what he can to pull us down.
Philip Henry

It is impossible to be a true soldier of Jesus Christ and not fight.
J. Gresham Machen

There can never be peace in the bosom of a believer. There is peace with God, but constant war with sin.
Robert Murray M'Cheyne

You will not get leave to steal quietly to heaven in Christ's company without a conflict and a cross.
Samuel Rutherford

There is no holiness without a warfare. *J. C. Ryle*

The Christian life is not a playground; it is a battleground. *Warren Wiersbe*

STEWARDSHIP

(See also: Giving; Tithing)

The fundamental truth in the matter of stewardship is that everything we touch belongs to God.

We are to get, not just in order to have, but in order to give. *Anon.*

It was not an accident that seventeen of the thirty-six parables of our Lord had to do with property and stewardship.
William James Dawson

Poor stewardship amounts to nothing less than withholding from the Lord that which is his.
Frank Gabelein

Stewardship is what a man does after he says, 'I believe'.
W. H. Greaves

Stewardship is not the leaving of a tip on God's tablecloth; it is the confession of an unpayable debt at God's Calvary.
Paul S. Rees

The use of our possessions shows us up for what we actually are.
Charles Caldwell Ryrie

SUBMISSION

(See also: Abandonment; Consecration; Zeal)

He who abandons himself *to* God will never be abandoned *by* God. *Anon.*

Nothing on earth do I desire,
But thy pure love within
my breast;
This, only this, will I require,
And freely give up all the
rest.
Antoinette Bourignon

If you lay yourself at Christ's feet he will take you into his arms.
William Bridge

All life should be subject to the kingly rule of God.
Martin Buber

One of the miracles of the grace of God is what he is able to do with the torn nets of lives surrendered to him.
G. B. Duncan

Submission to God is the only true balm that can heal the wounds he gives.
Nathaniel Emmons

Make this simple rule the guide of your life: to have no will but God's.
François Fenelon

Refuse nothing to God.
François Fenelon

Promotion, publicity, personality, politics, popularity and even prosperity we have in abundance. But there is a dearth of God-empowered men and women with a deep love for the Saviour, unconditional commitment to him and complete indifference to their own well-being. *James R. Graham*

There is nothing got by scuffling with God.
William Gurnall

Terms with God must always be *his* terms, not yours. *John Hercus*

If you don't surrender to Christ you surrender to chaos. *E. Stanley Jones*

We get no deeper into Christ than we allow him to get into us.
J. H. Jowett

My times are in thy hand;
My God, I wish them there;
My life, my friends, my soul I leave
Entirely to thy care.
William Freeman Lloyd

Let God have your life; he can do more with it than you can.
D. L. Moody

I want nothing for myself; I want everything for the Lord. *Watchman Nee*

Men must choose to be governed by God or they condemn themselves to be ruled by tyrants.
William Penn

There are times when God asks nothing of his children except silence, patience and tears.
Charles Seymour Robinson

The awesome purchase price of the very life of the Son of God should be more than ample motivation to make every child of God eagerly want to yield back to the Lord the very freedom which his death bought.
Charles Caldwell Ryrie

The capital of heaven is the heart in which Jesus Christ is enthroned as King.
Sadhu Sundar Singh

When all that you are is available to all that God is, then all that God is is available to all that you are.
Ian Thomas

Father, I wait thy daily will;
Thou shalt divide my portion still;
Grant me on earth what seems thee best,
Till death and heaven reveal the rest.
Isaac Watts

May the mind of Christ my Saviour
Live in me from day to day,
By his love and power controlling
All I do and say.
Katie Barclay Wilkinson

SUCCESS

If the devil cannot use failure to drag you down, he will use success.

Always expect to succeed, and never think you have succeeded.
Thomas Arnold

Men of great honour and worldly glory stand but in slippery places.
Thomas Brooks

The dangers to our spiritual welfare from success are far greater than the dangers from failure.
Arthur C. Custance

Try not to become a man of success but rather try to become a man of value.
Albert Einstein

There is a glare about worldly success which is very apt to dazzle men's eyes.
A. W. Hare

It is difficult to be high and not to be high-minded.
William Jenkyn

SUFFERING

(See also: Pain; Sickness; Trials)

God would sooner we had holy pain than unholy pleasure.

Pain and suffering are not necessarily signs of God's anger; they may be exactly the opposite.

God sometimes has to put us on our backs in order to make us look up.
Anon.

The face of Jesus must be very near our own when the thorns from his crown of suffering are pressing our brow and hurting us.
Anon.

We can sometimes see more through a tear than through a telescope. *Anon.*

There is as much difference between the sufferings of the saints and those of the ungodly as there is between the cords with which an executioner pinions a condemned malefactor and the bandages wherewith a tender surgeon binds his patient.
John Arrowsmith

Suffering times are teaching times. *William Bridge*

Suffering times are a Christian's harvest times.
Thomas Brooks

Out of suffering have emerged the strongest souls; the most massive characters are seared with scars.
E. H. Chapin

The soul would have no rainbow had the eye no tears. *John Vance Cheney*

Sufferings are but as little chips of the cross.
Joseph Church

God sometimes washes the eyes of his children with tears in order that they may read aright his providence and his commandments. *T. L. Cuyler*

Suffering prepares us for glory. *David Kingdon*

God whispers to us in health and prosperity, but, being hard of hearing, we fail to hear God's voice in both. Whereupon God turns up the amplifier by means of suffering. Then his voice booms.
C. S. Lewis

The real problem is not why some pious, humble, believing people suffer, but why some do not.
C. S. Lewis

There is nothing the body suffers that the soul may not profit by.
George Meredith

Good men are often great sufferers.
William S. Plumer

Saints should fear every sin, but no sufferings.
Vavasor Powell

There are no gains without pains. *J. C. Ryle*

Outward weaknesses are oft a means to restrain men from inward evils. God usually sanctifies the pains and griefs of his servants to make them better.
Richard Sibbes

I would . . . suggest that some form of suffering is virtually indispensable to holiness.
John R. W. Stott

A man is not known by his effervescence but by the amount of real suffering he can stand.
C. T. Studd

The Bible has a great deal to say about suffering and most of it is encouraging.
A. W. Tozer

Calvary is God's great proof that suffering in the will of God always leads to glory.
Warren Wiersbe

SUICIDE

No man must let the tenant out of the tenement till God the landlord call for it.
Thomas Adams

Suicide is a grave sin and scandal in a Christian, such as even throws doubt on the sincerity of his Christian profession. But there is no reason to think that the old man, still dwelling in the flesh of the regenerate, is quite incapable of such an act. *Roger Beckwith*

We must cast the world out of our hearts, not cast ourselves out of the world.
N. Bifield

Man was not born for his own pleasure, neither must he die at his own lust.
Henry Smith

No creature but man willingly kills itself.
Thomas Watson

SUPERSTITION

Superstition is godless religion, devout impiety.
Joseph Hall

The devil divides the world between atheism and superstition. *George Herbert*

Superstition is not, as has been defined, an excess of religious feeling, but a misdirection of it, an exhausting of it on vanities of man's devising.
Richard Whately

SYMPATHY

Sympathy is two hearts tugging at the same load.
Anon.

Sympathy is no substitute for action.
David Livingstone

Empathy is your pain in my heart.
Halford E. Luccock

TELEVISION

If a man's leisure-time exercise consists only of changing channels, it is not only his legs that will become atrophied.

If you have half a mind to turn on television, it is all you will need for many programmes.
M. R. De Haan

All television is educational television. The only question is, what is it teaching? *Nicholas Johnson*

TEMPTATION – Avoiding and Resisting

It takes two to make a successful temptation, and you are one of the two.
Anon.

Most people who fly from temptation usually leave a forwarding address.
Anon.

We have many leaders into temptation, but it is our fault if we follow them.
Thomas Adams

If you don't want the devil to tempt you with forbidden fruit, you had better keep out of his orchard. *Doug Barnett*

Better shun the bait than struggle in the snare.
John Dryden

What makes resisting temptation difficult for many people is that they don't want to discourage it completely.
Franklin Jones

Christ will not keep us if we carelessly and wantonly put ourselves into the way of temptation.
F. B. Meyer

Weak doctrines will not be a match for powerful temptations.
William S. Plumer

To pray against temptation, and yet to rush into occasion, is to thrust your fingers into the fire, and then pray they might not be burnt. *Thomas Secker*

If you hold the stirrup, no wonder if Satan gets into the saddle.

William Secker

Temptation rarely comes in working hours. It is in their leisure time that men are made or marred.

W. T. Taylor

TEMPTATION – Blessing

Every temptation is an opportunity of our getting nearer to God.

John Quincy Adams

Temptations discover what we are.

Thomas à Kempis

It is good to be without vices, but it is not good to be without temptations.

Walter Bagehot

Temptation provokes me to look upward to God.

John Bunyan

Temptations are a file which rub off much of the rust of our self-confidence.

François Fenelon

If it takes temptation and sin to show God in his true colours and Satan in his, something has been saved from the wreck.

Michael Green

My temptations have been my masters in divinity.

Martin Luther

One Christian who has been tempted is worth a thousand who haven't.

Martin Luther

Nothing is so conducive to real humility as temptation. It teaches us how weak we are.

Donald MacDonald

TEMPTATION – Certainty

Temptation is something we must never excite, but always expect.

There is no order so holy, no place so secret, where there will be no temptation. *Thomas à Kempis*

God promises a safe landing but not a calm passage.

Anon.

Temptations are everywhere, *and so is the grace of God.* *Anon.*

How daily, hourly, is the struggle with sin and fear

and temptation – it is never over! *J. J. Bonar*

Jesus was tempted, not because he was bad, but because he was important.
G. B. Duncan

There is no devil so bad as no devil.
Ralph Erskine

The best of saints may be tempted to the worst of sins. *Matthew Henry*

The greatest temptation out of hell is to live without temptation.
Samuel Rutherford

You are not tempted because you are evil; you are tempted because you are human.
Fulton J. Sheen

TEMPTATION – and Satan

(See also: Satan)

Satan, like a fisher, baits his hook according to the appetite of the fish.
Thomas Adams

Even on the brink of Jordan I find Satan nibbling at my heels. *Anon.*

Temptation is the tempter looking through the keyhole into the room where you are living; sin is your drawing back the bolt and making it possible for him to enter.
J. Wilbur Chapman

No player hath so many dresses to come in upon the stage (with) as the devil hath forms of temptation. *William Gurnall*

O Lord, help us to hear the serpent's rattle before we feel its fangs.
Thomas De Witt Talmage

Satan never sets a dish before men that they do not love. *Thomas Watson*

TEMPTATION – and Sin

Temptation always promises more than it produces.

No degree of temptation justifies any degree of sin.
Nathaniel Parker Willis

Temptation is not sin; it is the call to battle.
Frederick P. Wood

THANKSGIVING

(See also: Gratitude)

No duty is more urgent than that of returning thanks. *Ambrose*

Thanksgiving is the vibration of the soul's heart-strings under the soft touch of God's benevolence.
Anon.

A thankful man is worth his weight in gold.
Thomas Brooks

A thankful heart has a continual feast.
W. J. Cameron

Those blessings are sweetest that are won with prayers and worn with thanks. *Thomas Goodwin*

Joy untouched by thankfulness is always suspect.
Theodor Haecker

Prayer without thanksgiving is like a bird without wings.
William Hendriksen

Thanksgiving is good but thanks-living is better.
Matthew Henry

Every furrow in the book of Psalms is sown with the seeds of thanksgiving.
Jeremy Taylor

Hearty thanks must be given to God: such as cometh not from the roof of the mouth but the root of the heart. *John Trapp*

The Christian is suspended between blessings received and blessings hoped for, so he should always give thanks. *M. R. Vincent*

THEOLOGY

(See also: Bible; Doctrine)

We must never let our theology rob us of our responsibility.

All my theology is reduced to this narrow compass – Christ Jesus came into the world to save sinners.
Archibald Alexander

Beware of a theology produced by spontaneous generation. *Anon.*

Every question is ultimately a theological question.
Hilaire Belloc

Theology can never be a science, on account of the infirmities of language.
Horace Bushnell

I have not the slightest interest in a theology which doesn't evangelize.
James Denney

The truth of God is a boundless expanse. Definitions were made for man, not man for definitions.
A. A. Hodge

The more we know of God, the more unreservedly we will trust him; the greater our progress in theology, the simpler and more child-like will be our faith.
J. Gresham Machen

Your theology is what you are when the talking stops and the action starts.
Colin Morris

If we pursue theological knowledge for its own sake, it is bound to go bad on us. It will make us proud and conceited.
J. I. Packer

Never study theology in cold blood.
E. G. Robinson

No Christian can avoid theology. *R. C. Sproul*

Rest assured that there is nothing new in my theology except that which is false. *C. H. Spurgeon*

Loose theology leads to loose morality.
R. A. Torrey

THOUGHTS

(See also: Imagination; Mind)

A man is not what he thinks he is, but what he thinks, he is. *Anon.*

In company, guard your tongue – in solitude, your thoughts. *Anon.*

Thought is a kind of sight of the mind. *Augustine*

A man's thoughts dye his soul. *Marcus Aurelius*

As the image on the seal is stamped upon the wax, so the thoughts of the heart are printed upon the actions.
Stephen Charnock

Thoughts are the immediate spawn of the original corruption.
Stephen Charnock

Think all you speak but speak not all you think.
Patrick Delaney

A man is what he thinks about all day long.
Ralph Waldo Emerson

Thy thoughts are vocal to God. *John Flavel*

It is bad to think ill, but it is worse to speak it.
Matthew Henry

More souls are lost through want of consideration than in any other way.
Robert Murray M'Cheyne

At every point right living begins with right thinking.
Bruce J. Milne

We cannot afford the luxury of careless thinking.
Irwin Moon

The spiritual battle, the loss of victory, is always in the thought-world.
Francis Schaeffer

Vain thoughts defile the heart as well as vile thoughts. *William Secker*

Thoughts are the seeds of actions. *Richard Sibbes*

God will not live in the parlour of our hearts if we entertain the devil in the cellar of our thoughts.
C. H. Spurgeon

The secret of clean living is clear thinking.
John R. W. Stott

Jesus is no stranger to your thoughts.
Geoff Treasure

TIME – and Eternity

The world began with time and time with it.
Thomas Adams

Time is but the fringe of eternity. *Anon.*

What we weave in time we wear in eternity. *Anon.*

The great weight of eternity hangs upon the small wire of time. *Thomas Brooks*

Time cannot be infinite.
Stephen Charnock

Time is the chrysalis of eternity.
Jean Paul Richter

God hath given man a short time here upon earth, and yet upon this short time eternity depends.
Jeremy Taylor

You cannot kill time without injuring eternity.
Henry David Thoreau

I am not careful for what may be a hundred years hence. He who governed the world before I was born shall take care of it likewise when I am dead. My part is to improve the present moment.
John Wesley

TIME – Misuse

To waste time is to squander a gift from God.

Kill time and you murder opportunity. *Anon.*

Lost time is never found.
Anon.

Do not squander time, for it is the stuff of which life is made.
Benjamin Franklin

Those who dare lose a day are dangerously prodigal; those who dare misspend it, desperate. *Joseph Hall*

Time and money are the heaviest burdens of life, and the unhappiest of all mortals are those who have more of either than they know how to use.
Samuel Johnson

We are always complaining that our days are few and at the same time acting as if they would never end.
Seneca

TIME – Urgency

Today is the tomorrow you worried about yesterday.
Anon.

Tomorrow is a post-dated cheque. Today is cash.
Anon.

What is past cannot be recalled; what is future cannot be insured.
Stephen Charnock

Time goes, you say? Ah, no! Alas, time stays, *we go*! *Henry A. Dobson*

Time is not a commodity that can be stored for future use. It must be invested hour by hour, or else it is gone for ever.
Thomas Edison

We live by demands when we should live by priorities.
J. A. Motyer

Time is the deposit each one has in the bank of God and no one knows the balance.
Ralph W. Sockman

TIME – Use

We speak of spending time, the Bible speaks of buying it.

Give me a Christian that counts his time more precious than gold.
Joseph Alleine

Life is too short for us to do everything *we* want to do; but it is long enough for us to do everything *God* wants us to do.
Anon.

Spend your time in nothing which you know must be repented of; in nothing on which you might not pray for the blessing of God; in nothing which you could not review with a quiet conscience on your dying bed; in nothing which you might not safely and properly be found doing if death should surprise you in the act.

Richard Baxter

Time is not yours to dispose of as you please; it is a glorious talent that men must be accountable for as well as any other talent. *Thomas Brooks*

I count that hour lost in which I have done no good by my pen or tongue.

John Bradford

There is nothing puts a more serious frame into a man's spirit than to know the worth of his time.

Thomas Brooks

Those to whom God has taught the value of time feel that it has little need to be 'killed'; it goes away from us all too quickly without that.

Robert Johnstone

The year is made up of minutes. Let these be watched as having been dedicated to God. It is in the sanctification of the small that the hallowing of the large is secure.

G. Campbell Morgan

Great men never complain about the lack of time. Alexander the Great and John Wesley accomplished everything they did in twenty-four hour days.

Fred Smith

I do not have time to be in a hurry. *John Wesley*

TITHING

(See also: Giving; Stewardship)

The tithe is not meant to be a ceiling at which we stop giving, but a floor from which we start.

If God gave you ten times as much as you give him could you live on it?

Anon.

Giving a tenth is nothing to brag about.

Samuel Chadwick

God demands the tithe, deserves the offerings, defends the savings and directs the expenses.

Stephen Olford

It could be argued that in the Old Testament tithes were *paid*, and therefore do not, strictly speaking, come under the heading of giving at all. Christian giving only begins when we give more than a tenth.

Kenneth F. W. Prior

TRIALS – Blessings

(See also: Pain; Sickness; Suffering)

I have learned more from life's trials than from its triumphs.

The trials of life are meant to make us better, not bitter.

Times of affliction are usually gaining times to God's people.

Joseph Alleine

Affliction is God's shepherd dog to drive us back to the fold. *Anon.*

Fire is the test of gold, adversity of strong men.

Anon.

Our great Teacher writes many a bright lesson on the blackboard of affliction. *Anon.*

The gem cannot be polished without friction, nor man perfected without trials.

Anon.

The water that dashes against the wheel keeps the mill going; so trial keeps grace in use and motion. *Anon.*

The purpose of the tests of life are to make, not break us.

Maltbie Babcock

Prosperity is the blessing of the Old Testament; adversity is the blessing of the new. *Francis Bacon*

Night brings out stars as sorrow shows us truths.

Gamaliel Bailey

The brook would lose its song if you removed the rocks. *Fred Beck*

Troubles are often the tools by which God fashions us for better things.

Henry Ward Beecher

Affliction is an excellent comment upon the Scriptures. *Thomas Brooks*

Afflictions are but as a dark entry into our Father's house. *Thomas Brooks*

Afflictions ripen the saint's graces. *Thomas Brooks*

The grand design of God in all the afflictions that befall his people is to

bring them nearer and closer to himself.
Thomas Brooks

Thou art beaten that thou mayest be better.
John Bunyan

As threshing separates the wheat from the chaff, so does affliction purify virtue.
Richard E. Burton

Afflictions ought ever to be estimated by their *end*.
John Calvin

The brightest crowns that are worn in heaven have been tried, and smelted, and polished, and glorified through the furnace of tribulation.
E. H. Chapin

We often learn more under the rod that strikes us, than under the staff that comforts us.
Stephen Charnock

In prosperity, our friends know us; in adversity we know our friends.
Churton Collins

Afflictions . . . are as necessary for our waftage to heaven as water is to carry the ship to her port.
William Gurnall

God's wounds cure; sin's kisses kill. *William Gurnall*

God sometimes snuffs out our brightest candle that we may look up to his eternal stars.
Vance Havner

The Lord doesn't take us into deep water to drown us but to develop us.
Irv Hedstrom

Sanctified afflictions are spiritual promotions.
Matthew Henry

Sometimes God teaches us effectually to know the worth of mercies by the want of them and whets our appetite for the means of grace by cutting us short in those means.
Matthew Henry

Let prosperity be as oil to the wheels of obedience and affliction as wind to the sails of prayer.
Philip Henry

Affliction is the medicine of the mind.
John P. K. Henshaw

The great blows of God are designed to make a man stand up.
John Hercus

As the wicked are hurt by the best things, so the godly are bettered by the worse. *William Jenkyn*

Only in the hot furnace of affliction do we as Christians let go of the dross to which, in our foolishness, we ardently cling.
David Kingdon

This school of trial best discloses the hidden vileness of the heart and the vast riches of a Saviour's grace. *Henry Law*

I never knew the meaning of God's Word until I came into affliction.
Martin Luther

Affliction is the whetstone of prayer and obedience.
Edward Marbury

Trouble is the structural steel that goes into character-building.
Douglas Meador

Affliction is the school in which great virtues are acquired, in which great characters are formed.
Hannah More

One breath of paradise will extinguish all the adverse winds of earth.
A. W. Pink

Afflictions often possess remarkable power to remind us of our sins.
William S. Plumer

It is a blessed thing when our trials cure our earnest love for things that perish.
William S. Plumer

By afflictions God is spoiling us of what otherwise might have spoiled us – when he makes the world too hot for us to hold, we let it go. *John Powell*

I have never met with a single instance of adversity which I have not in the end seen was for my good – I have never heard of a Christian on his deathbed complaining of his affliction.
Alexander M. Proudfit

Grace grows best in the winter.
Samuel Rutherford

Affliction is a searching wind which strips the leaves off the trees and brings to light the bird's nests.
J. C. Ryle

Afflictions should be the spiritual wings of the soul.
Richard Sibbes

After conversion we need bruising, to see that we live by mercy. *Richard Sibbes*

As Jacob was blessed and halted both at one time, so a man may be blessed and afflicted both together.
Henry Smith

In shunning a trial we are seeking to avoid a blessing. *C. H. Spurgeon*

Stars may be seen from the bottom of a deep well, when they cannot be discerned from the top of a mountain. So are many things learned in adversity which the prosperous man dreams not of.
C. H. Spurgeon

The anvil, the fire and the hammer are the making of us. *C. H. Spurgeon*

There are some of your graces which would never be discovered if it were not for your trials.
C. H. Spurgeon

Jesus was transfigured on the hilltop, but he transforms us in the valley.
J. Charles Stern

It takes a world with trouble in it to train men for their high calling as sons of God and to carve upon the soul the lineaments of the face of Christ.
J. S. Steward

A sanctified person, like a silver bell, the harder he is smitten, the better he sounds.
George Swinnock

We are safer in the storm God sends us than in a calm when we are befriended by the world.
Jeremy Taylor

For a Christian, even the valleys are on higher ground.
D. Reginald Thomas

Better be preserved in brine than rot in honey.
John Trapp

Troubles are free schoolmasters. *John Trapp*

Is it any injustice in God to put his gold into the furnace to purify it?
Thomas Watson

Jonah was sent into the whale's belly to make his sermon for Nineveh.
Thomas Watson

The whale that swallowed Jonah was the means of bringing him safe to land.
Thomas Watson

Whilst I continue on this side of eternity, I never expect to be free from trials, only to change them. For it is necessary to heal

the pride of my heart that such should come.
George Whitefield

Among my list of blessings infinite stands this the foremost – that my heart has bled. *Edward Young*

TRIALS – Certainty

A saint is often under a cross, never under a curse.
Anon.

There never yet was an unscarred saint. *Anon.*

The Christian life *is* a bed of roses – thorns and all. *Doug Barnett*

Saints have their winter seasons. *Thomas Brooks*

As we are adopted in Christ we are appointed to the slaughter.
John Calvin

Spiritual believers are honoured with warfare in the front line trenches.
Lewis Sperry Chafer

The Scriptures show conclusively that tribulation is a natural by-product of genuine Christianity.
William E. Cox

Afflictions are in the covenant, and therefore they are not meant for our hurt but are intended for our good. *Matthew Henry*

The corn of God's floor must expect to be threshed by afflictions and persecutions. *Matthew Henry*

Testing is important, inevitable . . . because we must be revealed to ourselves.
J. Russell Howden

Every Christian is a cross-bearer. *Martin Luther*

A believer is to be known not only by his peace and joy, but by his warfare and distress.
Robert Murray M'Cheyne

Why should I complain
Of want or distress,
Temptation or pain?
He told me no less;
The heirs of salvation,
I know from his Word,
Through much tribulation
Must follow their Lord.
John Newton

God promises no immunity from crosses.
Richard Sibbes

There are no crown-wearers in heaven that were not cross-bearers here below.
C. H. Spurgeon

He that escapes affliction may well suspect his adoption. *John Trapp*

Life and trouble are married together. *Thomas Watson*

TRIALS – God the Sender

God may call you to endure difficulties, but he will never cause you to experience defeat.

The storms of life no more indicate the absence of God than clouds indicate the absence of the sun.

God promises a safe landing but not a calm passage.
Anon.

God sometimes puts his children to bed in the dark.
Anon.

The pressures of life are the hands of the Potter.
Anon.

Wherever souls are being tried and ripened, in whatever commonplace and homely way, there God is hewing out the pillars of his temple.
Phillips Brooks

God's way of answering the Christian's prayer for more patience, experience, hope and love often is to put him into the furnace of affliction.
Richard Cecil

God measures out affliction to our need. *Chrysostom*

Count each affliction, whether light or grave, God's messenger sent down to thee.
Aubrey T. De Vere

God sometimes brings his people into a wilderness that there he might speak comfortably to them.
Matthew Henry

There may be love in Christ's heart while there are frowns in his face.
Matthew Henry

God will not look you over for medals, degrees or diplomas, but for scars.
Elbert Hubbard

Adversity is the diamond dust heaven polishes its jewels with.
Robert Leighton

Let God lay on a burden, he will be sure to strengthen the back. *Thomas Lye*

Afflictions are but the shadow of God's wings.
George MacDonald

If God sends us on stony paths he will provide us with strong shoes.
Alexander MacLaren

Affliction by itself does not sanctify; it exhausts and embitters, it depresses and entices. It is the presence of God and the use made of it by him, as he relates it to our lives as a whole . . . that makes adversity salutary.
Donald MacLeod

God will never permit any troubles to come upon us unless he has a specific plan by which great blessing can come out of the difficulty. *Peter Marshall*

It is true that God *tempts none*, as temptation formally leads into sin; but he *orders temptations.*
John Owen

The whole of life is a test, a trial of what is in us, so arranged by God himself.
William S. Plumer

There is no cross or misery that befalls the church of God or any of his children, but it is related to God.
Samuel Rutherford

Let no man think himself the better because he is free from troubles. It is because God sees him not fit to bear greater.
Richard Sibbes

The Lord gets his best soldiers out of the highlands of affliction.
C. H. Spurgeon

The refiner is never very far from the mouth of the furnace when his gold is in the fire.
C. H. Spurgeon

Mountains are God's methods.
J. Charles Stern

While the storm gathers let us by faith rejoice in our place behind the shut door – in Christ.
J. Charles Stern

God tempers the wind to the shorn lamb.
Laurence Sterne

God's wounds are better than Satan's salves.
John Trapp

Affliction is a badge of adoption.
Thomas Watson

God doesn't save people from punishment or pain. He saves them by giving them the strength and the spirit to bear it.
Leonard Wilson

We may feel God's hand as a Father upon us when he strikes us as well as when he strokes us.
Abraham Wright

TRIALS – Response

God has done a mighty work in our hearts when we can praise him in every pain, bless him for every burden, sing in every sorrow and delight in every discipline.

We are called upon to reflect the love of God as much in trial as in tranquility.

Reckon any matter of trial to thee among thy gains.
Thomas Adams

Adversity does not make us frail; it only shows us how frail we are.
Anon.

If you meet with misfortunes, consider that you merit greater ones.
Petrus Blesensis

In the day of prosperity we have many refuges to resort to; in the day of adversity, only one.
Horatius Bonar

I do not pray for a lighter load but for a stronger back. *Phillips Brooks*

It is a genuine evidence of true godliness when, although plunged into the deepest afflictions, we yet cease not to submit ourselves to God.
John Calvin

Afflictions are blessings to us when we can bless God for afflictions.
William Dyer

It lightens the stroke to draw near to him who handles the rod.
Tryon Edwards

A cross which comes from God ought to be welcomed without any concern for self. *François Fenelon*

Shall light troubles make you forget weighty mercies?
John Flavel

We should be more anxious that our afflictions should benefit us than that they should be speedily removed from us. *Robert Hall*

Days of trouble must be days of prayer.
Matthew Henry

While the fire is hot, keep conversing with the Refiner.
F. B. Meyer

No affliction would trouble a child of God if he knew God's reasons for sending it. *G. Campbell Morgan*

A Christian should never let adversity get him down except on his knees.
Mae Nicholson

We ought as much to pray for a blessing upon our daily rod as upon our daily bread. *John Owen*

There is a strange perversity in men concerning their trials in life, and only grace can cure it.
William S. Plumer

Many a man has thought himself broken up, when he has merely been made ready for the sowing.
Hugh Redwood

Praise God for the hammer, the file and the furnace!
Samuel Rutherford

When I am in the cellar of affliction I look for the Lord's choicest wines.
Samuel Rutherford

Cast your troubles where you have cast your sins.
C. H. Spurgeon

Nothing influences the quality of our life more than how we respond to trouble. *Erwin G. Tieman*

TRIALS – Temporary Nature

When God's hand is on thy back, let thy hand be on thy mouth, for though the affliction be sharp it shall be but short.
Thomas Brooks

Though your life be evil with troubles, yet it is short – a few steps and we are out of the rain.
William Gurnall

How soon you will find that everything in your history, except sin, has been *for* you. Every wave of trouble has been wafting you to the sunny shores of a sinless eternity.
Robert Murray M'Cheyne

It was well worth standing a while in the fire, for such an opportunity of experiencing and exhibiting the power and faithfulness of God's promises.
John Newton

No pain, no palm; no thorns, no throne; no gall, no glory; no cross, no crown. *William Penn*

God does not mock his children with a night that has no ending; and to every man who stands resolute while the darkness lasts there comes at length the vindication of faith and the breaking of the day. *James S. Stewart*

He that rides to be crowned will not think much of a rainy day. *John Trapp*

Affliction may be lasting, but it is not everlasting.
Thomas Watson

TRUTH

(See also: Honesty; Integrity)

Whatever you add to the truth subtracts from it.

He who sets one great truth afloat in the world serves his generation.
James W. Alexander

Truth is not the feeble thing which men often think they can afford to disparage. Truth is power; let it be treated and trusted as such. *Horatius Bonar*

If a thousand old beliefs were ruined in our march to truth we must still march on.
Stopford A. Brooke

Truth is always strong, no matter how weak it looks, and falsehood is always weak, no matter how strong it looks. *Phillips Brooks*

Every parcel of truth is precious as the filings of gold; we must either live with it, or die for it.
Thomas Brooks

When truth is silent, false views seem plausible.
Walter J. Chantry

Truth is incontrovertible. Panic may resent it; ignorance may deride it; malice may distort it; but there it is. *Winston Churchill*

If all heretical doctrines and ways and the memory of them were rooted out of the world, the heart is bad enough in one day to set them all on foot again; therefore guard the truth. *John Collins*

Truth is the foundation of all knowledge and the cement of all societies.
John Dryden

If God were able to backslide from truth, I would fain cling to truth and let God go.
Meister Eckhart

Godliness is the child of truth, and it must be nursed . . . with no other milk than that of its own mother. *William Gurnall*

News may come that truth is sick, but never that it is dead. *William Gurnall*

Some people live their whole lives just around the corner from the world of truth. *Carl F. H. Henry*

The truth makes us free *from* our spiritual enemies, free *in* the service of God, free *to* the privileges of sons. *Matthew Henry*

Truth is always as honest in its recognition of darkness as it is exultant in its understanding of light.
John Hercus

Every truth, like a lease, brings in revenue the next year as well as this.
William Jenkyn

Peace if possible, but truth at any rate. *Martin Luther*

It is truth alone that capacitates any soul to give glory to God. *John Owen*

There are no victories like those of truth.
William S. Plumer

Let us rejoice in the truth, wherever we find its lamp burning.
Albert Schweitzer

Truth is always the strongest argument. *Sophocles*

A thousand errors may live in peace with one another, but truth is a hammer that breaks them all in pieces. *C. H. Spurgeon*

Long ago I ceased to count heads. Truth is usually in the minority in this evil world.
C. H. Spurgeon

Men to be truly won must be won by truth.
C. H. Spurgeon

The shining of truth, like the shining of the sun, wakens insects into life, which otherwise would have no sensitive existence. Yet, better for a few insects to quicken than for the sun not to shine!
Augustus M. Toplady

Truth is like our first parents — most beautiful when naked. *John Trapp*

Truth must be spoken, however it be taken.
John Trapp

The truth is sometimes daunting but always worth knowing.
Thomas Winning

UNBELIEF

(See also: Atheism; Impiety)

If you are an unbeliever when you die, Christ did not die for you.
Ambrose

Unbelief in the face of evidence is either stupidity or sin. *Anon.*

All unbelief is the belief of a lie. *Horatius Bonar*

Infidelity is always blind.
John Calvin

Our own unbelief is the only impediment which prevents God from satisfying us largely and bountifully with all good things.
John Calvin

Unbelief was the first sin, and pride was the first-born of it.
Stephen Charnock

Alongside getting faith out of a heart that is utterly hostile and unbelieving, making a silk purse out of a sow's ear or getting blood from a turnip is child's play.
John H. Gerstner

Unbelief is at the bottom of all our staggerings at God's promises.
Matthew Henry

Unbelief is the shield of every sin. *William Jenkyn*

Unbelief is not failure in intellectual apprehension. It is disobedience in the presence of the clear commands of God.
G. Campbell Morgan

For the most part we live upon successes, not promises. Unless we see and feel the print of victories we will not believe.
John Owen

The errors of faith are better than the best thoughts of unbelief.
Thomas Russell

It is unbelief that prevents our minds from soaring into the celestial city, and walking by faith with God across the golden streets. *A. W. Tozer*

A great many believers walk upon the promises at God's call in the way to heaven even as a child upon weak ice, which they are afraid will crack under them and leave them in the depth.
Robert Traill

Infidelity is the mother of apostasy. *John Trapp*

UNCERTAINTY

(See also: Doubt)

The fact that a Christian is uncertain does not mean that he is insecure.

Nothing in the world causes so much misery as uncertainty. *Martin Luther*

The only thing people are certain about is their uncertainty.
George Bernard Shaw

UNIVERSALISM

Universalism is the curse of the universe.

Universalism abstracts from the radical condition of man as a sinner before God.
Jakob Jocz

Universalism is the evangelist's 'By-Path Meadow'. We shall do well to stick to the road. *J. I. Packer*

URGENCY

We must take the opportunity of a lifetime in the lifetime of an opportunity.
Anon.

God says 'today'; the devil says 'tomorrow'. *Basil*

Now if ever, now for ever, now or never, up and be doing, lest you be for ever undone.
William Dyer

Harvest time is always the ever-present *now*!
Billy Graham

We shall have all eternity in which to celebrate our victories, but we have only one short hour before the sunset in which to *win* them. *Robert Moffatt*

There is only one time that is important – *now.*
Leo Tolstoy

VICTORY

Be careful that victories do not carry the seeds of future defeats. *Anon.*

We will be controlled either by Satan, by self or by God. Control by Satan is slavery; control by self is futility; control by God is victory. *Anon.*

A victory inside of us is ten thousand times more

glorious than any victory can be outside of us.
Henry Ward Beecher

Let us be as watchful after the victory as before the battle. *Andrew Bonar*

The more anyone excels in grace, the more he ought to be afraid of falling.
John Calvin

There is only one answer to defeat and that is victory. *Winston Churchill*

A victorious Christian life is not a superior brand of Christianity reserved for the elite of the elect. It is the normal Christian life for every Christian.
Ronald Dunn

God's victories are won only on the battlefield of the human heart.
H. H. Farmer

God has not called us to fumble through life.
Stephen Olford

There is no more dangerous moment in our lives than that which follows a great victory. *Stephen Olford*

There can be no victory where there is no combat.
Richard Sibbes

The first step on the way to victory is to recognize the enemy.
Corrie Ten Boom

God wants us to be victors, not victims; to grow, not grovel; to soar, not sink; to overcome, not to be overwhelmed.
William A. Ward

VIGILANCE

The permanent presence of the old nature guarantees that in the Christian life there is no victory without vigilance.

Many a saint, for want of keeping a tight rein, and that constantly, over some corruption which they have thought they had got the mastery of, has been thrown out of the saddle.
William Gurnall

Our enemies are on every side, so must our armour be. *William Gurnall*

Set a strong guard about thy outward senses. These are Satan's landing-place, especially the eye and ear.
William Gurnall

The humble Christian is the wary Christian.
William Gurnall

Those whom God has promised to save he has promised to render watchful. *Charles Hodge*

Eternal vigilance is the price of liberty.
Thomas Jefferson

The best way never to fall is ever to fear.
William Jenkyn

No stage of experience takes away the need for vigilance. *J. A. Motyer*

Unless we keep a strict watch, we shall be betrayed into the hands of our spiritual enemies.
John Owen

True conversion gives a man security, but it does not allow him to leave off being watchful.
C. H. Spurgeon

A wandering heart needs a watchful eye.
Thomas Watson

VIRGIN BIRTH

(See also: Incarnation – Jesus Christ)

Those who deny that Jesus was without a human father must explain how he was without human failure.

The God who took a motherless woman out of the side of a man took a fatherless man out of the body of a woman.
Matthew Henry

As bread is made of wheat, and wine is made of the grapes, so Christ is made of a woman. His body was part of the flesh and substance of the virgin.
Thomas Watson

WAR

A great war leaves the country with three armies – an army of cripples, an army of mourners and an army of thieves. *Anon.*

The tragedy of war is that it uses man's best to do man's worst. *Anon.*

If there is anything in which earth, more than any other, resembles hell, it is its wars. *Albert Barnes*

War is a tragedy which commonly destroys the stage it is acted on.
Matthew Henry

War is not an act of God but a crime of man.
Cordell Hull

Mankind must put an end to war, or war will put an end to mankind.
John F. Kennedy

War is a specific product of civilization.
Louis Mumford

Let men who delight in the cruelties of war remember that their day is coming.
William S. Plumer

Truth is the first casualty in any war.
John Nevin Sayre

War is the slaughter-house of mankind, and the hell of this present world.
John Trapp

WEALTH

(See also: Luxury; Materialism; Money; Possessions; Prosperity; Riches)

Wealth can do us no good unless it help us toward heaven. *Thomas Adams*

Wealth is no harm, but the inability to give it up is deadly. *Anon.*

Wealth is not only what we have, but what we are.
Anon.

Our wealth is often a snare to ourselves and always a temptation to others.
C. C. Colton

Wealth consists not in having great possessions but in having few wants.
Epicurus

Poor people are as much in danger from an inordinate desire towards the wealth of the world as rich from an inordinate delight in it.
Matthew Henry

The real measure of our wealth is how much we'd be worth if we lost all our money.
John Henry Jowett

Glory and glitter are not synonymous terms.
J. McIlmoyle

The wealthiest man is he who is contented with least. *Socrates*

Many a man's gold has lost him his God.
George Swinnock

WILL

(See also: Free Will)

When the will is won, all is won. *Thomas Brooks*

To will is human, to will the bad is of fallen nature, but to will the good is of grace. *John Calvin*

All the wickedness of the wicked world is owing to the wilfulness of the wicked will. *Matthew Henry*

The will is the basal, fundamental force in personality. *John Henry Jowett*

If there were no will there would be no hell. *Christopher Nesse*

God looks more at our wills than at our works. *William Secker*

The sinner in his sinful nature could never have a will according to God. *J. Denham Smith*

The will is the deciding factor in everything that we do. In every sphere of life it settles alternatives. *Frederick P. Wood*

WILL OF GOD

(See also: Guidance; Providence)

Nothing is right for a Christian if it is not God's will for him.

The will of God is the measure of things. *Ambrose*

The study of God's Word for the purpose of discovering God's will is the greatest discipline which has formed the greatest character. *Anon.*

All heaven is waiting to help those who will discover the will of God and do it. *J. Robert Ashcroft*

Nothing, therefore, happens unless the Omnipotent wills it to happen: he either permits it to happen, or he brings it about himself. *Augustine*

If we would avoid a senseless natural philosophy we must always start with this principle: that everything in nature depends upon the will of God, and that the whole course of nature is only the prompt carrying into effect of his orders. *John Calvin*

Jesus taught us that we are to be obsessed with living according to the will of God. *Herbert W. Cragg*

Nothing lies beyond the power of man if it is within the will of God.
James E. Crowther

Perfect conformity to the will of God is the sole sovereign and complete liberty.
J. H. Merle D'Aubigné

God's will is not an itinerary but an attitude.
Andrew Dhuse

The will of God is not something we are just to understand; it is something we are to undertake.
G. B. Duncan

If you think that you know the will of God for your life . . . you are probably in for a very rude awakening, because nobody knows the will of God for his entire life. *Elisabeth Elliot*

Make this simple rule the guide of your life: to have no will but God's.
François Fenelon

The revealed will of God is either manifested to us in his Word or in his works.
John Flavel

Once the will of God to me was a sigh; now it is a song.
Frances Ridley Havergal

All moral obligation resolves itself into the obligation of conformity to the will of God.
Charles Hodge

God will always reveal his will to one who is willing to do it. *Hilys Jasper*

Most people don't want to know the will of God in order to do it; they want to know it in order to consider it.
William Pettingill

God's will is the law of universal nature.
William S. Plumer

To understand the will of God is my problem; to undertake the will of God is my privilege; to undercut the will of God is my peril. *Paul S. Rees*

Contentment with the divine will is the best remedy we can apply to misfortune.
William Temple

WISDOM

Humility is the hallmark of wisdom. *Jeremy Collier*

Modesty is the badge of wisdom. *Matthew Henry*

Unaided wisdom, with its strongest wing, can only flutter in the vale of vanity. No earth-born eye can catch a glimpse of God.
Henry Law

Surely the essence of wisdom is that before we begin to act at all, or attempt to please God, we should discover what it is that God has to say about the matter.
D. Martyn Lloyd-Jones

Wisdom opens the eyes both to the glories of heaven and to the hollowness of earth.
J. A. Motyer

Not until we have become humble and teachable, standing in awe of God's holiness and sovereignty . . . acknowledging our own littleness, distrusting our own thoughts, and willing to have our minds turned upside down, can divine wisdom become ours.
J. I. Packer

The kind of wisdom that God waits to give to those who ask him is a wisdom that will bind us to himself.
J. I. Packer

The greatest wisdom on this earth is holiness.
William S. Plumer

Wisdom is the knowledge which sees into the heart of things, which knows them as they really are.
J. Armitage Robinson

Wisdom is to the mind what health is to the body.
François Rochefoucauld

Wisdom is easy to him that will understand.
Richard Sibbes

Conviction of ignorance is the doorstep to the temple of wisdom.
C. H. Spurgeon

The sublimity of wisdom is to do those things living which are to be desired when dying.
Jeremy Taylor

It is a fact that those whose lives are daily being conformed to the Word and purposes of God will be given the ability to see issues more plainly.
Malcolm Watts

WITNESSING

(See also: Evangelism; Soul-Winning)

Christians should penetrate the world without ever becoming part of it.

The object in witnessing is not to win arguments but disciples.

The real mark of a saint is that he makes it easier for others to believe in God. *Anon.*

Witnessing is not something we do; it is something we are. *Anon.*

What I live by, I impart.
Augustine

A Christian is called to be a witness, not counsel for the prosecution.
Doug Barnett

Men may not read the gospel in seal-skin, or the gospel in morocco, or the gospel in cloth covers; but they can't get away from the gospel in shoe leather.
Donald Grey Barnhouse

A Christian's life should be nothing but a visible representation of Christ.
Thomas Brooks

The Bible calls the good man's life a light; and it is the nature of light to flow out spontaneously in all directions, and fill the world unconsciously with its beams.
Horace Bushnell

The Christian is the visual aid which God brings on to the stage when he begins to speak at an unconverted person.
H. W. Cragg

If you were arrested for being a Christian would there be enough evidence to convict you?
David Otis Fuller

The Christian's task is to make the Lord Jesus visible, intelligible and desirable. *Len Jones*

A witness in a court of law has to *give* evidence; a Christian witness has to *be* evidence. It is the difference between law and grace! *Geoffrey R. King*

Nothing locks the lips like the life. *D. L. Moody*

Faith is not created by reasoning, but neither is it created without it. There is more involved in witness than throwing pre-arranged clumps of texts at unbelieving heads.
J. I. Packer

Witnessing is the whole work of the whole church for the whole age.
A. T. Pierson

If it is possible for your closest contacts to be neutral about Christ then there is something wrong with your Christianity.
Alan Redpath

The sermons most needed today are sermons in shoes.
C. H. Spurgeon

The real problem of Christianity is not atheism or scepticism, but the non-witnessing Christian trying to smuggle his own soul into heaven.
James S. Stewart

Testimony is not a synonym for *autobiography*! When we are truly witnessing, we are not talking about ourselves but about Christ. *John R. W. Stott*

My heart is full of Christ, and longs
Its glorious matter to declare!
Of him I make my loftier songs,
I cannot from his praise forbear;
My ready tongue makes haste to sing
The glories of my heavenly King.
Charles Wesley

WORK

A dictionary is the only place where you will find success before work.
Anon.

I never did anything worth doing by accident, nor did any of my inventions come by accident; they came by work. *Thomas Edison*

God gives every bird its food, but he does not throw it into the nest.
Josiah G. Holland

A dairymaid can milk cows to the glory of God.
Martin Luther

Instead of letting a mob of hoodlum tasks surround and trample me to death, I force them into a single file and handle them one at a time. *Don Mallough*

WORLD

(See also: Worldliness)

Worldly glory is but a breath, a vapour, a froth, a phantasm, a shadow, a reflection, an apparition, a very nothing.
Thomas Brooks

The world is all appearances, like our clothes: the truth lies underneath.
Thomas Carlyle

This world is our passage and not our portion.
Matthew Henry

The world would not hate angels for being angelic, but it does hate men for being Christians. It grudges them their new character; it is tormented by their peace; it is infuriated by their joy.
William Temple

WORLDLINESS

(See also: World)

A man caught up with this world is not ready for the next one.

Jesus did not pray that his Father would take Christians out of the world, but that he would take the world out of Christians.

There is no surer evidence of an unconverted state than to have the things of the world uppermost in our aim, love and estimation. *Joseph Alleine*

If we loved the world the way God loves it, we wouldn't love it the way we shouldn't love it.
Anon.

If you are wise, let the world pass, lest you pass away with the world.
Augustine

I looked for the church and I found it in the world; I looked for the world and I found it in the church. *Horatius Bonar*

The two poles could sooner meet, than the love of Christ and the love of the world. *Thomas Brooks*

It is infinitely better to have the whole world for our enemies and God for our friend, than to have the whole world for our friends and God for our enemy. *John Brown*

There are Christians living on spiritual stale bread and mouldy cheese when they might be enjoying roast turkey from heaven!
A. Lindsay Glegg

The bee will not sit on a flower where no honey can be sucked, neither should the Christian.
William Gurnall

If you find yourself loving any pleasure better than your prayers, any book better than the Bible, any house better than the house of God, any table better than the Lord's table, any person better than Christ, any indulgence better than the hope of heaven – take alarm! *Thomas Guthrie*

When the night-club invades the sanctuary it ought not to be difficult for any Bible Christian to discern the time of day.
Vance Havner

Whoever marries the spirit of this age will find himself a widower in the next.
William Ralph Inge

It is better to trust in the Lord than in men or princes; whereas whoever will live on worldly principles must carry the same strain and care as does the man of the world.
G. H. Lang

The legitimate courtesies of life become positively sinful when they take priority over the interests of the Lord Jesus.
William MacDonald

The world is a dirty, defiling thing. A man can hardly walk here but he shall defile his garments. The men of the world are dirty, sooty creatures. We cannot converse with them but they leave their filthiness upon us.
Thomas Manton

The only ultimate disaster that can befall us is to feel ourselves at home on this earth.
Malcolm Muggeridge

Conformity to the world can be overcome by nothing but conformity to Jesus.
Andrew Murray

Worldliness and Christianity are two such ends as never meet. *Nehemiah Rogers*

It is dangerous dressing for another world by the looking-glass of this world.
William Secker

All earthly things are as salt water, that increases the appetite, but satisfies not. *Richard Sibbes*

He who has the smile of the ungodly must look for the frown of God.
C. H. Spurgeon

You might as well talk about a heavenly devil as talk about a worldly Christian. *Billy Sunday*

Worldliness is a spirit, an atmosphere, an influence permeating the whole of life and human society,

and it needs to be guarded against constantly and strenuously.
W. H. Griffith Thomas

It is scarcely possible in most places to get anyone to attend a meeting where the only attraction is God.
A. W. Tozer

Of all the calamities that have been visited upon the world, the surrender of the human spirit to this present world and its ways is the worst, without any doubt. *A. W. Tozer*

Pleasure, profit, preferment are the worldling's trinity.
John Trapp

There is not a minute to waste in getting the world out of the church and the church into the world.
Foy Valentine

Make no mistake about it, the world with its unbelief is a spiritual ice-house, and too much contact with it will quickly cool the spirit.
Malcolm Watts

WORRY

(See also: Anxiety; Fear)

Worry and worship are mutually exclusive.

The devil would have us continually crossing streams that do not exist. *Anon.*

Worry is the interest we pay on tomorrow's troubles.
Anon.

Worry over tomorrow pulls shadows over today's sunshine. *Anon.*

Worry is an intrusion into God's providence.
John Edmund Haggai

Never attempt to bear more than one kind of trouble at once. Some people bear three kinds – all they have had, all they have now and all they expect to have.
Edward Everett Hale

Worry is sin against the loving care of the Father.
E. Stanley Jones

Worry has an active imagination.
D. M. Lloyd-Jones

A day of worry is more exhausting than a week of work. *John Lubbock*

Worry over poverty is as fatal to spiritual fruitfulness as is gloating over wealth. *A. W. Pink*

Worry is a thin stream of fear trickling through the

mind. If encouraged, it cuts a channel into which all other thoughts are drained. *A. S. Roche*

Worry is faith in the negative, trust in the unpleasant, assurance of disaster and belief in defeat.
William A. Ward

I dare not fret any more than I dare curse and swear.
John Wesley

WORSHIP – Blessings

Worship is to Christian living what the mainspring is to the watch.
Lawrence R. Axelson

It is only when men begin to worship that they begin to grow. *Calvin Coolidge*

In our worship there should be the power of the supernatural which brings home a sense of God.
Bryan Green

By doing obeisance we are learning obedience.
Matthew Henry

Worship liberates the personality by giving a new perspective to life, by integrating life with the multitude of life-forms, by bringing into the life the virtues of humility, loyalty, devotion and rightness of attitude, thus refreshing and reviving the spirit.
Roswell C. Long

In the most lofty devotion we become unconscious of self. *Austin Phelps*

There is more healing joy in five minutes of worship than there is in five nights of revelry. *A. W. Tozer*

I know of no pleasure so rich, none so pure, none so hallowing in their influences and constant in their supply as those which result from the true and spiritual worship of God.
Richard Watson

WORSHIP – Essence

True worship exalts God to his rightful place in our lives. *Anon.*

Christian worship is at once the Word of God and the obedient response thereto.
W. H. Cadman

Worship is transcendent wonder. *Thomas Carlyle*

To worship God is to realize the purpose for which God created us.
Herbert M. Carson

Worship is the declaration by a creature of the greatness of his Creator.
Herbert M. Carson

The dearest idol I have known,
Whate'er that idol be,
Help me to tear it from thy throne,
And worship only thee.
William Cowper

Reverence is essential to worship. *Frank Gabelein*

Worship is that to which we give our interest, our enthusiasm and our devotion.
Clarence E. MacCartney

Worship . . . is giving to the Lord the glory that is due in response to what he has revealed to us and done to us in Jesus Christ his Son.
Oswald B. Milligan

Worship is the adoring contemplation of God as he has revealed himself in Christ and in his Word.
J. Oswald Sanders

In true worship men . . . have little thought of the means of worship; their thoughts are upon God. True worship is characterized by self-effacement and is lacking in any self-consciousness.
Geoffrey Thomas

Worship is the submission of all our nature to God. It is the quickening of conscience by his holiness, the nourishment of the mind with his truth, the purifying of the imagination by his beauty, the opening of the heart to his love, the surrender of the will to his purpose.
William Temple

WORSHIP – Importance

(See also: Awe; Fear of God)

If we worshipped as we should, we wouldn't worry as we shouldn't.

Worship comes before service, and the King before the King's business.

What we worship determines what we become.
Harvey F. Ammerman

The first foundation of righteousness undoubtedly is the worship of God.
John Calvin

The man who does not habitually worship is but a pair of spectacles behind which there is no eye.
Thomas Carlyle

Carnal men are content with the 'act' of worship; they have no desire for communion with God.
John W. Everett

Nothing prepares the heart more for worship of the Lord than to contemplate his beauty and perfection.
Frank Gabelein

Public worship will not excuse us from secret worship. *Matthew Henry*

Worship is the highest function of the human soul.
Geoffrey R. King

We need to worship and adore as well as to analyse and explain. *Isobel Kuhn*

A man can no more diminish God's glory by refusing to worship him than a lunatic can put out the sun by scribbling the word 'darkness' on the walls of his cell. *C. S. Lewis*

Our whole life . . . should be so angled towards God that whatever strikes upon us, whether sorrow or joy, should be deflected upwards at once into his presence. *J. A. Motyer*

Our minds are so constituted that they cannot at one and the same time be stayed upon the Lord and fixed upon next winter's new coat or hat.
A. W. Pink

Worship is as much God's due as anything can be.
William S. Plumer

I am called to worship a God I cannot see, but not to submit to a God I cannot know and prove.
David Shepherd

We are called to an everlasting preoccupation with God. *A. W. Tozer*

I say that the greatest tragedy in the world today is that God has made man in his image and made him to worship him, made him to play the harp of worship before the face of God day and night, but he has failed God and dropped the harp. It lies voiceless at his feet.
A. W. Tozer

Worship, then, is not part of the Christian life; it is the Christian life.
Gerald Vann

To pray is less than to adore. *Clarence Walworth*

Posture in worship is too often imposture.
Thomas Watson

Man is not made to question, but adore.
Edward Young

YOUTH

Every adult Christian generation owes its young people a divine demonstration of the reality of what it believes and preaches. *Anon.*

Tell me what are the prevailing sentiments that occupy the minds of your young men and I will tell you what is to be the character of the next generation.
Edmund Burke

I believe young people are indifferent to the church today, not because the church has required too much of them, but because it has demanded so little.
Mort Crim

A young sinner will be an old devil. *William Gurnall*

Demoralize the youth of a nation and the revolution is already won.
Nikolai Lenin

When we are out of sympathy with the young, then I think our work in this world is over.
George MacDonald

Many teenage troubles are a revolt against an unfriendly world.
Alan Redpath

My character, tastes and ideals were, in the main, fixed by the time I reached the age of sixteen . . . the seed had been sown, and could only produce a growth of a certain species.
Bertrand Russell

ZEAL

(See also: Abandonment; Consecration; Soul-Winning; Submission)

It's easier to cool down a fanatic than warm up a corpse. *Brother Andrew*

Zeal is like fire; it needs both feeding and watching.
Anon.

I want my religion like my tea – hot! *William Booth*

Unless I go about my business of saving the souls of men with an energy and a zeal almost amounting to madness, nobody will take any notice of me, much less believe what I say and make everlasting profit out of it. *William Booth*

Attempt great things for God; expect great things from God. *William Carey*

Give me the love that leads the way,
The faith that nothing can dismay,
The hope no disappointments tire,
The passion that will burn like fire.
Let me not sink to be a clod;
Make me thy fuel, Flame of God.

Amy Carmichael

Men ablaze are invincible. Hell trembles when men kindle. *Samuel Chadwick*

It is better to wear out than to rust out.

Richard Cumberland

In those things in which all the people of God are agreed, I will spend my zeal; and as for other things about which they differ, I will walk according to the light God hath given me, and charitably believe that others do so too. *Philip Henry*

Oh, that I was all heart and soul and spirit to tell the glorious gospel of Christ to perishing multitudes!

Rowland Hill

The disgrace of the church in the twentieth century is that more zeal is evident among Communists and cultists than among Christians. *William MacDonald*

No divinely sent opportunity must elude us.

Watchman Nee

Misplaced zeal is zeal *for* God rather than the zeal *of* God.

William L. Pettingill

He who has no zeal has no love to God.

William S. Plumer

If by excessive zeal we die before reaching the average age of man, worn out in the Master's service, then glory be to God, we shall have so much less of earth and so much more of heaven.

C. H. Spurgeon

The supreme need of the church is the same in the twentieth century as in the first: it is men on fire for Christ.

James S. Stewart

No craze so great as that of the gambler, and no

gambler for Jesus was ever cured, thank God.
C. T. Studd

Zeal without knowledge is like wild fire in a fool's hand. *John Trapp*

A fanatic is a person who loves Jesus more than you do. *George Verwer*

Zeal is as needful for a Christian as salt for the sacrifice or fire on the altar. *Thomas Watson*

My talents, gifts and graces, Lord,
Into thy blessed hands receive;
And let me live to preach thy Word,
And let me to thy glory live;
My every sacred moment spend
In publishing the sinners' Friend.
Charles Wesley

Get on fire for God and men will come and see you burn. *John Wesley*

I am never better than when I am on the full stretch for God.
George Whitefield

Subject Index

Subject Index